SALMAN THE SOLITARY

YASHAR KEMAL was born in 1923 in a village on the cotton-growing plains of Chukurova. He received some basic education in village schools, then became an agricultural labourer and factory-worker. His championship of the poor peasants lost him a succession of jobs, but he was eventually able to buy a typewriter and set himself up as a public letter-writer in the small town of Kadirli. After a spell as a journalist, he published a volume of short stories in 1952, and in 1955, his first novel, *Memed, My Hawk*, which won the Varlik Prize for the best novel of the year, and has been translated into every major language.

Yashar Kemal was a member of the Central Committee of the banned Workers' Party. In 1971 he was held in prison for twenty-six days, then released without being charged. More recently he has again been placed on trial for action in support of the Kurdish dissidents. Among the many prizes and honours he has received internationally, in recognition of his gifts as a writer and of his courageous fight for human rights, are the French Légion d'Honneur and the Prix du Meilleur Livre Etranger. Kemal is Turkey's most influential living writer and, in the words of John Berger, "one of the modern world's great storytellers".

THILDA KEMAL is the author's wife; virtually all of his work to have appeared in English has been in her translations.

Kemal

SALMAN
THE SOLITARY

Translated from the Turkish
by Thilda Kemal

THE HARVILL PRESS
LONDON

First published in Turkish with the title *Kimsecik I*

First published in Great Britain in 1997
by The Harvill Press,
84 Thornhill Road,
London N1 1RD

First impression

Copyright © Yashar Kemal, 1980
English translation copyright © Thilda Kemal, 1997

Yashar Kemal asserts the moral right to be identified as the author of this work

A CIP catalogue record for this book is available from the British Library

ISBN 1 86046 389 4 (hbk)
ISBN 1 86046 390 8 (pbk)

Designed and typeset in Imprint at
Libanus Press, Marlborough, Wiltshire

Printed and bound in Great Britain by Butler & Tanner Ltd
at Selwood Printing, Burgess Hill

Translator's Glossary to
Salman the Solitary

agel   Kind of circlet tied round *keffiyeh* (Arab cotton head-dress)

ayran   Drink made from watered yoghurt

Bairam   Holiday, religious festival

bedel   Sum paid for exemption from military service

bora   Black squall

börek   Kind of pastry

bulgur   Type of wheat that has been parboiled, cracked and dried

chardak   Summer sleeping place built on stilts

cura   Smallest stringed instrument in Anatolian folk music

dolama   Woman's over-garment

dönüm   Quarter acre (940 square metres)

Düldül   Name of prophet Mohammed's white mule

ezan   Muslim call to prayer

gövend   Kurdish country dance

halay   Group folk dance

Halil Ibrahim   The Patriarch Abraham, an important figure in Islam. Urfa has a traditional story of his life which is at variance with that given in the Bible but can be found in the Talmud

han   Inn or caravanserai

Hidrellez   Fortieth day after the spring equinox, May 6, popularly considered the first day of summer

inshallah   God willing

jerid   Game played in Muslim countries on horseback with blunt wooden javelins

jijim   Embroidered hand-woven rug

jingir   Local name for species of red eagle

Kadir   Holy night in month of Ramadan

katana   Breed of Hungarian horses

kaymak   Kind of clotted cream

kilim   Pileless rug

köçek   Boy dancer dressed as a woman

kurban   Sacrifice or offering to God

madimak   Spring plant a little like spinach

mashallah   Expression of admiration and wonder, also to avert the evil eye

mashlak   Open sleeveless coat

namaz   Muslim prayer performed five times a day

Party, the   The Union and Progress Party

Pasha, the   Mustafa Kemal Ataturk, President of the Republic

saz   (Plural: *sazes*) Stringed musical instrument

semah   Folk dance more particular to the Bektashis and Alevis
shalvar-trousers   Baggy trousers
Sorani   Kurdish dialect
sumac   Kind of spice
tandir   Oven made in a hole in the ground
tarhana   Wheat mixed with yoghurt and sun-dried
tespih   Prayer beads
Yilankalé   Castle of the Snakes
yörük   Name for nomadic tribes
yufka   Unleavened bread in thin sheets

SALMAN
THE SOLITARY

1

BRIGHT MOONLIGHT FLOODED the valley where the village lay. In a corner of the courtyard Salman stood, stiff and motionless, singing a strange old-time song in a muffled undertone. The village children were playing at hidie-hole again. Hidie-hole is a kind of hide-and-seek that is played only on moonlit nights. Two teams are made up and, while the one tries to hide in the most unexpected nooks, the other has to flush them out. They would toss heads or tails for which team should hide first and it was always Colt Mustafa who called the coin. This was his undisputed privilege.

Salman's shadow, two, three times his size, fell dark and long, over the dust of the yard, and the children could distinguish the rifle slung over his shoulder. Even in the very heat of the game, they could not help glancing at that huge dark shadow, and each time they would scamper off as far as they could to avoid seeing it.

Salman had flaxen hair that stuck out stiff as a hedgehog's spines. His eyes were a cold poison green; they were very tiny, and sunk deep in their sockets. He hardly ever spoke, never laughed, and this added to the harshness of his sunburnt features. His nose was sharp. It twitched and quivered as though somebody had tacked it onto his face only a moment ago. A squat man with bow-legs, he had wide shoulders and very long arms that reached almost to the ground. His German rifle was burnished bright, stock and barrel glistening under the moon as though in broad sunlight. During the day, when he was not sleeping, Salman spent most of his time taking care of this rifle. He oiled the stock, the barrel, the cartridges – yes, even the cartridges –

using all sorts of strange fragrant greases, he wiped and polished, then set the rifle before him and gazed at it, spellbound. Now and again, as in a waking dream, a rapt smile, a fleeting happiness suffused his face, then he picked up the rifle and started oiling and polishing it afresh. At last, he would stand it against the cactus hedge opposite the gate of the big house. The blue sheen of the rifle would blend in a steely flashing radiance with the spiny cactus hedge, tall as a man and dotted with white, yellow, blue, pink and orange flowers.

Salman always had six gold-embroidered bandoliers strapped about his body and never was a single cartridge missing in any one of them. Four were crossed over his chest and two bound round his waist. There were days when the number of bandoliers increased until he was covered with them up to the throat. A huge pair of binoculars hung from his neck and two identical Circassian daggers with silver-nielloed hafts dangled against his hips. His gold-embossed, ivory-handled Nagant revolver, reputed to be of inestimable value, hung, unholstered, at his right thigh and his hand was seldom away from it.

Salman could have been anything from twenty to thirty years old. It was impossible to tell. He had a set of milk-white teeth, rarely seen, and a reddish moustache that drooped about his chin like the silks of a corncob.

On the right of the thick-growing cactuses that circled the crags was a very ancient pomegranate with branches that spread as wide as a plane tree's. Beneath it Salman stood, motionless, his dark shadow swaying and lengthening. And to escape the sight of that looming figure the children glided silently away between the mud-daubed dwellings and reed huts and headed for the far end of the village. At times, Salman's shadow followed them relentlessly. They would then take to their heels and start playing again only when they came to Sheldrake Rock on the banks of Jeyhan River.

But not in the winter, not on those freezing winter nights when the north wind, descending from the mauve rocky mountain, swept through the village, keen as a sword. On such nights, moonlit or not, the village was quite deserted, not a living soul abroad, only a few cats and the wild wind howling in the solitary emptiness, the only signs of life some faint lights filtering through the hand-sized windows and thatched reed walls of the huts, and also Salman, wrapped in a felt cloak, standing there on the edge of the cactuses in Ismail Agha's courtyard, his shadow stretching out in front of the pomegranate tree.

Everyone knew that Ismail Agha kept another two men to guard his house, but somehow no one ever noticed them. It was Salman, and Salman only, whose dark shape was to be seen, filling the whole yard, the whole night, and those huge sheep-dogs, each one as large as a horse, asleep at his feet, never once barking, never even lifting their heads so long as Salman did not move.

The Tick counted the boys. They were just nineteen beside himself. "Minstrel Ali's one too many," he declared.

"Well, I won't play then," Minstrel Ali said, crestfallen. He was one of the oldest boys, more than ten years old.

"Let's team up," Mustafa said. He was a tall slender boy of about seven with large luminous dark eyes and the only one of the group to wear shoes.

After a good deal of noisy wrangling two teams were formed.

"I'm not playing . . ." Minstrel Ali's voice broke. He was taking it very hard.

"Wait," Mustafa said. "Let's toss heads or tails first." He cast up the coin and the boys clustered around to see. "It's for us to hide," he announced, "and Minstrel Ali will come with us."

The Tick was the oldest of them all, almost sprouting a moustache already. He never joined in any of these games, but not for one moment did he part from the boys, always watching from a distance, thoroughly engrossed, as though in a happy dream. And when they were playing at hidie-hole, he would sit on a large graven marble slab and act as a kind of umpire. He never tolerated foul play and was quick to detect any cheating. The children trusted him. Now, as the ten boys scampered off to hide, he lined up the rest facing the reed fence of a barn, so as to keep them there until the others had quite vanished from sight.

The rule of the game was that every one of those who had gone into hiding must be tracked down, but some boys found such good caches that it took quite a while to uncover them, and so the game could go on for many nights. And when finally the "hiders" had all been brought to light, they would have to give presents to the "seekers", handkerchiefs, slingshots, bird snares and many another gift. Also a feast would be spread at the expense of the losers. And if three of the "hiders" could not be found for a whole week then it was for the others to distribute gifts.

5

"Are you all facing the fence?" the Tick shouted.

"Yes, yes, don't you worry," Wiggler Yusuf assured him.

Yusuf was the son of Wiggler Hüseyin, the only immigrant from Thrace to have settled in the village. On his arrival, even before entering his house or unpacking his belongings, Hüseyin tackled the villagers who had come to welcome him. "See here, neighbours," he said, "my name, I'll have you know is Wiggler. That's how they called me in the old country, Wiggler of name and fame. Is there anyone here who goes by this name?"

The villagers took it all in their stride. "No, no," they said. "How could there be!"

"Sure, you're very welcome, Wiggler."

"Sure, we could do with a Wiggler here."

"It's too bad there wasn't a Wiggler before in our village."

"But it's all right now . . ."

"We've got a Wiggler at last!"

"And one Wiggler's more than enough for one village."

"Why, you could search the whole Chukurova and not find another Wiggler!"

"That, you couldn't," Wiggler Hüseyin laughed. Then he turned to his wife. "See here, woman," he said, "you start toting our things inside. I'm going to have a chitchat with our new neighbours. This looks like a good place the government's chosen for us." From the red sash at his waist, he produced a tobacco pouch, a lighter and a holder. "Come here, fellows, come," he called as he squatted against the reed wattling and began to roll a cigarette.

"No, no," they cried, "the first cigarette's on us." Cigarettes rained in front of him, tinderboxes sparked and, squatting in a circle, they all fell to smoking.

"It's really a good thing there's no other Wiggler here. Always best to be the one and only. But I'm a smith too, you know, and a cartwright as well. Is there anyone here who's a smith and a cartwright as well?"

"No, no," they assured him.

"Woman, you hear that? No smith, no cartwright here! That's even better than not being any Wiggler."

"Much better," the villagers laughed.

"D'you do any ploughing around here?"

"Oh yes!"

"And you use ploughshares and harrows?"

"Yes, yes."

"And carts, d'you have carts?"

"Every house owns one."

"Splendid! Woman, every house in this village owns carts and shares and harrows."

"Well, good for you, man! You should be pleased indeed . . ."

"You can start now," the Tick announced. "They've all hidden."

Wiggler Yusuf was off like an arrow. "Let them hide," he boasted. "I'll soon unearth them."

Colt Mustafa and Bird Memet were standing behind Mad Poyraz's barn. There was a tall spineless cactus hedge a little beyond, and the space between the barn and the hedge was over-hung by a dense blackberry bush. This was where Mustafa and Memet always went to hide and where Wiggler Yusuf never failed to find them.

"Look, Mustafa," Bird Memet said, "don't let's go in there. Wiggler's sure to get us again. Why, he's already caught Scabby Mistik. I can hear him screaming."

"Mistik's always the first to get caught. He does it on purpose. Now he'll join up with the others and help them find us, the rat!"

"Look, we can't just stand here talking."

"Let's get in under that bush."

"It's not safe," Bird Memet objected. He drew Mustafa into the cleft of a rock. "This is better, but . . . Look, why don't we nip over to the Narrow Pass?"

"It's crawling with snakes there," Mustafa protested. "We'll get bitten, we'll die!"

"No one would think of looking there. No one would even dare come near the Narrow Pass."

"Let's hide on the river bank, under the cliff," Mustafa suggested.

"Hush!" Bird Memet warned. "Can't you hear their footsteps?"

They pressed back into the cleft, holding their breaths.

Wiggler's voice came from somewhere near the barn. "I'll dig Mustafa out from under the blackberry bush in a jiffy. He's such a scaredy-cat he'd never hide anywhere else."

"Oh, but he would!" Mustafa chuckled. The downy leaves of a spurge plant were tickling his face.

Then they heard Wiggler again. "What's this, what's this? He's not here! Where else would he hide, that Mustafa?"

"They're coming this way now," Bird Memet whispered.

"No, no, they're going away. Look, I'm stuck here, I can't move!"

"Me too," Bird said.

They had squeezed so far into the cleft that struggle as they might they could not get free. A dusty odour of bitter thyme and sun-baked rock rose to their nostrils.

"I'm out, Mustafa," the Bird said at last. He took a deep breath. "I thought I was going to die."

"Pull me out," Mustafa urged.

The Bird dragged him out by the shoulders. They were all in a sweat. "Listen, Wiggler's after us. What a pest! We must hole up somewhere so he'll burst and never find us."

"Wiggler's got an eagle," Mustafa said.

"Oh-ho, he's got everything that one!" the Bird said. "His father's a cartwright and the carts in this village are so old, half a dozen of them break down every day. But you have a lot of things too, don't you? Even horses, Arab horses . . . They say your father's brought them over from Aleppo."

"Wiggler's eagle is huge, with wide wide wings . . ."

"Quick, get back inside, here they come again," the Bird hissed.

This time it was Slyboots prowling nearabouts. "Where can he have got to, that Mustafa?" Slyboots grumbled.

"He never hides anywhere further off than this," Mistik said.

"But he's got the Bird with him this time," Slyboots said. "D'you know, those two were born on the same day, at the crack of dawn. They were neighbours even then, before Mustafa's father built this mansion. They cried out at the same time . . ."

"The Bird twittered and the Colt neighed," Scabby Mistik said.

"They're both milksops. I'll find them even if they're hidden in the Narrow Pass," Slyboots vowed.

"Oh no, never! Why, it's swarming with snakes there!"

Bird Memet nudged Mustafa. "Why don't we go there, then?" he said. "Let's see him find us!"

"No, no, the snakes . . ."

"What about Memik Agha's mulberry tree? He'd never dare go near the place."

"We wouldn't either," Mustafa said.

"Suppose we hid near the cactus hedge in your yard . . ."

"Not on your life!" Mustafa exclaimed.

"But that's the only place they would never go, not when Salman's standing there."

"Would you dare?"

"I would if you're with me."

Slyboots was talking to Mistik. "You wait here, Mustafa's sure to turn up."

"We must get away," Mustafa whispered.

"The cactus hedge, then. Salman will never notice us."

"He will, he will!" Mustafa shouted.

Scabby Mistik heard him. "They're here, Slyboots," he yelled. "Quick, they're here, but I can't see them."

Memet grabbed Mustafa's hand and drew him away. Swiftly, on all fours, they squeezed through the cactus hedge, the thorns tearing at their flesh, and fled, threading among the huts and hedges. And when they lifted their heads, there was Salman, right above them, still as a statue, not fifty paces away. He was standing on a tall marble slab, his rifle, bandoliers and daggers glinting in the moonlight.

"Stop," Mustafa quavered. "Stop, Memet." He was shaking in all his limbs. Suddenly, they bolted, running for their lives, and stopped only on the brink of the Narrow Pass, where the earth smelled strange and was coloured blue, yellow, green, crystalline. The pass yawned darkly beneath them.

"Shall we go down?" the Bird asked doubtfully.

"Let's . . ."

But they wandered back into the village again. Keeping to the shadow of the huts and hedges, they came to Memik Agha's mulberry tree. This tree was charred on one side and all leafy on the other, and the charred part showed up very black even in the night. Owls were hooting in the mountain. Above the pointed rocky peak eagles soared, faint black specks in the sky. Only for a moment the boys stood there, staring at the tree, breathing hard. Then they rushed away, past Salman's huge shadow that fell over the ruined castle fort and on again to the ravine. It was very dark, very deep . . .

Over the ravine they whirled in a great rustling mass, the eagles, the vultures, the buzzards, the rufous kites, wing to wing, beak to beak, all steeped in blood, then suddenly plunged scrambling over each other to the bottom of the pit where Long Osman's naked body lay, feet in the water, the water red . . . Eagles swarmed over the body, tore off a piece of flesh and started up, while others fell over it again in hundreds. All around the pit, the villagers were trying to drive them away with staves and rifles and sticks of dynamite and the deafening beating of drums and tin cans. Nothing could arrest the swooping eagles, some of which, huge black ones, even attacked the crowd. Wings thrashing, jostling, rising and falling, the eagles kept at it fiercely until, though it lasted no longer than the time to smoke a cigarette, all that was left of the corpse was a skeleton of white bones. Then the eagles glided off and began wheeling above. Yet it was several days before the villagers could recover Osman's remains, for the vultures, long-winged and bald, sluggish and aged, had assembled on the edge of the pit, keeping an obstinate watch. The village hunters shot at them from a distance. They killed a great many, the pit was full of them, the stench in the summer heat was unbearable, and still the vultures remained there for many and many a long day after . . .

High above the Narrow Pass, eagles were wheeling in the moonlit sky. The shadow of the stately castle keep on the peak of the crags grazed the outlying houses of the village and fell over the glittering river that flowed along the level plain as though skimming through the air. Of one accord the two boys ran swiftly back to where Salman's dark figure loomed larger than ever. His silver-nielloed bandoliers flashed in the moonlight. He had drawn out his two daggers and was playing a strange game, the dagger in his left hand held upright, the other swivelling around it at lightning speed, emitting dazzling sparks. At times the right hand would slow down, dropping the dagger, only to retrieve it deftly before it touched the ground.

"Let's get past him to that corner," Bird Memet whispered, but Mustafa had already fled. Memet rushed after him and they found themselves at the foot of the crags facing Memik Agha's mulberry tree. Overhead, above the mauve rocky peak of the mountain the eagles were still wheeling, and below, Jeyhan River, flowing in a silvery haze, seemed to be soaring even higher in the air. The shrill call of a bird sounded intermittently, echoing back from the pale walls of the castle. Suddenly they leapt to their feet.

"Look, Memet!" Mustafa cried. "D'you see the tree?"

On the burnt side of the trunk millions of tiny sparks were crawling up, ant-like, dying away among the branches, only to sprout again at once from the roots of the tree.

"Run, Memet, run . . ."

As though swept up in a storm, crazed with fear they darted from the tree to the Narrow Pass, from the Pass to Salman, and back to the tree again, now flying like the wind, now creeping low, cat-like, so as not to be seen by Salman or by the vultures or the jinn. Round and round the village, forgetting the game of hidie-hole, forgetting everything, their homes, their parents, sleep . . . Drenched in sweat, their eyes starting from their sockets . . .

Shots burst out on the mountain, volley after volley, nearer and nearer and stones clattered down, raising thunderous echoes in the night. All the villagers, in nightshirts or underpants, half-asleep, were out of their houses.

"It's the bandits," someone said. "They've surrounded Memik Agha's house and killed his three armed guards."

It was not long after the late evening prayer and people had only just gone to bed.

Zalimoglu was shouting: "Come out, Memik Agha. Today's the day, my day! Come out and let's settle accounts man to man. Don't you trust in the gendarmes. I've posted five of my men on every road leading here."

There was no sound from inside the big house.

"Come out, Memik Agha! Your sons, your brothers, your men too. Let's have it out right here in the open, at the foot of this old castle. Don't hide like a woman!"

From where he had taken cover behind a rectangular stone which bore an ancient inscription and in relief the head of a straight-nosed frizzy-haired woman with huge eyes, Zalimoglu went on hurling abuse at Memik Agha until all of a sudden – it was past midnight by now – bullets started whizzing through the air, bombs exploded, the earth shook.

"Out, out Memik Agha! I'll never let you go."

Horses neighed, cows and oxen bellowed, dogs howled, cocks crowed of one voice, children bawled, people yelled, the uproar thundered against the rocks and the castle walls, all hell was let loose in the night. And above the din Zalimoglu's voice rang out ever more vengeful, blazing with anger.

"Out, out Memik Agha! I'm going to finish you off tonight at all costs, you should know that. Don't make me kill innocent people as well. If you won't give yourself up, I'll set fire to your house, and everyone in it from seven to seventy will be burned alive. People will say that Zalimoglu's a godless tyrant who kills even small babes . . ."

On and on Zalimoglu shouted until it was almost dawn, but the only answer he got was a hail of bullets, hit or miss, bursting at intervals from ten or fifteen rifles all at once.

"I'm setting fire to the house, Memik Agha. The whole village is witness that I waited all night here for you to come out, that I begged you even . . ."

A huge flame flared up at the front portal. As the east began to pale the big house was ablaze and Zalimoglu had stopped shooting. He crouched there, vigilant, behind the large slabstone, staring at the head of the beautiful woman with the straight nose, the huge eyes and the hair like coiled snakes, cold in the half light. God knows who she was, he wondered, in her lifetime, this woman surely long dead and turned to ashes, who knows how proud of her beauty that she had her living likeness engraved upon this stone so that people should admire her for ever, and now the stone itself is buried under the earth and she herself long forgotten, lying here in the dung of the village, her eyes of stone open wide in a bewildered avid stare, unconscious of Memik Agha's bullets . . .

Mustafa had woken up screaming, he had rushed out of the house like a madman, without even putting on his clothes, straight to Memik Agha's house and had crouched behind another slabstone with another woman's head in relief. His father, his father's men had seized their weapons and taken up well-covered positions in the courtyard of their house. Only Mustafa's mother was about, oblivious of the flying bullets, running this way and that, looking for Mustafa.

After a while Bird Memet joined him behind the stone. He had seen Mustafa dashing out of his house and only chains could have kept him from his friend.

"Your mother's after you again, Mustafa," he said. "What a fusspot of a mother she is!"

"Who cares?" Mustafa said incensed. "Let her look!"

Flames surged from the doors and windows of the big house, from the chimneys, from between the roof tiles. It was light now, though the sun had not yet risen. The villagers had gathered at a safe distance up among the crags and were watching in silence, when suddenly they saw Memik Agha emerging from the flaming doorway with his rifle in his hand, dazed, like a man walking in his sleep, and after him his sons and his men, blinking in confusion, like sleepwalkers too. Taken off his guard, Zalimoglu hesitated, trigger-ready, while the men, nine of them, stood reeling to and fro as though in a trance. Only for a moment. Zalimoglu was the first to react. With one bullet he shot down Memik Agha's youngest son, Ismet, a university student. Next he hit Hassan, who came from Jigjik village, and then Ali. Ali was wounded. He fell screaming, then leapt up and flung himself back through the flaming doorway, emerged almost at once, looked about him for an instant and fled inside. Memik Agha, who had not moved up to now, followed him as he rushed back into the house. The rest of the inmates tumbled in and out of the flames, as though performing some kind of fire worship, and every time they came out, Zalimoglu shot one of them down. Bellowing, the man rolled on the ground, a mass of flames, and then was quite still. One after the other they fell until only Memik Agha was left. In and out of the house he shuttled, his clothes on fire. Zalimoglu had stopped shooting now. One last time, Memik Agha appeared, his whole body in flames, his eyes fixed in an empty gaze. Then he threw himself inside. Zalimoglu, the villagers waited and waited, but Memik Agha did not come out again.

The sun rose, the mountain tops brightened and the flowing river took on a silvery sheen. Memik Agha's big house was now a smouldering ruin and the outhouses were all aflame. Mopping his brow, Zalimoglu left without another look behind him. As soon as he was out of sight the villagers rushed up to gather the dead and put out the fire in the outhouses. A mulberry tree near the house was smouldering too and clinging fast to it, clawing at the trunk, was Memik Agha's negro Arab, bleeding from a bullet wound.

It took the efforts of several men to prise him away or he would have been burned to ashes. Anyway, he did not live long after this.

Well, this charred tree, the only thing left standing in Memik Agha's yard, is known to bleed every night at the hour when the eagles wing above the flinty peak of the mountain. The blood flows down the trunk as from a spring and owls perch on the tree, and vultures too, old and bald, foul, repulsive, and there are nights when the tree moans, it moans all night through, like a baby being strangled.

It was Mustafa who had first seen the tree bleeding. Struck with terror he breathed the news into the ears of his friends. Night after night the boys kept up a watch and in the end they, too, saw the blood streaming down the trunk, heard the tree howling like a wounded wolf. Next the women of the village, then the old people, and finally the men were witness to this miracle. All saw the blood and heard the moaning . . .

"The tree's bleeding," Mustafa said.

"It's moaning, d'you hear?" Bird Memet whispered.

"I'm going to cut this tree down," Mustafa said, shivering.

"Your hands will wither," Bird Memet said. "This tree comes from the good folk. It's human."

"As though no one's ever killed a human being!"

"Just let me see you cut it then," Bird Memet defied him.

"I'll do it, I will!" Mustafa shouted.

The tree was drawing nearer. And suddenly Wiggler Yusuf was upon them. "Stop!" he cried triumphantly. "You're caught."

Mustafa and Memet were all in a sweat. They had long forgotten the game of hidie-hole and it was with relief that they came to.

"We've found every one of you now!' Wiggler said.

"Tomorrow morning, I'll have mother make honey cakes for you all," Mustafa promised, "and I'll give each of you a glass marble. If you like, I can even get dates and dried fruit from the shop."

"A glass marble for everyone from me too," Bird Memet said. "You've earned it."

Wiggler was highly gratified at so much generosity, but a little baffled as well, for as far as he could make out these two had not hidden at all. They were panting like a bellows, both of them, as though they had been running hard all the time.

As the boys straggled back home, both winners and losers well pleased with the game, Mustafa held Memet back. Memet guessed at once what was coming and he went cold all over. "But I'm afraid," he protested. "Everyone's afraid of Salman. You go alone. It's your house after all."

"Memet, I'm dying of fear," Mustafa implored. "It's me he's going to kill, not anyone else."

"He'll kill me too," Memet shouted. "And Wiggler, and Scabby Mistik, and . . ."

Mustafa clapped a hand on Memet's mouth. "Hush! Not so loud."

"That Salman may be your father's bodyguard," Memet said, lowering his voice, "but he's still worse than Zalimoglu. He'll burn everyone in this village and cut that tree down too. He'll kill me and my mother and my uncle as well . . ."

"But me, he's going to kill most of all," Mustafa said. He was crouching against the wall of the village mosque. For a time they did not speak.

Bird Memet was the first to break the silence. "I'll come with you," he said. "I have to, because if I don't that man will kill you. And me too, mind you. Look, I'll come up to the corner of the yard, but not a step further."

"All right, but don't go before I'm inside. Salman can't see you there."

"I'll wait," Bird Memet said. "Keep low as you go along the hedge."

A cloud came and hid the moon. What luck . . . Mustafa quickly glided along on all fours. "You can go now," he whispered. "He won't see me."

Bird Memet was a friend, a real friend. Though his teeth chattered with fear, he never moved until Mustafa was inside and the door closed behind him. That's what a real friend is like . . .

2

AS THE LITTLE snow-white clouds billow higher and higher up over the distant Mediterranean, the south wind begins to blow, cool and moist and smelling faintly of the sea. It rises in the afternoon, gentle at first, then gathering strength it whips up the dust of the roads and forms dust devils that it drives inland past the village and on towards the snow-patched Binboga, the Thousand Bulls Mountains, which lie leaning against each other, range after range, violet at first, then mauve, blue, paler and paler, the last ranges fading into the sky, quivering gauze-like, hardly visible.

Mustafa was sitting inside gazing idly at the glinting shaft of sunlight that fell through the window in a bright pool over the old Turcoman *kilim*. It was another of those torrid days and not a living creature was abroad. After a while he rose and skipped out onto the balcony. There was a swallow's nest there. He had counted the chicks, five in all, with pink bodies, goggling eyes and huge yellow mouths. When the mother swallow arrived their mouths gaped even wider, their necks stretched out so, it was unbelievable. And the clamour they raised! How could these tiny creatures make such a din? There were many things that amazed Mustafa in this world, but this was certainly the most wonderful. Every day, after spending hours gazing at the rugs spread over the floors and hung on the walls of the house, lost in contemplation of each intricate design, of this wealth of hues set like flowers in a garden, after watching the thousand and one scintillating colours in the shaft of sunlight that fell through the window, he would turn again to the swallow's nest. How they made him laugh, those quaint little chicks! With what a loud rumpus, what rapturous joy they greeted their mother! How Mustafa shared their joy! One day he even found himself stretching his neck as far as he could on the arrival of the mother swallow. How he laughed, then, holding his sides there, under the swallow's nest.

In the stable under the big house was a white stallion and six other thoroughbreds, while eleven Arabian steeds were lodged in the long stable at the foot of the crags. Mustafa loved to go to the stables, but he was afraid of Salman who was also very often there. Of the three mares in the long stable, the loveliest was the bay filly, with her shimmering coat, rufous, paler in the sunlight, and different, blood-red in the gloom of the stable.

One day, Mustafa had seen Salman doing something to the bay filly from behind and he soon guessed what, for he had once come upon the white stallion mounting a mare, huge teeth clutching the mare's mane, while she stood there, passive, very small, apparently unconcerned. The stallion, on catching sight of the mare, had reared and neighed and stamped frenziedly, and when after long efforts he thrust in his member, his legs, his whole body quivered for a while, his rump was all puckered. Then he fell back, ears flagged, all his ardour spent. Like the stallion Salman was stuck to the bay filly's croup, sweating and panting. At last, he fell away, smaller somehow, holding his limp penis, casting fearful glances to right and left as though he did not know what to do next. Suddenly, he drew up his *shalvar*-trousers, tied the cord and hurried to the door. Mustafa was terrified, he almost fainted. Just then, Süllü, the head groom, appeared in the doorway. He was a thin bandy-legged man who always wore breeches and top boots. His head on the long wrinkled neck was just like a bird of prey's.

"What's this, Salman?" he said. "The stable's become your second home. D'you have something to do, or is it that you've been smitten by some dark-eyed beauty here?"

Salman did not answer, he did not even turn to look at him.

It was very hot outside. The sky was bleached white, the rocks, the houses, the castle, trees, bushes and fields were steaming in a milky whiteness and the sluggish river winding along the plain seemed about to evaporate.

Mustafa's father, Ismail Agha, was asleep in the next room with the door locked. He would often take a nap during the day when his work allowed it, for he slept very little at night, and always when he slept his right hand rested on his revolver, while his shining German carbine was thrust under the pillow.

He had been asleep a long while now. Ah, if only he would wake up and take Mustafa to the castle where it was so cool among the crags. Up and down the long room Mustafa wandered, stamping impatiently, making all sorts of noises. His mother, his uncle's wife and her two children, Salman and the two other watchmen, Hassan and Hüseyin, were all next door, in the other house which was not so large and did not have so many beautiful *kilims*. Here the floors and walls were entirely lined with *kilims* of every colour and design, and so were the divans that were set against the walls.

Mustafa had not told anyone about this business of Salman's with the bay filly. For all his dread, he still kept a watch, and whenever the young man went to the stable he stole after him and stuck his eyes to a crack in the brush wall. Once it seemed as though Salman had detected him. Mustafa sank to the ground almost dead with fright, and for a long time he crouched there, unable to get up, his heart pounding, his hands and feet ice-cold in the summer heat, certain that Salman would kill him. After that, Mustafa swore that he would never spy on Salman again and for a time he did keep his word, though whenever he saw him making for the stable he was eaten up with curiosity.

One day, late in the afternoon he spotted Salman looking warily to right and left. He was going to the stable, that was sure. His right hand kept fiddling with his pants. Suddenly, Mustafa was seized with a strange fever, a pleasant tremor shot through his body and his penis hardened. As Salman entered the stable an irresistible force drew him to the crack in the brush wall. Salman was already at work behind the bay filly. She was pressing her haunches gently against his groin, gazing back at him, a long sad look, mute, compassionate, like a human being. How very very happy Mustafa was to watch the bay filly like that with Salman.

She seemed happy too, the way she tensed her limbs and then, when it was over, opened her legs wide and pissed long and loud, while Salman bent down as though to breathe in the smell. Mustafa resolved to do this thing just like Salman when he was as old. Watching Salman he had learnt exactly how it was done.

And as he crouched there, holding his penis, strange thoughts flitted through his mind. What if Salman had a child by the bay filly? A foal . . . What would Salman do with it? Maybe the bay filly would give birth not to a foal but to a baby. A baby that looked like Salman . . . Maybe the baby would be half horse, half human, with the head of a horse on a human body . . . Then, when it cried would it neigh like a horse? Or suppose it had a human head on the body of a horse? There used to be horses like that in the old days, hadn't Ferhat Hodja himself told his father so? Most probably there were also many then, like Salman, who took mares to wife. Yes, now the bay filly was Salman's wife, that was certain, though no one but Mustafa knew about it. Mustafa imagined the foal with the human head growing up and himself riding it and he started to laugh, then stopped short in dismay. Would Salman ever let Mustafa ride a child of his? Never mind, the foal might turn out to be a girl, and just as ugly as Salman! But what if Salman killed the foal with a baby's head as soon as it was born? No, no! From now on Mustafa would never let them out of his sight, not for a minute. He'd be there when the bay filly gave birth, he'd guess the exact time from her belly swelling. Ah yes, Salman would be sure to kill the foal so as to avoid disgrace. Well, if he did, Mustafa would tell his father, he would raise hell, even if Salman were to make mincemeat of him, he would go to the government, to the gendarmes, even to the big bey, the one who had a motorcar, he'd tell them everything, how his father and Salman had plotted together . . . That is, if his father were to side with Salman . . . And Mustafa was afraid of that. The two of them, fearing the scandal, would kill the baby foal, stuff it into a sack and cast it into the river and the poor thing would be devoured by those huge-mouthed catfish, each one as large as two men. But maybe his father would have pity on the baby, maybe he would love this tiny foal with a human head. Especially if it did not resemble Salman, especially if it was a beautiful girl . . . Maybe it would take after the bay filly, with eyes like hers, huge and sad and wondering, as she turned again and again to look at Salman. First he had to tell his father. No, no, he'd speak first to Hassan and Hüseyin. They were really kind people, in spite of their handlebar moustaches. Hassan had wide black eyes that saw everything far and wide. He must have seen what Salman did to the bay filly, but he was a close one, he wouldn't tell. Maybe he, too, was afraid of Salman . . . Ah, everyone feared Salman . . .

* * *

Black specks on the incandescent sky, swallows skimmed and darted here and there like arrows. Mustafa clung to the railings of the balcony, on the look-out for the mother swallow. He would cry out with the chicks when she arrived and maybe his father would wake up then. But that father of his did not love him as he used to. Before, Mustafa could do anything, and all his father would say was, there's my good boy, there's my lion of a lad . . . Before, oh how well Mustafa remembers, even when he went on horseback, his father would take him up on his shoulders. Once, they had gone like that all the way to Dörtyol and though Mustafa's legs ached so he could hardly walk when they got there, he had set his teeth and never breathed a word of complaint for fear his father would not carry him piggyback again. At Dörtyol they had visited an orange grove and stayed in a beautiful white-washed mansion. There was a girl there with flaxen hair, rippling bright, and a wizened woman in a snow-white kerchief, with eyes of the bluest blue. All around them oranges and lemons gushed from the green of the trees and in the middle of the grove was a pile of oranges tall as a mountain. The white-bearded Agha, a Cretan, his father's friend, had clear blue eyes too. An invigorating scent, unfamiliar to Mustafa, pervaded the orange grove, reminiscent of a pine forest with mint-scented springs bubbling over white pebbles . . .

Sick of waiting for the mother swallow, Mustafa had drifted back inside and what should he see but a bumblebee buzzing away furiously along the shaft of sunlight that fell through the window. It was no end of fun observing such angry bees. Mustafa squatted down, rested his chin in his hands and began to watch, so absorbed now that he forgot all about his father. The bee kept whizzing from the window to the *kilim*, unable to tear itself from the sunbeam, unable to find the opening in the window, mad with rage, vanishing in a blue crystalline scintillation of wings. Its buzzing filled the air, now rising to a long thin whine, its wings invisible, now sinking to its lowest pitch. Through the sunbeam the bee traced brief streaks of tiny blue, red and purple sparks that whirled and spilled over the *kilim* in heaps of steely blue or bright red. Mustafa would open his eyes wide and the bee's glittering flight, its buzzing became different. Then he closed them tight and when he opened them again the bee, its wings, the bright red glitter would be quite, quite different.

It was heaven for Mustafa when he could come upon a bee like that, trapped in a shaft of sunlight. Sometimes, a whole group of them would fall into the sunbeam, the buzzing, the sparkling would merge and cascade over the *kilim* in heaps of tiny glittering pinpoints, bright blue, red, orange. Some days the bees would go on like this from morning to night and Mustafa, beside himself, would forget food and drink, lost in a blissful dream, gliding along the sunbeam with the bees, the scintillation gathering and spreading within him, his heart fluttering with joy. All was erased from his mind, his father, Salman, Osman devoured by the eagles, Zalimoglu, the bleeding, ever-bleeding mulberry tree . . . But when he came to, the terror would return, the hellish dread, the trembling.

His father's voice drew him out of his reverie. He was there, at his side, smiling, calm. Ismail Agha was a huge man, people thought him fearless, but Mustafa knew better. He knew it when his father was afraid and a pang of fear would shoot through his heart. A shadow would pass over Ismail Agha's face, over his eyes, his hands, and Mustafa would shiver with alarm. Long ago, when his father heaved him up on his shoulders and took him riding on the white horse, Mustafa would be scared stiff. But his father would be afraid too, though he never showed it. Even the horse would be quaking . . . At first, Ismail Agha had not believed in the bleeding mulberry tree, nobody in the village believed it, but Mustafa had seen it. Maybe in a dream, maybe . . . The village children had dreamed of it too like Mustafa, then the women, Mother Hava first, then the old people, the men, and all had been scared stiff. People had taken turns to watch, night after night, and though no one actually saw the rivers of blood, they all believed it in the end. Even that bandit, Zalimoglu, heard of it up in his mountain lair and he was mad with rage. "Even if all the trees bleed night and day," he said, "even if the rocks and stones, the grass and streams run with blood, I'm going to butcher all the Memik Aghas there and all the Memik Aghas in the world, parents and kin, down to the last one. I've made a vow to root out the evil ones in this world."

Mustafa looked at his father. Ismail Agha was always afraid of something, some calamity, death perhaps, but Mustafa never felt so safe as when he was by his side. Today, as he bent over Mustafa, there was no trace of anxiety on his face. "Come my Mustafa, come my brave son," he said. He drew him up to his bosom. Mustafa threw his arms round his neck and kissed him. His father smelled so good, like the bees, the honey bees. There were two smells Mustafa adored, his father's which never failed to hearten him, and that of the bees. "We're going up to the castle."

Far to the south the snow-white clouds called sails were swelling up into the sky and gliding inland as the south wind gathered force. Ismail Agha made Mustafa put on his blue pin-striped trousers, which had been carefully ironed, his white shirt of pure Bursa silk and his best patent-leather shoes. Then he took him by the hand and led the way up to the castle ruins. There, in the shadow of the huge crags that dropped in a sheer dizzy descent beneath the castle, was a long dark cave, its mouth wide and lined with smooth red-veined rock, and from its depths at times, there issued an eerie soughing moan. Swarms of bats inhabited it, hanging by their feet, upside down, and at night, it was well known, if they caught a child they would bleed him white. The crags were strewn with children's bones, so they said . . . Mustafa, and all the other children too, were terrified of this lowering cave that panted like a giant, shaking the crags and the ruins. Whenever he passed along on his way to the fields, he would close his eyes and run for his life and never stop until he reached the fields, his heart in his mouth, bathed in sweat, trembling in all his limbs. Then, looking back at the steep precipice, the majestic castle fort above and the tenebrous cave, he would break into a song of relief and walk on through the growing grain towards their own field at Adaja. Like Mustafa, like all the children, the grown-ups too shivered as they walked along the path beneath the cave, only they were careful not to show their fear.

Salman had followed them and when they came to the shadow of the crags he went up a little way towards the castle and settled in his usual place on a stone shaped like a step, his rifle clasped tight in his hands, his eyes fixed on the distant Gavur Mountains. In the afternoon, when the south wind was blowing, it was pleasantly cool up here in the shadow of the crags. The wind carried the scent of dried thyme and sage and asphodels, of scorched earth and grain. Here Mustafa and his father too forgot the village and their troubles. It was as though they had drifted into another world, a world composed of scents and flavours.

Ismail Agha always made his ablutions before coming up, so he could settle at once for his *namaz* prayers on the same flat rock which he first brushed clean of pebbles and grasses. Salman would sit on there, quite still, never letting go of his rifle. Now and again, as though impelled by a spring, he would bounce up and take a few turns around the rocks at a running pace, his binoculars wobbling, his long nielloed daggers dangling against his legs, the silver, gilt and bronze of the bandoliers sparkling in the sun. Then he would take up his post again, impassive, still as a statue.

While Ismail Agha said his prayers or afterwards, as he sat leaning against a rock, silent, lost in his thoughts, his hairy chest bared to the breeze, Mustafa played with the grasshoppers, the bees, the swallow chicks, there were so many swallow nests among the crags and Mustafa could easily clamber up and play with the fledglings, some still downy and featherless with yellow bills, some already feathered and ready to start flying. Often, he would come upon young swallows which had fallen from their nests in attempting to fly, some at their last gasp, others with wings outstretched as they tried to rise again. Some days there were so many of them that Mustafa got quite exhausted having to carry them all back to their nests. As he played, Mustafa never stopped singing. He would invent songs about the eagles in their eyries, the swallows and their chicks, the horned rattlesnakes that ate the chicks, the half-burnt mulberry tree that spurted blood, the bat-infested cave, the saint's shrine on the mountain top . . . One Hidrellez day, the whole village, dressed to the nines, had walked all morning to reach the shrine and there they had offered sacrifices and prayed and sung and danced, while five minstrels played the *saz*. That day Mustafa had not stirred from the minstrels' side, his eyes intent on the fingers flying over the strings of the instruments. Most of all he had loved the *saz* of Minstrel Rahmi who came from Yarpuz village, for its body was inlaid with mother-of-pearl which glinted bluely in the sunlight. Never would he forget Minstrel Rahmi, his long slim fingers, his tall frame, his dark beautiful face that broke into dimples when he smiled, his strong clear voice, the ancient laments like a cry of grief, the jolly songs that set one's feet a-dancing, and ever since as he improvised his songs he had tried to imitate the minstrel's voice.

His father had begun to perform his prayers and while Salman, his head held high, stared straight ahead, Mustafa sang a song about Mount Düldül with a recurrent refrain which he had improvised. Come, he said, walk over, oh mountain, come and sit right here between us and that castle . . . He never pronounced Salman's name, but what he meant was, come and sit between Salman and us, let him remain behind, in a ravine, deep, unscalable.

Several ranges of blue hills of varying height stretched between Mount Düldül and the castle on the crags. Beyond these hills, the mountain rose, a tall pink spire, coppery, streaked with red on one side, its sharp graceful peak enveloped in a pink and blue haze, cloudless, snowless, like a wisp of smoke rising to the sky. Its flanks broadened as they came to rest on the blue hills and its valleys were dark and shadowy, fraught with mystery and magic. The mountain seemed to advance and recede, pink, mauve, now huge, now a tiny reflection on the wings of the glistening scarab beetle that Mustafa had caught. At times it vanished in the haze and next its silhouette was mirrored in the river and it flowed along through the blue of the plain in a torrent of light at a crazy speed, then suddenly it was back in its place again, on the far side of the hills, trembling and smoking in a copper haze.

Salman also sang when he was alone, his wild throaty voice, surprising in one of so short a stature, raising echoes from the mountains. He sang in a language no one understood in these parts, not even the Circassians or the Kurds, songs that made you want to weep. That filled you with sadness and melancholy . . .

Bird Memet, Mustafa's friend, thinks himself brave! Indeed, when he loses his temper, oh mother, just let him not get mad! He can jump at a man's throat and kill him. He's afraid of nothing, not of the burnt mulberry tree, or Zalimoglu, or the ravine with the dead body, he wouldn't shut his eyes, that one, and run for his life as he passes in front of the cave below the castle, oh no, but of Salman he lives in dread. At the very sight of him, he looks for a hole to hide in. It is Salman's hands he fears most, those rugged hands twice the size of his head, and also his feet which break away in the night and scale the steep crags all by themselves, bodyless . . . As for Mustafa, why should he fear Salman who guards their house and keeps watch over his father so his enemies shouldn't kill him? . . . If there is one person Salman loves, it is Ismail Agha, and Ismail Agha trusts him implicitly. So why should Mustafa be afraid of Salman? But everyone is, everyone! Those eyes that look at nothing, not even at the mountain opposite, vitreous eyes, bloodshot, spinning like tops in their sockets, and when he talks – but who ever heard him say anything – the words roll in his mouth like grunts . . . Every day, every single day he goes down into the valley behind the mountain, his rifle in his hand, and keeps shooting from morning till night, he can hit a coin in the air, he can hit anything the eye can see, he destroys all the swallow nests he comes across and wrings the necks of the chicks, he even shoots them down from the telephone lines, and sometimes at midnight under the moon – Bird Memet has seen it with his own eyes, and the other children too – Salman whips out his daggers and performs a strange wild dance, he plants the daggers into the earth, stands on his head and spins around, on his head, on his hands, then falls back splayed on the ground, bounces up high in the air, kneels, straightens, curls himself into a ball and rolls over the cactuses, creaking like a spinning-wheel, he plunges the dagger into his belly and not a drop of blood comes out, his feet race up to the castle and he comes flying through the air after them, his legs, his whole body breaking into pieces and joining up again . . . His jutting cheekbones, his yellow stiff blond hair like nails stuck into his skull . . . Bird Memed fears him, so does Mother Hava and the bandit Zalimoglu and so does his father's enemy, the one Salman lies in wait for, should he come to kill Ismail Agha, the one who rides in a motorcar . . . Mustafa has seen it . . . Well, even that man fears Salman. Everyone does, even the rufous-winged eagles up on the crags don't dare to steal the chicks for fear of him. On summer nights, from up on the *chardak* Bird Memet has watched all Salman's antics. He has seen Salman kissing that bay filly, leading her in the moonlight behind the cactus hedge, making love to her, the bay filly fainting with bliss, kissing Salman, licking him. Madly in love they are those two . . . Bird Memet knows about these things, he keeps awake at night and spies on his mother and father. He knows everything. He's not like Mustafa.

Ismail Agha lifted his hands, palms up, murmured one last prayer and rose to his feet, a tall slim figure. Brushing his clothes, he turned to Mustafa. The boy was playing with a hard-winged green and red spotted scarab. Mustafa was the only child in the village to own real toys. His father, his father's friends from the big town, that man with the motorcar who wanted to kill him, all of them showered Mustafa with gifts. Once someone had brought him a large mosque made of sugar, all green, a replica of the Süleymaniye Mosque in Istanbul. Mustafa had licked at the tip of a minaret now and again, but by the time he got half-way down one of the minarets he had enough. He invited all the children to come and lick too, and so they did, stretching out in turns, group after group, and in no time there was no trace of the green sugar mosque.

Ismail Agha settled down in his favourite spot, a wide rock shaped like a chair, mauve, red-veined, spotted with green on its northern edge. From here he had a sweeping view of the white powdery road cleaving through the flat fields below, of the Adaja crags like a tiny island in their midst, of the other road that coiled snake-like around the mountain, the purpling spar of Kirmaji village's Hyacinth Rock, the Gökburun cliffs mirrored in the river below, and Osmaniyé town, always under a cloud of dust, the meandering Jeyhan River on the level plain, Toprakkalé Castle, Telkubbé, the white clouds sailing in from the Mediterranean, Sakarjalik village with its dark cluster of trees, Tejirli borough, and Yeniköy, the village of immigrants with its slender minaret, everything clear to the smallest detail.

Mustafa came over and sat beside Ismail Agha. But his large eyes were troubled and sad. Salman was always behind them like a shadow. Wherever they went, whatever they did, in the village or in the town, even when they went visiting or attended some festivity, he was there at their heels, his rifle in his hand, revolvers and all, his eyes fixed in a wide obstinate gaze or spinning wildly as though they would pop out of their sockets. He never left them alone. Mustafa knew that Salman was a small man, he had seen him naked many times, just a puny little thing. But at night, and particularly in the moonlight he grew and grew and turned into a giant. Even on winter nights, in the blustery north wind, in the beating rain, Salman would stubbornly stick to his post in the yard, never bothering to shelter under the eaves of the mansion. There were mornings when they found him there frozen stiff, teeth chattering, and had to wrap him up in blankets and make him swallow numberless glasses of tea before he could recover.

When appointing him as his bodyguard Ismail Agha had put Salman to many a severe test. Out in the rain, in the icy wind – some nights can be bitterly cold in the Chukurova – even if he was sick, burning with fever, he never once fell asleep, his attention never relaxed, he never failed to fire at any shadow that moved outside the yard. No one had died, but at least three men had been hit like this and lamed for life.

Ismail Agha loved Salman as much as he did Mustafa, perhaps even more, Mustafa knew it, yet he wasn't jealous. Why should he be? Ismail Agha was not Salman's real father. No, jealous he was not, but that did not prevent his being afraid. One night, sick with fear at the sight of Salman, Bird Memet had bawled out loud, I'm frightened Mustafa, I'm afraid of that man, and he had thrown up! Salman haunted the villagers even in their dreams, especially the children, and in the morning, before daybreak those children who had dreamed of him in the night would gather on the shingle at the riverside under the shelter of a steep bank and whisper their dreams to each other, but without ever mentioning Salman's name. How could Mustafa help dreaming too? And ever in these dreams Salman would be astride the bay filly driving her straight at the children and trampling them, most of all Mustafa, who would be mangled to bits. And just as the children were picking up the pieces of his body from the dust and dung, Mustafa would wake up screaming in anguish . . . Then the bay filly would speed to the top of the crags and on to Anavarza, riding through the skies, and Salman would jump off and, clinging to her rump, quivering, his legs dangling in the air, he would mount her while they glided between a seething mass of horned rattlesnakes, and the snakes would sail alongside, flame-red, coiling and uncoiling in long ribbons, and the bay filly would open her legs wide, her rump crimpling, fainting with plea-sure . . . But Salman withdraws his penis, a huge thing, large as a horse's, and the bay filly turns again and again, her eyes sad, questioning, and suddenly she snaps at Salman's penis and tears it off. Blood rains down, all the villagers rush out to watch the blood streaming from Salman's severed penis, very black in the bay filly's jaws. The people and houses, the mosque, the white castle ruins on the purple crags, the flowing river, all are steeped in blood.

Jeyhan River is aflame, flowing in a torrent of light, illuminating the whole Chukurova plain like a thousand suns, and from this brightness, from among the billowing clouds Salman springs forward, stark naked. He brandishes his daggers, drip-ping with blood, and performs a crazy dance, then returns to the house and stands at his usual post, stiff as a poker. Aghast, the

27

villagers take to their heels. They lie low in their houses, while overhead a dark horde of rapacious eagles, wing to wing, clamorous, their strident calls rending the skies, rise over the purple crags and sweep on to Anavarza and Yilankalé, right up to the white clouds over the Mediterranean, then swerve back like a seething stormcloud. Louder and louder they screech, deafening echoes rebound from the sultry crags, shaking the mountain to its base, and all at once they swoop down over the village, a shower of eagles, blanketing the banks of the river, the houses, the mosque, everything. Mustafa, Memet, the other children are crushed under the eagles, stifling, drowned in blood.

Suddenly, an eerie silence spreads over the whole world. The eagles are mute. Not a rustle, not even the hum of an insect . . . Only a bleak lifeless desolation, a pulsing silence, emptier than any void, that goes on and on, a month, a year, a thousand years . . . Then, like a thunderbolt slashing the sky as with a giant razor, a rooster crows on the rim of the world. The eagles are roused. They surge up, wing to wing, in a churning mass, breaking, gathering again, then making off for the Gavur Mountains. And Salman dons his *shalvar*-trousers, thrusts his penis inside and rigs himself up with his bandoliers, binoculars, revolvers and daggers. Brandishing a dagger that drips with blood, he pounces on the rooster, the singing rooster with glossy red, green and blue feathers, but the rooster escapes, it perches high up on the castle, flaps its wings and starts crowing again, louder than ever, and all the roosters in the world flap their wings too and break into a loud chorus of crowing, drowning all other sounds. The boundless blue plain swarms with roosters, so does the river, it flows in a blaze of blue, green and red feathers. And soon the eagles come thronging in from the Gavur Mountains, from Anavarza, from Mount Düldül . . . They swoop down gathered into tight balls, thousands streaking the sky, and charge at the roosters. Eagles and roosters grapple in a confused battle, crowing, screeching, feathers and pinions flying in the dust, and everything is plunged in darkness. Along comes Salman, his dagger held ready to strike. He is huge again, his shadow falls on the castle walls, it reaches across the river to the shores of the Mediterranean. First he slashes off the heads of the roosters, then of the eagles and casts them over the village. The severed heads shriek louder than ever as they swirl blindly through the air, bodyless heads, headless bodies . . . Warm blood rains over the village, feathers, severed heads crowing . . . Suddenly, a strong wind springs up, driving away heads, feathers and all in a dark blood-red turmoil, and Salman, tensing himself, swings his dagger. Sparkling, a stream of light in its wake, the dagger flies straight at the tall cactus in the yard where Ismail Agha is standing. Ismail Agha dodges behind the bush, the dagger pursues him, he races round and round the spiny cactus and the long long dagger whistles after him. Ever more quickly they go, in a shower of white spines, and the cactus bursts into bloom, yellow, orange, blue and red flowers adorn it from top to bottom, and all around the flowering cactus and the fleeing Ismail Agha, the dagger weaves a web of light, glowing, razor-sharp, impenetrable. Just then, a swarm of bees emerge from their hives, they are slashed in two, they drop to the ground in mounds, knee-deep, they cover the surface of the water. Ever more quickly Ismail Agha hurtles round the cactus, the dagger after him, and the swarm of bees too, thick as a wall, filling the air with their smell, bleeding, their wings quivering in a last shimmering agony. Speeding in its course the dagger traces long red streaks of bleeding bees, dead bee-wings, glittering, sharp, razor-edged . . . The cactus bush glows, streaked with red, lost in a scintillation of bee wings, incandescent. On, on the dagger flies, razor-sharp, fulgurating, drawing nearer and nearer to the roots of the cactus. A hundred daggers are after Ismail Agha now, a thousand, and rooster heads flutter among the daggers, dripping with blood. A loud buzzing fills the air as the daggers slash through the cloud of bees, then rise into the sky shuttling back and forth at a dizzying speed from the mountain peak to the castle.

Ismail Agha is growing tired now. Help, he cries desperately, help . . . All the world's roosters start crowing again, to and fro they go from the steel-blue mountain to the burning castle, and the daggers, all aflame, swish past severing their heads. Rufous eagles spread overhead, the sky is red, a crystal red. The purple mountain is overgrown with orange flowers, fragrant, intoxicating. Eagles gather in the sky, ever more of them, very black, and the world is plunged in darkness. Boom, boom goes the mountain. Boom go the orange-flowering crags. The other mountains begin to move, the Binboga and Gavur Mountains, Aladag, Demirkazik, Beritdag, Mount Düldül, they all come and stand in a circle around the village. Boom, boom the mountains resound, aflame like a forge. Louder, deafening the crowing of the roosters . . . Ismail Agha flees. Help, help! Ismail Agha's screams rise above the crowing of the roosters, the rumbling of the mountains, the whistle of the dagger, speeding, reaching him, boring into his breast, the flaming blade piercing his heart. Again and again the dagger stabs him. Ismail Agha shrieks, he tries to escape with the flaming dagger still stuck in his chest, but the mountains block his way, he turns back, he collapses at the foot of the cactus bush, dead, and his blood spurts out, green over the cactus leaves, while the flowery flanks of the mountains close in around him. And Salman bursts into Ismail Agha's house, he stabs the inmates, one after the other they fall down beside Ismail Agha's corpse in the last agonies of death. Salman rushes out again, mad with rage. All the world's roosters come fluttering back in a riot of dazzling colours. They perch on the mountain, crowing with one voice as Salman rampages through the village, striking his dagger at whoever he comes across. The dead lie strewn on the mountainside, shrivelled dry among the sun-baked crags. Salman keeps watch over them, sitting on his usual rock, his rifle in his hand. Clouds of green flies swarm over the dead bodies and, overhead, eagles are wheeling. An eagle swoops down, its wings drawn in tight, tears off a morsel of flesh and makes away. Salman sits on there, unheeding, staring straight ahead, and soon only skeletons are left lying about the mountainside.

Mustafa is cowering by his father's corpse beneath the cactuses, his skin tingling, steeped in blood, the blood caking on his body. He presses ever closer into the roots of the cactuses, and the bees weave an ever-thickening curtain between him and Salman. Suddenly, all is hushed, the curtain of bees fades away, the cactuses gather in their flowers and glide off snake-like into the crags, squirting spines, flowers and bees as they go, and Mustafa is exposed naked on a flat endless plain, desolate, not the hum of a bee, not the flutter of a swallow's wings. Then it is that Salman pounces on him and grips his throat. Mustafa's eyes are bulging, his body rigid. But he shakes himself free and runs for his life. Salman cannot catch up with him now. Mustafa streaks along the plain like the wind. Salman hurls his daggers after him, they whizz past his ears, only just missing him, and hit the rocks striking sparks as from a forge. Mustafa races on in a flurry of sparks, the rocks scraping his hands and feet, tearing his clothes, leaving him naked, bleeding. He hides behind a rock, but the daggers, leaving blazing trails, weaving sheer nets of red flame, surround him, their steely flashing blades pointed at him and he is caught in their midst, spinning like a top in a shower of sparks, unable to breathe. Up there, on a burning red rock, Salman laughs, he dances with glee, he mocks Mustafa, thumbs his nose at him, thrusts his tongue out, then leaping onto a horse, he starts shooting, a hail of flaming bullets . . .

Mustafa was taut to straining point.

"You, Memet, you're not afraid of anyone, are you?"

"Not of anyone, no," Bird Memet declared. "Not even of Zalimoglu, not even of Sal . . . Sal . . ." He stopped short.

Autumn was drawing on. The odour of sun-scorched grass and wild thyme was stronger now, more pungent. From the first days of August to the end of October, up there in the shade of the crags, the south wind that started early in the afternoon blew on till midnight, cool and gentle and laden with scents. And all through the summer, Ismail Agha would take Mustafa up to the castle ruins. He would first kneel on his usual flat slabstone among the wild thyme and perform his *namaz* prayers. Then he would sit with his back to a rock and, closing his eyes, he would start singing in a soft undertone. And Mustafa would crouch at his knees, listening entranced to the long-drawn-out sorrowful laments that his father sang in Kurdish and that were so different from the songs people sang here. There were days when father and son would sing on till nightfall, and Salman too would sit quite still a little further away, lost in a dream. Years ago, when they first came to settle in this village, it was Salman that Ismail Agha took by the hand to bring him up here. Then, too, he would lean against this same rock and start to sing and Salman would close his eyes and listen, spellbound. Salman also called Ismail Agha father, like Mustafa did. He took him for his own father . . .

Ismail Agha was quite capable of forgetting to eat or drink or even to make his *namaz* once he started singing. He would go on and on late into the night, and Salman would sit there, clasping his rifle and swaying backwards and forwards endlessly. And when Ismail Agha and Mustafa roused themselves from their trance, the moon would more often than not be past its zenith. Shadows would be falling over the level plain from the castle and the crags, and the glittering river that cleaved through the plain, meandering in a flood of light, would seem broader, brimming over, licking the crest of the trees as it speeded down into the heart of the night.

On certain nights when the world was bathed in moonlight, Ismail Agha would stop short on the stony path leading down to the village. He would turn back to their place up on the crags and stand awhile contemplating the distant shimmering slopes of the hills. Suddenly, he would sit down again, leaning against the rock which was pleasantly cool now. Salman, once more, would take up his post, crouched over his rifle, like an ancient sculpture, his shadow lengthening over the asphodels and mauve rock thistles.

There was no more singing now. Ismail Agha was quite silent, he never uttered a word, and Mustafa, his head on his father's knees, lulled by the stridulation of cicadas, was soon fast asleep. Bats flitted through the night. Once in a while an owl hooted in the mountain above. From the plain came the yawling of jackals and croaking of frogs. Now and then, the storks, clustering on the bastion of the castle like a white cloudbank, clattered their beaks all together in a fearful din. Towards daybreak eagles started up from their eyries on the snow-capped crags. Round and round the mountain top they wheeled, wing to wing, in hundreds, then glided off towards the Mediterranean. And after them rock doves soared into the air, only to plunge down abruptly like stones cast onto the plain. Mustafa lifted his head from his father's knee and stared dazedly about him. As his eyes rested on Salman, he started and shivered. Quickly, he looked away to the pale blue rise of the Gavur Mountains. Their whitening peaks reached high into the sky, gently swaying, and above, in a coruscating brightness, the dawn star shed its light over the earth. Wonderingly he gazed at this prodigious spinning ball of light. How often he saw it in his dreams, irradiating the level plain, the mountains, the whole world . . . But soon the first rays of the sun had struck the mountain peaks, and the brilliant star was fading to a blurred umbra, cool shadows stretched along the plain, the rare trees looming larger in this brief interval between moonlight and daylight. The hundreds of threshing floors dotting the plain stood out, bright green among the vaporous blue of the earth. Up on the castle the storks were quietly spreading their wings and drifting down into the plain. From the village came a confusion of sounds, crowing and mooing and neighing, carts creaking, harness bells tinkling, churns swinging . . . A few late owls hooted lengthily at the brightening east. The gentle dawn breeze wafted in odours of thyme, of sun-impacted wet earth and rock, of mauve thistles and dried asphodel stalks. It filled Mustafa with bliss. Carried away by some strange enchantment, forgetting his father and the dark statue of fear that was Salman, he rushed away, skipping over the crags, revelling in the first light of day, transported into another world. On and on until the cry of partridges sounded from the distant valleys and that of the francolins from the plain and his father was calling to him . . . Then suddenly the sun appeared, a perfect red orb, orange in the centre, white, deep, settling for an instant on the topmost peak of the Gavur Mountains, drowning the plain and the mountains in brightness. The River Jeyhan surged from its bed, winding above in the air like a torrent of light and, as the trees and shadows and hills gleamed and glinted, the sun tore itself away from the mountain peak and rose in the sky, drying the night dews, and the odours of thyme and other grasses became more pungent, burning the throat.

Autumn butterflies, orange, blue, large as a hand, flitted aimlessly up and down, sniffing at the crags, singly at first, then in couples, sheering in the sky, and the swallows started their twittering revelry, darting arrow-like right before them, scattering on the flanks of the mountains among the parched yellow grass, the dried asphodels and the green patches of holly oaks between the keen-edged crags.

In the dawning brightness Ismail Agha was so handsome, so dark and tall and straight, sturdy as a plane tree, such a safeguarding presence that Mustafa's heart leaped with sheer joy. He raced this way and that like a creature demented, shouting, singing, turning somersaults, playing hidie-hole all by himself, hiding in the cleft of a rock, then seeking and finding himself, until his eyes rested on Salman and his spirits sank like a punctured balloon. "I'm not afraid," he shouted at the top of his voice, and the sound echoed back from the castle and the mountain in lengthening waves, not – not – not – fraid – fraid – fraid . . . Mustafa was making a game of it. "Of no one," one – one . . . Then he stopped, recalling the roosters with slit throats as the crowing of the village cocks grew louder, echoing, re-echoing . . . Trembling in all his limbs, Mustafa screamed, "I'm afraid of no one, no one. Bird Memet's not afraid either." His cries mingled with the crowing of the roosters.

"None of the boys are afraid."

"Wiggler's not afraid . . . The Tick . . . Minstrel Ali . . . They're not afraid. My mother's not afraid, my father's not afraid. No one, not the roosters, or the swallows, the chicks, the flies, the bees . . . The bees . . . bees . . ."

Round and round he whirled, Mustafa, with outstretched arms like a dervish, yelling himself hoarse until his father caught him up in his arms.

"Mustafa, what are you doing? What's the matter?" The boy's hands and feet were frozen. Ismail Agha cradled him in a warm embrace. "Of course my son's afraid of no one. Why should he be when I'm here? My lion, my brave son . . ."

At last Mustafa calmed down. "I was just playing, father . . ."

"What kind of a game is that?"

"It's a game of being scared . . . We all play it in the village, like we play hidie-hole in the night."

"Are you afraid? Is there something that's frightened you and Bird Memet and the other boys?"

"I'm not afraid, I tell you," Mustafa almost shouted. "Bird Memet isn't at all afraid, not of anything, not even of him."

"Of whom?"

"No one . . ."

Ismail Agha did not press him further.

I'm afraid of nothing, I'm afraid of no one, Mustafa sang to himself, not of the snails, not of the centipedes, or the worms, or the black toads . . . Not of the bats that bleed children white, not even of the jinn in the old graveyard. Not of cats and flies and butterflies . . . Not of the swallow chicks . . . All the creatures he could think of, from the tiniest insect to the wild boar, all went into Mustafa's song. He was afraid of no one, nothing, not of the day, not of the night.

Ismail Agha took the boy's hand and led him down through the Narrow Pass. This pass was so deeply ensconced between the rock walls that only one person at a time could go through. On one of the rocks was an engraving in an unknown script, the same as on the rock face of a cave high up on the mountain where a sparkling spring dribbled lazily. No one knew what it was. Maybe some ancient magic spell, or the clue to some long-buried treasure . . .

On turning left after the defile, they reached the crags above their house and when they came to the pomegranate tree below they could catch already the odour of cooking, of boiling tea, warm milk and freshly churned butter. Mustafa was suddenly very hungry. Yet, when he looked back and saw Salman only a few paces behind as though tied to them by some inseverable chain, his mouth went dry and a lump settled in his throat. Salman would take his meals with them, but Mustafa would not once lift his head to look at him. Quickly, his hands working like a shuttle he would gulp down his food and slip away, unnoticed, making straight for Bird Memet's house. And the first thing he said was: "I'm not afraid Memet, not at all."

"I'm not afraid either," Memet replied quickly.

3

LAKE VAN IS surrounded by the mountains of Süphan, Nemrut and Esrük whose peaks, snow-capped all the year round, shed a white radiance on the mirror of the lake. Its shores as well as the mountain slopes are entirely bare, and so are the plains of Muradiyé, Patnos, Chaldiran and Van that stretch beyond.

The village was situated on the banks of the lake, just below Mount Esrük, at the approach to the Sor Valley. A long file of man-tall stones marched along this valley from Esrük to the lake. All the dwellings were underground. One descended into them through an opening like the mouth of a well. The sheep and goats, cattle and horses also went in through this entrance and slept inside along with the inmates. On freezing winter nights their breath warmed the whole house and their dried dung served as fuel for cooking. There was only one habitation above the ground and that was the Bey's two-storied, sixteen-roomed mansion, built of well-hewn stones culled from ancient edifices.

The Bey was a handsome, dark-complexioned man, very tall, with broad shoulders and a long white beard. His brothers and relatives resided in strange houses half buried in the earth, with no windows at all, only a largish hole on the mud roof which served both to let in the light and let out the smoke from the hearth.

The Bey had studied in Istanbul and Salonika. His brothers, too, were literate men, which was rare in these parts. Ismail Agha was the Bey's nephew, the eldest of three brothers, stalwart youths renowned all over the lake country for their good looks. Ismail Agha's father had sent him to high school in Van. He had felt oppressed, somehow, in this city of goldsmiths and jewellers, set right on the shores of the lake and surrounded by walls of sun-dried brick. Surmounting the city was the ancient citadel, its bastions of the same solid sun-dried brick as the city walls. Hundreds of years, thousands perhaps, had done nothing to impair these earthen walls and bastions, they had only grown sturdier with time.

Hüseyin Bey, the Bey's youngest brother, was a student at the Military Academy in Istanbul. He was Ismail Agha's only friend in the village and just as handsome. Together they would go riding to take part in a game of *jerid* and hunt for deer in the mountains. It was not only ties of blood that linked them, their friendship dated from their years at high school in Van where they had both stayed at the house of a relative. They were closer than brothers and had not parted until the day Hüseyin Bey left for Istanbul. After that Ismail Agha never set foot in Van again. He remained in the village, tilling his fields, growing melons and water-melons and hunting the deer. He would return from the hunt up on Mount Esrük, with huge-antlered deer, sometimes more than a dozen, and these were brought down by the mountain people. With the help of the village youths Ismail Agha would skin them and distribute the meat in equal parts to all the families in the village. Even the Bey never got more than his share. Winter was the season for hunting partridges. They flocked in from far and wide to shelter in the crevices of Sor Valley. However, it was not everyone who could tackle the drifts of snow that blocked the valley during the long winter months or brave the blizzards and the violent storms that never let up and could be heard way off from the shores of the lake like the rumble of distant thunder. But nothing could deter Ismail Agha. Penetrating into Sor Valley with a few dauntless companions, he soon uncovered coveys of partridges huddled in a shelter or scattered over the snow like buckshot. He and his men advanced towards them waving their arms and the partridges started up and alighted some five hundred paces further off. The men flushed them again and this time the birds settled less than two hundred paces away. At the third go, the partridges were unable to fly and Ismail Agha and his friends could gather them without further ado. Back in the village it would be a feast day. From every home rose the odour of partridges being broiled over acrid smouldering dried dung, and greasy fumes swirled through the air mingling with the smell of snow and of Lake Van which smelled like no other lake, not swampy at all, but more like a white-foamed spring surging from gnarled roots in a pine forest.

In the summer the village moved up into the high pastures of Mount Esrük, leaving Lake Van far below with its many shades of blue, shot with evanescent streaks of orange, and the snow-white reflection of Mount Süphan, and also Patnos plain with its flocks of cranes, its pelicans, its tall gracile poplars, and the snakes that swarmed in thousands in the white heat of the summer.

Long black tents of goat-hair were pitched on the plateaux between the tarns that abounded with red and blue speckled trout. The villagers, men and women, were expert at fishing for trout, for they had been doing it since their childhood. They caught so many that they could not eat them all and had to salt them away in barrels to take back down to the village.

A thousand and one flowers bloomed on Mount Esrük, the grass was knee-deep, a cool breeze blew constantly and gentle sunlight bathed the meadows. Musicians with pipes and drums flocked into the uplands and every day was a day of festivity. Half the villagers were Armenians, but they spoke Kurdish too and, until the killings and enmity, lived in perfect harmony with their neighbours. Moslem Kurds would dye eggs and cele-brate Easter together with the Armenians and the Armenians in their turn offered sacrifices along with the Kurds during the *Kurban Bairam*. So it had been for centuries. The Armenians would worship their own god in the mosque, and Moslems would perform the *namaz* in the church. For Ismail the time of the killings was the most painful in all his life. He could never forget his neighbour Onnik's face, stunned, distressed, incredulous . . .

"Save me, Ismail," he had cried, his eyes wide with fear. "They're after me. To kill! Our own Bald Riza! Riza with whom we grew up together! Riza who spent more time in our house than in his own . . . And now he wants to kill me!"

Ismail Agha had tried to reassure him, but Onnik was much too frightened and, that night while the household was asleep, he fled into the mountains.

"Why on earth d'you want to kill Onnik?" Ismail Agha had asked Riza.

"I'll kill him. I'll find him even if he's hiding in the pit of hell," was all he could get out of the man. He lost his temper. "If you kill him, then I'll kill you too," he shouted. "Just you try!"

* * *

On the flowering meadows youths and maidens, Kurdish and Armenian, dressed in bright-coloured clothes, lined up arm in arm for the *gövend*. Their bodies moved with incredible litheness, with joy and pride to the slow rhythm of this ancient dance. It was always Ismail Agha who led the dance, a handsome figure, tall and willowy, his large eyes shining like black diamonds in his swarthy face. And all the people of the uplands came to watch him and joined in the dance, swaying like a slumbering sea, delicate as a wisp of smoke trembling up into the sky . . .

Famous bards came from far and wide to visit the Bey's majestic seven-poled tent. They were installed on a throne-like elevation outside the tent and everyone crowded around on brightly-printed felt mats to listen to the telling of age-old epics. The most renowned of these bards was Abdalé Zeyniki, the Bey of Malazgirt's own private minstrel. Apart from his own ballads and songs, he recited traditional epics like no other bard ever could. Blind until the age of sixty, Abdalé Zeyniki had suddenly recovered his sight, and this he attributed to a miracle, which he celebrated in a ballad sung by all the minstrels of the region. The Bey had an immense respect for two bards. One was Abdalé Zeyniki and the other the Armenian, Hachik. He would rise to greet them, which he did for no one else, and never sit down until they had done so first. Indeed, these two bards were revered in villages and encampments from Kars to Van, from Van to Diyarbakir, Erzinjan and Erzurum. The household or village which they visited would ever after boast of their coming. Even Ismail Agha, the most modest of men, would proudly recall Abdalé Zeyniki's stay in their house. "This homestead," he would say, "has been honoured with the presence of the Abdal, the great Zeyniki . . ."

When Hüseyin Bey arrived from Istanbul to spend the summer in the high pastures, he would quickly shed his black city suit, so outlandish in these parts, to don the wide trousers and waistcoat of the local costume called the *shal shapik* and join with Ismail Agha in the merrymaking.

Were they happy, these people? Ismail Agha? Or unhappy? Such a thought never crossed their minds. Wars and massacres they had known, famines and pestilences that decimated men and beasts, and that was perhaps for them the meaning of unhappiness. But even then they still knew how to laugh and though there was much suffering, there were just as many joys.

Unhappy was a word Ismail Agha heard for the first time from the lips of Hüseyin Bey.

"I'm unhappy, Ismail," Hüseyin Bey said with a deep sigh one day after he had come from Istanbul.

Ismail Agha was puzzled. "You're not ill, are you?" he asked.

"Ill? No," Hüseyin Bey replied. "I wish I was . . . Consumptive, leprous, anything . . . I'm unhappy."

Ismail Agha concluded that this was a kind of sickness, and worse than any other. Indeed, as from that day Hüseyin Bey did not go back to Istanbul. He kept out of the village activities and was never heard to speak to anyone again, not even Ismail Agha.

East of the village were some tall crags that fell steeply into the lake. Each day Hüseyin Bey would get up before dawn, boil his milk and tea and eat his breakfast all alone. In the winter he would don a thick shepherd's cloak, in the summer his blue *shal shapik*, then he would make off for the crags, there to sit till nightfall, motionless, his huge dark eyes fixed steadfastly on the lake, and when it was too dark to see he would return home, eat the meal that was kept ready for him in front of the hearth and go straight to bed. Such had been Hüseyin Bey's whole existence for five or six years. Neither the snakes that swarmed over the crags in the scorching summer heat, nor the frost that cracked the rocks, the snows that hid even the telegraph poles, and the black *bora* that uprooted the trees could make him stir from his post on the crags. Vast as a sea, situated at five thousand four hundred feet above sea level and surrounded by mountains, Lake Van is sometimes swept by tidal bores, and waves as high as minarets beat against its shores. None of this seemed to touch the man nailed to his rock. At the most, as though on some blind impulse, he would move a little higher up the crags when a water spout sucked at the shore.

And so the story went . . .

Istanbul is a city on the sea, just like Van city, with many islands too. One day, on one of these islands, an island like Aghtamar Island on Lake Van, Hüseyin met a girl and it was love at first sight for both of them. They made love, but suddenly the girl drew away and rushed straight into the sea. Hüseyin caught a glimpse of her hair floating on the water before she sunk away out of sight. After this he was unable to drag himself from that island. He remained there for months on end, his eyes glued to the spot where the girl had disappeared, and one day the girl's head rose out of the water. In a rush of emotion Hüseyin Bey fainted away and when he came to, there was not a trace of the girl. But he waited, for days, for months he waited and then at last she appeared again. This time Hüseyin Bey jumped into the water. He was unable to catch her, but she spoke to him. I am a fairy, she told him, and I love you true. Go to Van. There, in the lake I have a sister. I'll come and join her and, though I won't be able to get out of the water, I'll be there where you can see me every day from dawn to nightfall. After the sun sets I must go back to my father, the Peri King who lives in Van Castle . . . Hüseyin was overcome with joy. Van Lake is where I live, he said. I know, the girl said. Van is my home too, that's where I first saw you, on the steep crags below Van Castle, and when you left for Istanbul I followed you . . . So that is why Hüseyin Bey hurried back home. That is why each day when the east begins to pale he goes to the lake and the girl's head appears on the surface of the water, so beautiful that Hüseyin Bey can never have his fill of looking at her. And the fairy, too, is so enraptured with Hüseyin's handsome countenance that she remains there all day long, oblivious of waves and storms and water spouts.

For days on end the villagers flocked to the shores of the lake, stealthily they hid among the rocks, not to be seen by Hüseyin Bey, eagerly they waited and watched, but no one ever saw the beautiful head of the fairy. At last they gave up. "She's visible to none but her lover," they concluded, and left Hüseyin Bey and his fairy love to themselves.

Cranes in bevelled formation wing through the sky, shedding their shadow on the blue of the lake. At every moment of the day Lake Van is imbued with a wealth of colours. On a sudden, a lightning flash of orange shoots across the water from east to west and the whole lake is an orange dream on which rests the head of the fairy. Next, a flash of mauve tinges the lake. Sweeping white-foamed wavelets before it, it reaches the flanks of Mount Süphan and casts a mauve blanket over the richly-flowering Patnos plain. Sometimes the rippling surface of the lake is bright red on one half and deep blue on the other and sometimes the majestic shape of Mount Süphan with its snow-capped peak soaring far into the sky, is reflected on the lake in a white immaculate splendour that irradiates even the darkest night.

And there he sits, Hüseyin Bey, singing in an undertone. He

sings for his fairy love whose head only he can see on the water and he sings to the unending columns of cranes flying past, sometimes very low, their wings skimming the surface of the lake, sometimes soaring high into the vast blue sky. He sings to the red earth and green pastures of Mount Esrük, and the breeze blows down to him from the mountain, laden with the fragrance of a thousand and one flowers and grasses. His sad eyes are riveted on the lake and over his pale mournful face flickers the reflection of the ever-changing colours of the waters, now foaming and tempest-tossed, now smooth and calm as though no wind had ever touched them. And as the sun sets, colours and lights, rocks and flying cranes fade into the gloom and out of the night rise the cries of wild beasts and birds, the noise of many waters and the booming of the mountain.

One night, Hüseyin Bey gave ear to an officer who had lost both feet in the war and for the first time in many years he was shaken to the core.

"Defeated!" the officer was saying. "Ninety thousand men left there on the snows of Sarikamish! And most of them devoured by lice. By lice! It's the lice defeated the Turkish soldiers, not the Russians. Lice!" he shouted, and repeated in Arabic, in Kurdish, in Syriac. "The great Ottoman Empire eaten up by lice, finished!" He hid his face in his hands and wept, then went on with a bitter smile. "The battle of Sarikamish will go down in history as the battle where the Turks were vanquished by lice. Ninety thousand men lying there, dead on the snow. Run, my friends, get away from here, the Russian army is coming, burning, destroying, killing, and before it, shielding it, is its greatest weapon, swarms of lice. Quick, my friends, empty the village, for when they arrive they will leave nothing standing, no one alive . . ."

The Bey and his guests stared at him as though he had gone out of his mind. How could the great Ottoman army be defeated? It was inconceivable.

A few days later survivors of the routed Hamidiyé regiment entered the village and at once began to plunder and kill. It was terrible. The dregs of the Hamidiyé regiment, the last remaining soldiers of Enver Pasha, had turned into a wild desperate horde, hounded by lice and the Russian army. All over the mountain, deserters ravaged the villages, making away with the cattle, abducting the women, stealing their gold necklaces, bracelets and rings, and burning those villagers who tried to resist. And so it was everywhere in the eastern provinces, swarms of marauders pillaging and killing, and most of all it was the Yezidis and Alevis and Armenians that they killed. The villagers themselves were not always idle. They struck at these remnants of the Ottoman army whenever they could.

At the first burst of cannon to be heard from behind Mount Süphan the deserters took to their heels. But still the stragglers came, weary now, sick, wounded, all skin and bones, with nothing human left about them. Their ragged capes were stiff with blood.

Then one evening just before sunset a cannonball fell plumb into the hot water spring that flowed in the middle of the village. The waters gushed high into the air and a deep pit was formed that soon filled up with water. After this, cannonballs began to fall all over the place. Pandemonium broke loose, people screamed, cattle bellowed, horses neighed and there were many killed and wounded. People lay around with severed legs and arms. Nothing could be done to relieve them and they just bled to death.

From where he sat by the lake Hüseyin Bey could hear the burst of cannon, but he never stirred. For all he cared, the cannonballs that exploded near him might have been so many autumn leaves falling. Only at his appointed hour, after the sun had set, he rose, stood a while as he always did, his eyes fixed on the darkening waters, then set off for the village, oblivious of the shells that whistled and fell about him, striking up flames from the trembling soil and raising columns of water poplar-high from the lake.

The Bey came to meet him half-way. "My dear Hüseyin," he said very gently, as he took his hand and drew him along, "we have to leave this place tomorrow before daybreak. The enemy is advancing, burning the villages, killing everyone, young and old. Can't you hear the shells hitting our village? So many killed already . . . Tomorrow morning you must not go to the crags for we shall be leaving very early. Who knows," he sighed, "if we shall ever see our home again, our village, the lake, our high pastures . . ."

Darkness fell and the shelling stopped. But the villagers did not sleep. They spent the night gathering their belongings and loading the packs onto donkeys, horses, cows and oxen. When they finally set out at daybreak, the cannonade started again and soon after, the first of the enemy advance guard entered the village.

The Bey anxiously sought out Ismail Agha. "What am I to do?" he said. "Hüseyin's nowhere to be found."

"He must be there by the lake," Ismail Agha said.

"But I told him not to go! He knew we were leaving."

"Don't worry, uncle. It's on our way. I'll run and fetch him and catch up with you all."

Utter confusion reigned in the countryside. Long trains of fugitives pressed on, shouting and wailing and moving slowly in the pale dawn light.

Ismail Agha quickly reached the crags, but he saw with sudden misgiving that for the first time in all these years Hüseyin Bey was not in his usual place. He looked around and his eyes fell on the figure lying prone on the water about fifty strokes offshore. It was Hüseyin, wearing his black Istanbul clothes and swaying gently on the pale blue of the lake. Ismail Agha plunged into the water and swam up to him. Hüseyin Bey's body was rigid, his eyes fixed in a bulging stare. The gold chain of his watch, a watch which he had not worn for years, gleamed dully in the water. Ismail Agha heaved him onto the shore and sat him down in his old place facing the lake, his back against the rock. And there he left him and ran back to join the trek. But there was something that troubled him, some change in Hüseyin Bey. The watch, he knew about. His shoes were the patent-leather shoes he had worn on his return from Istanbul, the shirt, embroidered, also from Istanbul . . . Then it came to him. The gold wedding ring on his long slim finger! Ismail Agha had never seen it before, neither on the day Hüseyin Bey arrived from Istanbul, nor at any time after in the years that followed.

The Bey gave a cry of pain when he saw Ismail Agha return alone. "Where is he?"

"He's gone," Ismail Agha said. "Maybe he's already ahead of us. We'll meet him on the way."

The tears ran down the Bey's face. "He's lost, alas," he sighed.

That night they did not stop to sleep, but were carried along with the flow of refugees, and it was only towards morning on the second day that they were able to slip away into a little valley and disburden the beasts under a spreading walnut tree. There they bethought themselves of food and cooked their first meal.

Ismail Agha's mother was an invalid and he had carried her

on his back up to here. His brothers had offered to take her in turns, but he would not let them. His younger brother was still a bachelor. The youngest, Hassan, was married though it was unusual in these parts for younger brothers to get married before their elders. Ismail Agha himself had taken a wife late in life and only very recently.

They remained there one day at the foot of the walnut tree, then set off again, the noise of cannon still ringing in their ears. Ismail Agha's mother was on his back again, silent, uncomplaining, bearing it all with the patience of a saint. Though over seventy she was still beautiful, her face without a single wrinkle. Her only worry now was that she had to be carried, that she was wearing down her son. She never showed her distress, but Ismail Agha guessed it and did his best to give her the lie. He laughed and sang and every now and then he repeated: "Why mother, how light you are. Just as if a bird had come to perch on my shoulder!"

A month and a half later they reached the plain of Diyarbakir. Thousands of refugees were streaming into this torrid plain, strewn with black incandescent rocks, its waters like warm blood, its swamps spreading malaria. People died like flies and the survivors did not have the strength to bury them. And still they came, fleeing, dying . . . The family had nothing left to eat. Some of their cattle had been stolen by the deserters, some they had to kill for food and the remainder were dropping dead in the blistering heat of Diyarbakir. The whole plain, the roads and ditches, the River Tigris reeked with the stench of carrion. People began to flee into the hills and to loot the villages up there. Famished hordes swooped down on the hamlets and small towns like swarms of locusts and when they departed there was not a morsel of food to be found, not a crumb of bread or a drop of water. The grass did not grow again on their passage. In the towns and hamlets the men armed themselves and massacred the invaders. But nothing could stop the human flood. Day after day, like a torrent overflowing its banks, this ragged famished multitude poured into the plains, the valleys, the hills, and pursuing them were the deserters, the fires, the roar of cannon. The war with the enemy, they had left behind in Van, but a fiercer war was raging in Diyarbakir and the surrounding provinces, a merciless war between the deserters and the refugees, between the local inhabitants and the invaders who scorched the earth they stepped on. Those whose homes had been plundered began to pillage other villages and towns, thus swelling the bands that fluctuated from the plain of Diyarbakir to the desert of Mardin, and from there to Urfa and the plain of Harran, naked, starving, dying, but ever more numerous. They had grown accustomed to the dead strewn on their way, to the putrid odours, intensified by the heat that hit them like a blow in the face, to the eagles and vultures and other birds of prey that fell upon the corpses, tearing them to pieces, their wings and beaks and talons red with blood. And the birds of prey, too, did not shy away from these exhausted half-dead creatures. The dead and the living, the eagles and vultures, all were merged in a constant flux. Throughout the southeastern lands and on the vast Mesopotamian plain, crazed multitudes milled around, sometimes walking a whole day for a drop of water, the weaker ones, the sick, falling or dragging themselves along. And when they found no one to despoil, these homeless, starving people attacked and killed one another until, scenting food in some town, they marched upon it, leaving nothing but desolation in their wake. They themselves were reduced by half, but others came to take the place of the dead.

Ismail Agha never recalled by what miracle they escaped from this inferno, nor how they reached the Gavur Mountains. One fine morning they found themselves in a pine grove by the side of a mountain spring. A year and a half had gone by since they had left their homeland. At Bitlis they had got separated from the Bey and the others. Ismail Agha's younger brother had died on the way. With bitter weeping and laments they had buried him there, south of Mardin, this handsome man, lithe as a gazelle, and left him under a mound on the wide plain. The father of Zéro, Ismail Agha's wife, had also died, and more were left behind to sleep their last sleep among the yellow thistles at the foot of the black-pocked rocks.

"There must be a village hereabouts," Ismail Agha said.

His brother Hassan was ever inclined to be contrary. "How could there be a village here on this mountain top?" he objected.

"But don't you see, Hassan, how pleasant this place is? The grass so green and the flowers and those great pines, this light . . . And the sun!"

"What if there is a village, we haven't any money left and we can't go looting, can we?"

Ismail Agha's eyes went to his wife. Zéro was not yet

seventeen. She was tall and slender, with large hazel eyes and curly black hair that gleamed greenly in the sunlight. A staunch spirited woman, she had been the one, more than her husband, to look after the family and tend to the sick during their long wanderings among that ocean of fugitives on the plains of Mesopotamia. Somehow, she had managed to feed them all. Ismail Agha to say the truth had been mostly taken up by his mother.

Zéro caught her husband's glance. Without hesitating, she unfastened the gold belt concealed at her waist and placed it before him. Ismail Agha froze, his eyes fixed on the belt.

"It's all right, Agha," Zéro said. "We can always buy another one. A gold belt's not a thing you can eat or drink!"

"No, it isn't . . ." Ismail Agha said with a bitter smile. "Well, I'm off to see if I can find a village or a town around here. I may be able to sell this belt and buy some food and a horse maybe."

Their horse had died the day before, as they reached the forest.

Ismail Agha's mother straightened up from her pallet under a pine tree and called to him. "Ismail," she said, "listen to me. If you come upon a town, you must rent a house, a good house, and take me there. I want to die with a roof over my head. Not like this, not like a stray dog. I want to be buried in a graveyard. With an engraved tombstone . . ."

"It'll be as you wish, mother," Ismail Agha said. "We won't always be wandering about like this. They say the enemy's stopped pursuing us, they say the war's over. So now we can find a place to settle . . ."

"And you must buy me a winding-sheet, white and clean and smelling of soap . . ."

"Everything will be just as you wish, mother," Ismail Agha said.

He walked off following the course of the stream. This little brook must lead me somewhere, he thought, and sure enough, after a while he came to a good road which ran through the valley. Here the brook flowed into a river spanned by an ancient bridge of solid black and white stones that traced a wide arch maybe a hundred and fifty paces long from one bank to the other. Ismail Agha leaned on the parapet and looked at the waters that surged and foamed deep down below, booming and echoing from the hills. He took pleasure in watching the river flowing through the pines and the flowering oleanders, now disappearing behind the rocks or in a clump of trees, now emerging as a cascading torrent, very deep in places, very green, then spreading out in shallow sheets over the white pebbles.

I ought to wait here on this bridge, Ismail Agha thought. Someone's sure to pass sooner or later. He could walk on, of course, and with luck come upon a village before long, but what would he do once there, who would he go to? Whereas one could always strike up a good companionship on the road. Maybe he could even touch the wayfarer for a hint about a likely buyer in these parts. He had hidden the belt under his shirt next to the skin and wound his Lahore sash tightly around it. Nobody could get that belt without killing him first. His hand went to the Nagant revolver that never left his side. His gold-embroidered cartridge-belt was full of ammunition. Still, it pained him to have to part with Zéro's belt. During their wanderings they had kept the wolf from the door by selling almost everything they had, including his mother's Georgian ruby-embossed gold necklace, Zéro's pearl anklets and the gold watch and chain that had belonged to his father, but somehow no one had the heart to sell this priceless gold belt which was engraved with suras. It had been a wedding present to Zéro from her outlaw brother, Mahiro. One evening as the drums were beating the rhythm and the young girls and youths were dancing the *gövend* arm in arm swaying like a gently flowing stream, Mahiro had appeared, followed by fifteen horsemen armed with nacre-inlaid rifles. The horses were all chestnuts with black manes and tails. Their coats glistened brightly and their saddles were embroidered with gold. Mahiro reined in before the dancers. He was a young man of about twenty with curly black hair, a thin moustache and an aquiline nose. He wore a striped dark blue *shal shapik* and bandoliers were strapped all over his body. He sat very straight on the horse which foamed at the bit and pawed the ground restively. A couple of men had rushed up to hold the bridle and invite him to get down. "Thank you, but we're in a hurry," Mahiro said. "Where's my sister?"

Zéro ran out in her wedding gown and threw her arms round her brother's neck as he leaned towards her. "Welcome, dear brother," she cried. "I knew you'd come, I knew you'd be here at all costs, my only brother, my brave one . . ."

Mahiro sat up again, his eyes full of tears. Zéro was weeping openly. The wedding guests had frozen in a circle around them.

Then, from his saddlebag Mahiro took out the belt wrapped in a silk shawl. He handed it to Zéro, kissed her once more and galloped off with his horsemen towards the bare mauve mountains. Nothing was heard from him again. Some said he had been killed, others that he was somewhere in Iran or Arabia or on Mount Ararat and that he exacted a toll from travellers who came his way. Until the war all kinds of rumours about him had reached them, but ever since leaving the village they had had no news of him at all. Maybe he would ride up to them again one day, slender as a young shoot on his chestnut horse . . .

Ismail Agha had realised at a glance the value of this belt. Who knows what rich Bey, Kurdish, Armenian, Circassian, Persian or Turkish, had had it fashioned with infinite care by some Armenian master goldsmith for the woman he loved, who knows how Mahiro had acquired it . . . ?

And who knows what beauty it will adorn now that we have to part from it, Ismail Agha was thinking as he stood there on the bridge, his eyes on the turbulent waters down below. Then, looking up, he saw a man on a horse come riding along the road and his spirits rose.

"*Selam* to you, friend," the rider greeted him, and Ismail Agha returned his greeting. The rider dismounted at once. "I'm tired," he declared. "Come and take a little rest with me under that tree there. What can you be waiting for here, on this lonely bridge?" He laughed, showing a set of gleaming gold teeth.

Ismail Agha laughed too. "I take a toll from passers-by," he answered. "Twenty aspers from those who pay and forty from those who don't."

Laughing they both walked to the tree. The man tethered his horse to a bush, took the feed bag hanging from the saddle and fastened it to the horse's mouth.

"Sit down here by me," he said to Ismail Agha as he leaned against the tree trunk. "You've chosen a good occupation, brother, but you ought to take one asper from those who cross the bridge and a thousand gold pieces from those who don't!"

"My calculations must have gone wrong somewhere," Ismail Agha said. "It's not easy work, guarding a bridge!"

"Excuse me, but what is your name? Where do you come from and where are you going?"

Ismail Agha replied as shortly as he could.

"Well, my name's Niyazi," the man said. "Contrabandist by profession."

"A good profession, but difficult . . ."

"This revolver at my waist is a Nagant," Niyazi said. "No old parabellum for me!"

"Very good," Ismail Agha said.

"And that's a German rifle you see there under the saddle. I've got a reserve of three hundred and thirty-two shells. With that, I can hold a whole regiment at bay . . . I'm a deserter, you know. Wasn't I right to desert?"

"Very right," Ismail Agha assured him.

"The other men in our village went to the war and not one of them returned, all dead, devoured by lice at Sarikamish. Think of it, a huge village, three hundred homesteads with all the women widows, and me the only male! I can take you there if you like. You're a stout fellow, bless you, sturdy as an ox. Come with me and I'll find you five widows and more if you want. Why, it's years now that the women of our village have been itching for the sight of a man!"

"Oh, but I'm sure those women are only just enough for you!"

Niyazi was highly gratified. "Right you are," he exclaimed. "What a good thing I did to desert! To think I might have been feed for lice too . . . You know why I deserted? Well, I thought it over, see? God's given us this head so we should use it, and so I did. Six of my uncles went to the wars and never came back, my grandfather perished in the Yemen, my father, my three elder brothers, my cousins . . . Not one of them survived. Well, I'm no fool. Motherland, fatherland, that's all very well, I said to the men of my village, but are we the owners of this country? This country belongs to his majesty the Sultan, and also to Kurdish Hashmet Bey. Let them go and fight for a change. Why should we poor people die for them, isn't it so? Did you ever join the army?"

"Never."

"Of course not! How stupid of me! What a thing to ask! Why, if you had you'd never be here now! You'd have been eaten up by lice too, and your bones swept into some gully by the torrents of the thaw. Here, roll yourself a cigarette. And don't tell me you don't smoke!" He held out an engraved tobacco case and a lighter. "There isn't the like of this tobacco in all the land of Antep or Marash or Adana. I cater for all the beys from here to Aleppo and Damascus. Hashmet Bey himself I supply, and he sends some to

Istanbul to the commander-in-chief of the army, Enver Pasha. Oh yes, it's this very brand that Enver Pasha smokes! Come on, Kurdish son, try Enver Pasha's tobacco. You may be a bey too, for all I know. I've never come across a Kurd dressed like you, with a vest embroidered in gold. Kurds wear slit-sleeved jerkins of goatskin, the poor ones, and the rich, calfskin cloaks. You look like a different kind of Kurd to me."

Ismail Agha rolled his cigarette and lit it after one or two strokes.

He inhaled the smoke contentedly, his eyes closed. "Pure tobacco," he remarked as he blew out the smoke.

"Yellow Maid," Niyazi said. "Ever so finely shredded. Look!" He picked up a pinch and let it drop into the case, all fine and golden. "I'm taking this lot to Hashmet Bey. He's the bey of all the Kurds in Adana, Marash and Antep. His son's just come back from the front, the only one in these parts. He fought at Çanakkale, lost an arm there, but what does it matter, he's still alive, isn't he? Hashmet Bey went crazy with joy when he returned. They tell of Hashmet Bey that for years he had no son and so he made a vow that if God gave him a son he wouldn't make use of the *bedel* to buy him clear of the army. So when the time came, the lad went to the wars, like anyone else."

Niyazi rattled on, talking nineteen to the dozen about Hashmet Bey who had recently betrothed his son to the daughter of the Bey of Pazarjik and was in a hurry for the wedding to take place. Such a dowry he had paid the Bey of Pazarjik! Enough to load a mule! And now he was looking for some precious ornament to offer his daughter-in-law, something so rare that no one would have seen the like, and for this he had sent emissaries on horseback to the jewellers in Adana, Antep and Marash and others by train to Istanbul.

"A rare ornament?" Ismail Agha's eyes lit up.

"Yes, indeed," Niyazi said. "And do you know, Hashmet Bey won't have the wedding before he's found it!"

"Is he really so rich, this Hashmet Bey?"

"Prodigiously rich. Why, one large room of his mansion is crammed with jars full of gold!"

"How did he come by all this gold?"

"Oh-ho, brother Ismail, the things you ask! That's a real palace he's got, Hashmet Bey."

"Well, what of it?"

"Why, it took sixty-one master craftsmen, all Armenians, and ten thousand masons seven years to build! And with the idea it might one day fall in ruins and his descendants be poverty-stricken, he had jars full of gold coins buried at the four corners of the foundations. See what I mean now?"

"Yes indeed . . ."

"That's the kind of beys we have around here, proud as eagles."

"And rich too . . ."

"Rich? Swimming in gold, they are! Why, there's a certain Mad Memet Agha in Adana, oh mother! He's had a harrow made of pure gold, not to use, of course, just as a symbol, so as to say, I can make all my harrows of gold if I wish. And what do you know, he had a plough made of pure gold too and hung it in front of the Great Mosque in Adana. Do you have beys like these where you come from?"

"There are some, but not as illustrious as these you tell me about . . ."

"They can't be!" Niyazi cried. "This is the land of Antep, of Marash, of Adana, of the Gavur Mountains. And also the land of the Chukurova where the soil is so rich that the seed you sow today will yield a hundredfold in three or four months. The land around here is enough for seven kingdoms, and it all belongs to the beys. And mostly to Hashmet Bey."

Ismail fixed a keen searching gaze on his companion. Niyazi was taken aback. He faltered and stopped short. "Niyazi," Ismail Agha said, "is it true that you're on your way to this Hashmet Bey and that he is marrying his son?"

"Oh yes, yes," Niyazi cried.

"Then get up and let's go to him together."

There was such an air of authority about him that Niyazi leapt to his feet and rushed to the horse. "Here, Ismail Bey, you ride him," he offered, holding the stirrup.

"You ride your own horse," Ismail Agha ordered him. And so they set off, Ismail Agha walking in front and Niyazi riding behind.

Silent now, his eyes riveted on Ismail Agha's wide shoulders, Niyazi was filled with misgivings. What if this Kurd had pulled a hoax on him? What if he wasn't from Van at all, but one of the beys hereabouts? Those clothes! Did he look like someone who'd fled before the enemy, who'd left home and country and had been

52

wandering for a year and a half, a prey to hunger and thirst? What if when they got to the manor house Hashmet Bey welcomed him with open arms, what if the fellow mentioned the jars of gold at the four corners of the house, to say nothing of the room crammed with gold? Hashmet Bey with his handlebar moustache, his wild eyes . . . Wouldn't he summon Niyazi and say, why you scoundrel, is this how you talk of us all over the place? You, a common smuggler like your father was before you. What's all this about deserting from the army? Didn't I myself take you from that captain's hands, didn't I save your life only so you should provide me with good tobacco . . . ? Ah, where would this foolish Niyazi hide then . . . ? And worse, what if the man should turn out to be a relative of Hashmet Bey's? A fine pickle you're in, Niyazi, he muttered to himself. Why can't you ever hold your tongue? Do you have to go babbling and bragging to everyone you come across? Ah, you fool Niyazi, ah you blithering idiot . . . On and on he fretted and fumed until they came in sight of Hashmet Bey's mansion.

Ismail Agha stopped and stared. "It's magnificent indeed," he said, turning to Niyazi. The man was deathly pale and his lips trembled. "Why, what's the matter, Niyazi Effendi?"

"Nothing . . ." Niyazi said, thoroughly dejected now.

"Isn't the Bey at home?"

"Yes, yes. He's expecting me. Or rather his tobacco . . ."

"Let's go then," Ismail Agha said.

From close by, the manor house was even more imposing, with its intricate stonework and wide windows. Two lions sculpted in black granite towered on each side of the gate, man-tall, identical, with ferocious mien, bulging eyes and long fangs. Both had one huge paw extended with open claws as though ready to tear their prey to pieces. They had been taken from some ancient monument in Marash and they struck fear into all who entered the courtyard.

Hashmet Bey was standing on the wide gallery of the upper floor, leaning over the delicately-chiselled walnut balustrade. "Niyazi, you wretch," he shouted as soon as he spied the two men coming through the gate, "wherever have you been? I'm dying for a cigarette. I haven't had a smoke since yesterday. You know I can't stand any other tobacco."

Niyazi flung the reins over the horse's neck, grabbed the saddlebag and rushed up the stairs. "Here you are, Bey," he panted. "I'm sorry I'm late, but I met a fellow on the road, look, he's down there, a tall fine man . . . He waylaid me and insisted that I bring him to you. He's a bey too, a Kurdish Bey like you. And he speaks just like you . . . A beautiful voice, straight from the heart, just like you. Kill me, he said to me, plunge your hands in my blood, but first take me to our Bey. So I brought him along. Is that all right?"

Hashmet Bey was not listening. He had already opened one of the blue tobacco packets. With trembling fingers he quickly rolled himself a cigarette, lit it and drew a couple of puffs. "What were you saying, Niyazi?" he asked at last.

Niyazi was discomfited. "A Kurdish bey . . . Downstairs . . . A relative of yours, Bey . . . All beys are related to each other and even if they aren't, they like each other, don't they? This one's got his own fortress in Van. He didn't say so himself, but I heard it from Kurds camping in tents around here. He didn't say he was a bey either, but . . . He doesn't say much . . . You know beys never talk too much . . . So there you are, Bey. He's down in the yard, look!"

"A guest? Waiting outside?" Hashmet Bey roared. "What d'you mean? Quick, bring him up at once!"

Niyazi bounded down the stairs. In the yard and outside along the walls a number of men armed with rifles and daggers and equipped with binoculars were pacing up and down. "Come in, quick, you nearly caused my death. The Bey was furious, how dare you let my guest wait at my door like some poor waif, he shouted. You heard him. Quick!"

Without hurrying, Ismail Agha mounted the stairs while Niyazi whispered anxiously into his ear. "For heaven's sake, don't mention to the Bey all I said about him. He'll be angry I told you . . ."

Hashmet Bey was waiting at the head of the stairs. He greeted Ismail Agha in Kurdish. It warmed Ismail Agha's heart to be addressed in his own tongue. As for Niyazi, he was delighted. "Didn't I say so? Didn't I guess you'd turn out to be relatives?" he repeated as he danced around them.

Hashmet Bey was impressed by Ismail Agha's handsome countenance and his neat even elegant attire, surprising in these times of war and famine. He took him cordially by the arm and led him into a wide reception room with brightly-polished walnut panellings and intricately carved cabinets. Low divans covered with orange and green rugs lined the walls. On the floor a single *kilim* with a design of legendary bluebirds was spread from wall to wall. On the wall, in a gilt frame was a photograph of a youthful Hashmet Bey wearing a handlebar moustache.

"You're very welcome, my friend. Would you favour me with your name?"

Ismail Agha introduced himself and sat down on the edge of the divan, his hands resting respectfully on his knees.

"Do be comfortable, Ismail Bey! Make yourself at home."

"Thank you Bey, but I am not a bey."

"Ismail Agha then." Hashmet Bey turned to the servant who was waiting for orders. "Bring us some refreshment. Our guest must be hungry. And tell Niyazi to come too. Well, Ismail Agha, where are you coming from and where are you going?"

Ismail Agha gave the Bey an account of their misfortunes, and told in his deep beautiful voice, it sounded more like some epic poem recited by an ancient bard. Hashmet Bey flushed and paled in turns, his eyes filled and he lifted his hands to the sky. "Oh my God, oh my God the things men have to suffer . . ." he repeated. "D'you think the enemy will come as far as here?"

"They say the war is over," Ismail Agha said. "And it must be so, because the flow of refugees has stopped."

"They have killed them all," Hashmet Bey said sadly. "All our soldiers . . . Ninety thousand frozen at Sarikamish . . ."

"Some say even more . . ."

Niyazi entered the room. "Ninety thousand, a hundred, three hundred thousand, frozen!" He too was speaking Kurdish now. "Frozen! Thank God . . ."

"Why thank God, Niyazi?" Hashmet said sharply. "What's there to thank God about?"

"Because the soldiers were frozen, yes, but so were the lice that had been devouring them. The Ottoman nation got its revenge on the lice at least." Niyazi laughed. "Who knows how many millions, how many billions of lice lived on those ninety thousand soldiers . . ."

"That Enver Pasha's crazy," Hashmet Bey said. "I worked with him in the Party. Ignorant as well, and quite irresponsible. He's brought this country to ruin. What's to stop the enemy from overrunning the rest of the land? What will we do then?"

"We'll breed lice," Niyazi said. "And when the enemy's asleep, our spies will tell us when, we'll cast these lice at their tents.

By morning our lice will have devoured them all, just like they did the Ottoman army."

Hashmet Bey did not laugh. His hands moved nervously. Niyazi knew that Hashmet Bey's anger showed first by his hands and he bitterly repented having made such a jest. If the Bey exploded now, it would be all over with Niyazi. He would grab him by the neck, so you dare speak like that of your betters, eh? Well, I'm sending you straight to Sarikamish, to the army, feed for lice you'll be . . .

But it was not at Niyazi that Hashmet Bey's anger was directed. "You're right Niyazi, even you have the right to mock the Ottoman. This state has fallen into the hands of ignorant upstarts, God protect us from worse . . . Ismail Agha, please go on . . ."

Their descent into the Mesopotamian plain, the chaotic flight of the hordes of refugees, killing and plundering, more pitiless even than the enemy, the dead strewn all over the vast plain, men and beasts stinking and rotting . . .

"Another kind of war is still raging in all its fury on the banks of the Euphrates and the Tigris. People are butchering each other for a morsel of bread, a drop of water. I don't know how we managed to escape. For a year and a half we've been tossing and turning in a circle of death . . ."

A young manservant brought in the meal-mat and spread it on the *kilim* with the bluebirds. The mat was lined with an immaculate white cloth that smelled good of soap, and in the centre were the spoons and slices of *yufka*.

They were served first with *tarhana* soup topped with melted butter and fresh mint, then a pilaff cooked with vermicelli, then roast chicken and venison stewed in tomato sauce. To drink they had *ayran* in tall crystal glasses and for dessert honey with thick *kaymak* cream.

"And where are you going now, Ismail Agha?" Hashmet Bey asked as they sat on the divan again drinking their coffee.

"I don't know," Ismail Agha said.

"Your family, have they got enough food?"

"Enough for the next few days . . ."

"And tents?"

"Yes."

"Good," Hashmet Bey said. "I don't ask you to settle on my farmland, because the war may reach us even here. You had better go on to the Chukurova where you'll find plenty of abandoned farms and houses. I've got a good friend there, a Turcoman Bey. I'll send you to him." Hashmet Bey explained about the Armenians, how they had been persecuted and forced to abandon their belongings and flee from the Chukurova.

"It was the same back home," Ismail Agha said. "And now I must leave you, Bey. But first I would like to ask something of you." He hesitated.

Hashmet Bey cast a glance at Niyazi who left the room at once. Then he produced a few gold coins from his belt. "Please accept these, Ismail Agha," he said.

"Thank you, Bey . . ." Ismail Agha did not take the money, although Hashmet Bey pressed him until he was breathless. In vain. Ismail Agha kept his eyes fixed on the bluebirds of the *kilim*. Hundreds of bluebirds were whirling in his head, wing to wing, screeching. At last, he raised his eyes. "You want to do something for me?" he blurted out almost reluctantly.

"Anything . . ."

Ismail Agha unfastened the belt hidden at his waist and laid it before the astounded Bey. "What you can do for me, Bey, is to buy this belt," he said.

"But my whole fortune wouldn't be enough for this!" Hashmet Bey exclaimed. "Though I own this manor, though my flocks and herds abound on this plain, though the land from Güneshli to here is mine with all its farms and villages . . ."

"Give me what you can," Ismail Agha said.

"Look, I'll lend you as much money as you need, but don't sell this belt. Not even Mad Memed Agha in Adana could give you its full value."

"I must sell it, Bey," Ismail Agha said resolutely.

"But do you realize what you've got here, Ismail Agha? Do you know where this comes from? From Caucasia . . ."

"Yes, from Georgia," Ismail Agha said. "I have to sell it, Bey. Sooner or later . . . The war, emigration, it hasn't been easy. And now we've got to settle somewhere . . ."

"Very well then, I'll buy it," Hashmet Bey said as though accepting a challenge. "But on one condition. As soon as you make money, which I know you will, and a lot of money too, you're an honest man and you've got a heart as pure as a child's, then you'll give me back the money and take your belt. Will you promise me this?"

Ismail Agha laughed and held out his hand. "I promise," he said.

Hashmet Bey picked up the belt and hurried to the harem to show it to his wife and his sister-in-law. "The world has never seen the like of this!" he wondered. "I knew at once that it came from Caucasia. Armenian craftsmanship . . ."

His wife was the daughter of the Bey of the Amik-plain Turcomans, a woman who knew about rich jewellery. Her face froze in an expression of sorrow.

"What is it, Lady?" Hashmet Bey asked.

"Nothing, Bey. It's made me sad, that's all. Who knows whose waist this belt adorned. We should never boast of what we are today for we never know what we shall be tomorrow . . . Who knows how proud he was, the man who had this belt made long ago, how happy the woman who wore it . . . How in their days of gladness they thought the whole world was theirs . . ."

Hashmet Bey sighed. "I didn't want to take it, but . . ."

"Is it your guest's? The tall one . . ."

"Yes. He comes from Van with his family. Refugees . . ."

"Sad, very sad," his wife said, "but this is the perfect present we want for our son's bride."

"It's a very old piece. Just what I was looking for . . ."

"Well, buy it then," his wife said. "Life's like this, full of ups and downs. If you don't buy it, someone else will."

Hashmet Bey went back to his guest. Ismail Agha was standing. His face was very pale. This did not escape Hashmet Bey's eye. He looked at the belt, then at Ismail Agha and again at the belt.

Ismail Agha laughed. "No, no, Bey," he said. "It's not what you're thinking. This belt belongs to my wife."

"God forbid, God forbid," Hashmet Bey cried, all in a flurry of embarrassment. He laid the belt on the divan where the large diamond on the buckle sparkled briefly and left the room. Soon after he was back carrying a bag of embroidered green satin. He sat down on the divan, plunged his hand into the bag, drew out a red money pouch and began to count the gold coins it contained. Ismail Agha stood by with an air of detachment as though all this had nothing to do with him. "One, two, three . . ." The gold coins flowed from the Bey's fingers. "Twenty, twenty-one . . ." When the pouch was empty, he opened another one, then another, until there were no more pouches left in the bag. In front of him was a glittering mound of gold. "This is yours, Ismail Bey," he said. "It's all I have for the present."

Just then his wife came in. "Bey, I've got something too," she said and held out a purse. "Please take this, Ismail Bey."

Ismail Agha recoiled as though his fingers had touched live coals. The gold-embroidered silk purse fell to the ground with a dull clatter. "No, no," he protested. "This is enough. More than enough . . ."

Hashmet Bey bent down and picked up the purse. His wife stood by, her eyes fixed curiously on this handsome stranger with the large dark eyes. "He won't take it, wife," Hashmet Bey said. "Let's not insist on something that may embarrass our guest." He filled up the pouches again, put them in the satin bag and handed it to Ismail Agha. "Are you armed?" he asked sharply.

Ismail Agha showed him his Nagant revolver.

"How many men are you?"

"Two. We were nine when we left . . ."

"The roads are infested with bandits," Hashmet Bey said grimly. "You're sure to be robbed. I'm going to give you two men. You can depend on them. Jemshid and Resul are known to belong to my household, so no one will dare trouble you. They'll accompany you right on to the Chukurova. And now, go and fetch your people. Let them be my guests here for a few days. Then, I'll give you a letter and you'll stay in the Chukurova until the war ends." He clapped his hands and the young manservant waiting outside stepped in. "Go and fetch Jemshid and Resul," he ordered.

In a little while Jemshid and Resul, two tall stalwart fellows with handlebar moustaches and armed to the teeth were standing at attention before the Bey. "Saddle a few horses and give mine to my guest."

"No, no, Hashmet Bey," Ismail Agha protested as though gravely affronted. "They could chop my head off before I ride your horse. Don't even think of it."

"Well then, the black horse . . . You're to set out at once with Ismail Agha and bring back his family. You'll put them in the guest house."

Ismail Agha held out the bag with the gold. "I'd better leave this here," he said.

"Certainly not," Hashmet Bey said, rising. "You must keep your money with you. Get a saddlebag for our guest," he called to the servants.

The old mother, Zéro, Hassan, all were struck dumb at the sight of Ismail Agha with two strange men and so many horses.

"A rich Kurdish Bey . . ." Ismail Agha explained almost strangling with excitement. "Hashmet Bey . . . A lord in these parts. His mansion is quite near. He's invited us all."

"What about the belt?" his mother asked.

"That's all settled." Ismail was calmer now. He showed her the saddlebag. "Chock full," he announced, "and all gold. From Hashmet Bey."

The old woman dipped her hand into the bag and snatched it back as though it had touched fire. "God be praised," she murmured, and lifting her hands to the sky she began to pray.

For the next fortnight they stayed as guests in Hashmet Bey's mansion. If it was up to him he would never have let them go, but Ismail Agha was impatient to get to the Chukurova as quickly as possible. So one morning just before sunrise the family set out all on horseback, with Jemshid and Resul accompanying them. Ismail Agha was on the black horse, a present from Hashmet Bey, and his mother rode pillion behind him.

By easy stages, camping here and there, they made their way down to the Chukurova. In his pocket Ismail Agha carried the letter Hashmet Bey had dictated to his clerk and sealed with his golden seal. It was addressed to the most powerful Bey of the Chukurova asking him to extend his aid to the travellers, though with all the gold Hashmet Bey had given him, the whole family could live in the Chukurova for a dozen years without doing a stroke of work. Ismail Agha's joy was infectious. All along the road, the family talked and joked, and the old mother holding on to her son's waist and sitting on a soft cushion broke into a merry song.

They reached the German's spring. Here the path broadened into a well-frequented road. Jemshid had told them that below in the plain was a flourishing little town called Osmaniyé, set among gardens and vineyards. Ismail Agha decided to halt by the spring. He gave Jemshid a gold coin, asking him to buy a lamb from the Yörük nomads close by. But Jemshid returned accompanied by an aged Yörük agha who handed back the gold to Ismail Agha. "Please take this, Ismail Agha," he said. "You're my guest. Hashmet Bey's friends are always welcome with us. Do come to my tent."

"Thank you, Agha. Favour me with your name."

"They call me Old Tanish," the nomad replied. He had a long

red beard and wore *shalvar*-trousers of maroon serge with a Persian sash at his waist. On his head was a mauve conical bonnet.

The large Yörük pavilion was a veritable garden of Eden, with its nacre-inlaid poles, seven of them, its embroidered tent walls, its colourful rugs and sacks, satin cushions and mattresses. Entering it was like being suddenly transported into another world, all serene and secure. The Yörüks were handsome people, radiating health and good cheer, the product of a different civilisation, an unspoilt world. Arab horses were tethered in front of the tent and a little further off a few dromedaries squatted, their ornamented packsaddles shining bright.

Here, Ismail Agha and his family tasted their first real happiness since leaving their homeland. Old Tanish fussed about them like an excited child. The food his wife offered them was delicious. Lamb kebab, yogurt, *tarhana* soup, a rare fresh cream made from beestings, and virgin honey which is the first honey from a newly settled swarm and tastes like no other honey on earth.

That night Old Tanish would not let them go. In a spacious room, one of the seven partitions of the tent, they slept soundly in soap-scented feather beds. Ismail Agha's bed was spread in Old Tanish's very own room where all night through a huge wax candle was left to burn with a sweet smell. Old Tanish's tent was pitched in the middle of an encampment of hundreds of tents. It was guarded at night by armed men and enormous sheepdogs, some white, some tawny.

Old Tanish and Ismail Agha fell to talking and did not sleep the whole night.

"It's the end for us," the old man said with a deep sigh. "The end of the nomad life, the death of a glorious world. These forests, these flowery springs, these mountains will be forbidden to our children. It's no use resisting. We have to settle in the Chukurova in the end. This world is changing, we are heading for something unknown. Ours has been a wonderful existence, but it will fall to those who come after us to pay the price for it."

Outside each tent, perched on a forked stake was a hunting bird, falcons, hawks, even eagles. In the morning as Old Tanish and Ismail Agha were drinking their coffee in the main room of the tent, Old Tanish noticed Ismail Agha's eyes fixed on the birds. A bitter expression crossed his face. "We shall fly them soon, all of them. They will be free to go to their own mountains," he said. "And that will be the end of us. We too will become villagers." He took Ismail Agha's hand and pressed it. "Whatever became of *your* birds?" he asked.

Ismail Agha looked away. "We flew ours long ago, Tanish Agha," he said. "Maybe fifty years now . . ."

Old Tanish had a present for each one of them as they left. For the old mother it was a beautiful deerskin.

"What d'you think of all this, mother?" Ismail Agha asked as they rode away.

She was settled behind him again. "God rewards the good man in the end," she replied.

"And did you ever see such a tent?"

"God has given them what he took from us . . ."

"Well, soon God will take it away from them too. We had a long talk with Tanish Agha last night. They won't let us live on like this, he said, we shall have to let our falcons go . . ."

"I remember my mother telling me how we, too, had to let our hunting birds go. And nothing was ever the same after that . . ." The old woman went on talking about the past, the days of nomadism, their lost paradise, when suddenly she stopped. "Listen! I hear a sound, like someone crying . . ." And indeed a faint moaning came from under the trees on their right. "Go and look there among the bushes. There's somebody in trouble, wounded perhaps . . ." The moaning had stopped. They strained their ears, but there was no sound to be heard.

"I'm sure it was a human being," the old woman insisted. "There! Hear it? It's started again. Like someone who's dying . . ."

Jemshid and Hassan dismounted and retraced their steps, rummaging in the undergrowth as they went. It was not long before they came upon a little boy huddling in a thicket. He was nothing but a pack of bones, his neck stretching thin as a rope, his head covered with purulent sores, his tattered clothing barely covering the shrivelled skin that hung loosely about the bones.

Jemshid and Hassan set the boy down by the roadside and stood about uncertainly.

"What are you staring at?" the old mother cried sharply. "Have you never seen a wounded body in your life? One of you carry the child until the next halt. I'll take care of him there."

"Hassan," Ismail Agha said to his brother, "you take him."

Reluctantly, grimacing with disgust Hassan mounted his horse and rode off at a trot, one hand clutching the child, the other, the one with the reins, held to his nose. At the first spring he came to, he reined in, dumped the child down quickly and fled downstream. But he could not escape the fetid odour of putrid purulent flesh. He washed his hands and feet, scrubbed his face, mopped the saddle, rubbed it with fragrant pennyroyal, wiped the horse's coat again and again. In vain, he could not get rid of the smell. At last he sank down among the pennyroyal and lit a cigarette. The child whimpered now and again, and each time Hassan called down curses on his head. All along the way he had felt like throwing up and even now, among the sweet-smelling pennyroyal, the fetid odour would not leave him.

"Damn you! I thought we'd seen all the worst there was to see, but now I've got you to bear," he grumbled. "Damn you! This smell wouldn't leave me even if I had my skin flayed. Damn you! You'll die, that's for sure, but I'll be all done in by that time. Why, a corpse of forty days wouldn't smell that much . . ."

Hassan had ridden so fast that he was well ahead of the others. As he waited he kept swearing and grumbling, never once looking at the child. He expected him to die any minute and at every weak moan he fell into a fresh rage. "Damn you, you'll never die, you filthy skunk, you'll live on to be a burden to us in our exile . . ."

Just then he saw Ismail Agha come riding through the trees. He rushed up to him. "That thing stinks," he gasped. "The smell's enough to make your lungs burst, enough to choke a man to death. Look, I leant him against that tree and now the tree stinks, it'll stink a thousand years. The spring stinks, the pennyroyal, the pine trees . . . What are we to do?"

"Be quiet, you wicked man!" his mother cried. "It's sinful to talk like that."

Hassan was about to answer her when Ismail Agha intervened.

"Think, Hassan!" he said severely. "We could have been like him, you and I. Remember what we've gone through . . . Don't say things you'll regret. We'll wash the poor thing right away."

"Don't you bother," his mother said. "I'll just warm up some water . . ."

"Wait, mother," Zéro said. "Let me wash him. You can see to his sores afterwards. We won't let him die."

"Thank you, my good daughter, my tender-hearted Zéro."

Hassan's wife, Péro was still on her horse, watching in silence, a sulky look on her face.

"I'm going to help my sister Zéro," Jemshid said.

They all dismounted and unloaded the packs. Ismail Agha had to admit that Hassan was right, a really foul smell of putrid flesh came from where the child lay at the foot of a plane tree. He spread his mother's bedding as far from him as possible, while Zéro went to fetch water at the spring.

"Ismail," his mother said, "you must go and gather the herbs and flowers that I tell you."

"But mother, I wouldn't know the herbs around here. We don't have such a forest at home."

"But I do, little mother," Jemshid cried. "I know them all! My mother makes medicines with the herbs and flowers and roots of these forests . . . Look, little mother . . ." He took a small box from his pocket and opened it. A fragrant aroma overcame for a moment the smell of the moaning child. The mother's face brightened as she inspected the ointment in the box. "It's a good balm," she said. "For bullet wounds, I think . . ."

"Yes indeed," Jemshid said. "How did you guess, little mother?"

"At home, the wounded and the sick never went to the physician," Ismail Agha said. "They always came to my mother. Her balms and potions would revive the dead!"

The old woman beckoned Jemshid to her side. He kneeled down on the edge of her bedding while she told him the kind of plants she wanted. Jemshid nodded. "I'll soon be back with everything you need, little mother," he assured her.

An hour later when he returned, he found Zéro and Péro busy washing the child, Zéro soaping the skeletal body covered with wounds and sores, while Péro poured basin after basin of water over him. After long efforts they had him clean at last. Zéro wrapped him up in a large sheet and laid him down on a pallet that Ismail Agha had prepared near his mother. The child seemed to be ten or eleven years old, though it was difficult to say, so thin and emaciated was his body.

"He hasn't got a chance, mother," Zéro said. "Look at that wound in his head, crawling with worms, each one as big as a finger . . . And he doesn't talk at all, his jaws are clamped tight."

"Will you melt some butter and honey, my good daughter? Try and make him swallow it. And you," she said turning to Jemshid, "put all those herbs you've brought into a pan, add some honey and also your mother's balm, and boil the lot until I tell you to stop."

Jemshid lit a fire among the pennyroyal near the spring. He placed three stones in a triangle about it and balanced the pan over the stones. As he stirred the boiling mixture of herbs a penetrating odour spread through the air, redolent of all the plants and trees of the forest.

Péro had lit another fire and was cooking the *bulgur pilaff* and *tarhana* soup for their dinner. Ismail Agha stood leaning against a pine tree, silent, lost in thought. Hassan had gone to sleep, he was invisible among the tall pennyroyal. They could hear him snoring. Resul sat near the spring watching the little fish that shot here and there in the clear rippling water.

Suddenly Zéro's voice rang out joyously. "Mother! Mother, the boy's opened his eyes! And his mouth too. He's swallowing the butter and honey."

"He'll be all right," the old woman rejoiced. "Especially with my ointment . . . Children recover quickly. If what he's gone through hasn't killed him, a cannonball won't after this. Jemshid, keep on stirring the pan until the brew thickens. How good it smells! Sweet-smelling balms are the best healers. Whatever smells good adds life to life. When death comes it is always accompanied by evil smells . . ."

She dragged herself up to the pallet where the boy lay, his eyes open, quiet now after swallowing a bowl of buttered honey. "Get me some rags," she said.

Zéro pulled a petticoat out of her pack and tore it into strips. "Here you are, mother."

"We'll have to pick those worms out of the head wound . . . Only he must be shaved first."

Jemshid produced a large penknife from his pocket and began stropping it on his belt. Only when it was sharp enough to cut the hairs on the back of his hand did he start to shave the boy's head. The child uttered weak plaintive cries. "Hush, little one, hush," Jemshid said. "These worms will devour you if I don't take them out. Whatever's left of you, that is, you poor mite . . ."

The old woman saw that the boy was gritting his teeth. "There's my brave lad!" she cried. "He won't let himself die! Jemshid, when you've finished, apply my ointment to his wounds with those skilful hands of yours, very gently, try not to hurt him." She had pushed herself up in her excitement, but now she staggered and sank down huddled on her bedding as though suddenly very cold.

That evening, his wounds bandaged and attired in one of Ismail Agha's shirts that fell far below his feet and made him look as though they had put him into a sack, the boy ate so much that they were amazed. Where, how could such a puny little creature put away all that food?

Ismail Agha's sister, Hazal, who had kept aloof up to then, suddenly spoke out. "That child's going to live. Yes indeed! And I'm going to take care of him from now on."

Ismail Agha laughed. "What were you waiting for all this while?"

"Why should I bother with a dying child? Much better do something about a live one, isn't that so, brother?" Hazal was sincerely glad now.

The boy's eyes, full of doubt, moving very slowly in their sockets, went round and round again and again, and each time came to rest questioningly on Ismail Agha.

That night they slept there by the spring among the odours of pine and wild mint and yellow everlastings. The next morning they began the descent into the plain and by short stages they came to Osmaniyé where they stayed a couple of days with a relative of Jemshid's in a pleasant house with a wide garden shaded by vines that were entwined all over the poplars and fig trees. Their host urged Ismail Agha to settle right there. "I've got many farms, gardens and houses here," he told him, "and I need someone clever like you. I've no one to help me. We can work together . . ." But Ismail Agha refused. He must first deliver Hashmet Bey's letter.

"Well, you have a home here, whenever you may need it," his host assured him.

They set off again and came to Toprakkalé.

"Are we in the Chukurova at last?" the mother asked.

"Yes, mother, this is the Chukurova," Ismail Agha said.

"Then we're settling in this town."

"But mother, what are you talking about? The place we're going to is two days' journey away . . ."

"This is my place, Ismail."

"But mother . . ."

"Listen to me, Ismail." She pointed to a two-storied white-washed house. "You must rent us just such a house, now, here, at once. Let Zéro, Péro and Hazal sweep and clean it and you go and buy good sheets smelling of soap . . ."

Ismail Agha knew that his mother would never take no for an

answer. He turned to Jemshid. "Do you know anyone here?" he asked. "Can we find a house?"

"I think so," Jemshid replied. "Most of the people are up in the hills for the summer. Besides, Hashmet Bey has a foster brother here, Salih Bey, who owns a dozen good houses in the town. He's the Bey of the Jerit tribe."

They unloaded their packs in a field. A little further away were the railway tracks, and up on a hill, the citadel and its ramparts stood out black against the western sky. The old woman waited expectantly, her eyes fixed on the road that Ismail Agha and Jemshid had taken. In the afternoon, as the south wind began to blow and the little sail-clouds to rise in the sky, they were back accompanied by a paunchy stocky man with gold teeth and a huge moustache. He wore top boots and a necktie.

"Mother, this is Salih Bey," Ismail Agha said. "The Bey of the Jerit tribe."

"You're very welcome, son," the old woman said in her broken, almost incomprehensible Turkish.

"Salih Bey's got a house for us, mother, much nicer than these ones here."

"Oh-ho, a house is no problem," Salih Bey exclaimed. "Anything for Hashmet Bey's friends. Just tell me what else you need. The whole of Toprakkalé town is at your service."

"God bless you, Salih Bey, my good son," the mother said. "God grant you long life on your lands." And to her great joy, when they arrived a little before sundown they found the house swept and cleaned, all spick and span, ready for them. As they were settling in, she summoned Zéro to her side. "My daughter," she said, "you and your husband have borne a lot all these months because of me. Do me one last favour. Put some water to warm in a large cauldron and wash me properly with a good perfumed soap smelling of lemon."

Just then, Jemshid and Resul came up to take their leave. "Godspeed to you, my good sons," the old woman said as they kissed her hand. "And absolve me now of all your claims on me . . ."

Ismail Agha accompanied them to the Osmaniyé road. It was dark when he returned. Zéro had washed and dried his mother. She was nothing but skin and bones, Zéro easily carried her to the bed she had prepared on a divan with the soap-scented sheets that Salih Bey had sent.

"Thank you, daughter," the old woman said. "Now get me my nose-ring, my anklets, my necklace. Help me to put on my green dress and tie my silk scarf over my hair. Give me my beads too, for I'm going to spend this night in prayer."

Food and dishes had been sent over to the travellers from Salih Bey's house. They all sat down to eat. The old mother's face was smooth and lovely, rejuvenated. After the meal she settled down on her deerskin in a corner of the room. "My son," she said to Ismail Agha, "I am well pleased with you. No other son could have been so good to his mother. It makes me happy to have given birth to one whose heart is so pure and I know that a good son will also be a good husband. Zéro's got a kind heart too and she's proved herself during the hell we've gone through. God willing, she will give you children, but even if she doesn't, don't leave her. Always treat her well. Hassan will never grow up, he'll always be like an artless child. You'll have to keep an eye on him all your life and on your sister too. Hazal's simple-minded, and so tall maybe she won't ever find a husband . . . And now, I've got one last thing to ask of you. When you go to that town and decide to settle, don't ever do so in one of the houses or land that the Armenians were forced to abandon. A forsaken nest bodes no good. No bird will find rest in another's blighted nest . . . As for me, if I die, bury me in the graveyard here. I like this place."

"Now, mother! What kind of talk is this?" Ismail Agha protested. "God grant you long years of life yet."

She began telling her beads and did not say another word, though her lips moved silently.

Ismail Agha slept only fitfully that night. There was a weight on his heart. Each time he woke, his mother was in the same position, huddled over her prayer beads. Towards morning he saw that she had leant against the wall, her head had fallen to one side and the beads hung limply from her fingers. She was quite still. "Zéro!" he cried tremblingly. "My mother . . ."

Zéro was up in an instant, fully dressed. Ever since they had set out a year and a half ago, she had made it a habit not to undress for the night. At the mother's side she wept and intoned a funeral lament and Péro and Hazal soon joined her. The news travelled to Salih Bey's house and it was not long before the room filled up with white-kerchiefed Turcoman women whose keening in Turkish mingled with the Kurdish laments.

Salih Bey took care of the funeral and the old mother was

buried in the afternoon when the white sail-clouds puff up over the Mediterranean and the flowers and grasses of the sun-scorched Chukurova earth yield their heady scents. Fresh green myrtle branches were laid over her before they filled up the grave.

A few days later they rented a carriage and set out for their last stop, Ismail Agha riding in front on the black horse that Hashmet Bey had given him. After a night in the little borough of Tejirli, they crossed a river on a raft and entered the town on the second day. The carriage set them down in a pomegranate garden at the foot of a hill. The place was teeming with war refugees, speaking many different languages, Arabic, Kurdish or its Zaza dialect, Georgian, Circassian . . . Among them they came across a relative of theirs.

"A whole month I've been waiting here," he told Ismail Agha. "Every day I go to the Settlement Commission and every day it's, come back tomorrow. My family will soon be dying of hunger. I myself haven't eaten anything for two days."

"Don't you worry," Ismail Agha comforted him as he slipped some money into his pocket. "Tomorrow, we'll go to the Commission together. Everything will be all right."

The president of the Commission was none other than Arif Bey, the person to whom Hashmet Bey had written his letter. He was a small emaciated man. As soon as he read the letter he hurried up to Ismail Agha and took him by the arm. "A friend of Hashmet Bey's! You're more than welcome! A noble Kurdish bey like you, recommended by the powerful Hashmet Bey, the descendant of the noble Gökoguz . . ." He ordered coffee and then proudly introduced Ismail Agha to the other members of the Commission. "And now," he said, "let's get down to our business. So you come from Van, so? You've lost your home and domains, yes? Well, considering your family's high standing, our all-powerful state will show you every facility. Therefore, I'm registering in your name the former house of the wealthy Armenian Kendirliyan, a large twelve-room mansion. Is this all right with you, gentlemen?" he asked the other members.

"Quite, quite," they approved.

"I don't want that place," Ismail Agha protested.

"Well then, you can have Semail's farm if you like," Arif Bey said soothingly. "Nothing's good enough for Hashmet Bey's noble friend. Though, really, Kendirliyan's mansion is the most splendid in this town. My friends can bear witness to it. But if it's not big enough, I can always allocate another one next to it. For Hashmet Bey, such a noble descendant of the Gökoguz line . . ."

"Thank you, Bey, but I will have no Armenian house or farm or land."

Arif Bey lost his temper. "Then why have you come to me, Effendi?" he snapped.

"I only want a little place. Something I can afford. Besides, it was Hashmet Bey who told me . . ."

"What's wrong with Armenian houses and farms?" Arif Bey interrupted, trembling with wrath.

"A bird cannot find rest in another's blighted nest."

"We're talking about Armenians, not birds!" Arif Bey shouted. He stamped his foot. "What's all this about birds, you fool Kurd? Are you mad? Armenians aren't birds, nor are their houses nests."

"They *are* birds," Ismail Agha flashed. He was getting worked up too. "And their houses are nests."

"Birds! What birds, you idiot Kurd? They're Armenians, Armenians!" Arif Bey screamed, beside himself with rage.

"They're birds," Ismail Agha retorted, really angry now. "Birds, birds, birds!" His deep voice carried far and wide.

Arif Bey attempted to shout him down. "Armenians, Armenians, I tell you!" he bellowed frantically. "Birds indeed! What next? Armenians, Armenians . . ."

The members of the Commission did their best to calm him down. They ordered coffee for him and made him drink a few cups.

Mopping his brow, Arif Bey looked at Ismail Agha almost imploringly. "Ismail Bey, brother, friend of my friend . . . Hashmet Bey's friend means more to me than my own life . . . Tell me now, you did say an Armenian, didn't you, and not a bird? I did get you wrong, didn't I?"

"I said bird," Ismail Agha said stubbornly. "A bird who destroys a nest will see its own nest destroyed. A bird who settles in a plundered nest will never find rest."

"That's enough!" Arif Bey roared. "I'm going to send you to a place where you'll see what's what. A hell of a rocky hillside, no birds there, not even insects. A month of that and you're sure to kick the bucket. So, by order of this Commission that's where you're going to live and two gendarmes will see that you go there."

Ismail Agha's relative was waiting for him outside.

"It's no use, Ömer," Ismail Agha said. "They're banishing me from this town."

"Take me with you," Ömer pleaded. "I want to be wherever you are banished."

Ismail went back inside.

"What do you want now?" Arif Bey snapped, adjusting his glasses.

"This friend of mine here, a relative, would like to be settled along with me."

"Very well, he can go too. Wait outside. The gendarmes will be here any minute." Just then two gendarmes came into the room. Arif Bey pointed to Ismail Agha. "Take this man and his family to that rocky burning hell of a village, the one infested by snakes," he ordered. "Do you wish to set out now?" he asked Ismail Agha.

"Now, at once," Ismail Agha replied.

4

THE NEXT MORNING the gendarmes brought them to the village and handed them over to the Muhtar.

"Suit yourselves," the Muhtar said. "You can see all there is to see of the village. Settle wherever you wish."

"We need a house," Ismail Agha said.

"No empty houses for the moment . . ."

"But you must find us a house. Arif Bey, the head of the Settlement Commission has banished us here. I'm obliged to stay here."

The Muhtar was a dark wizened man with foxy eyes and a hard-boiled look. "Why did Arif Bey send you here?" he asked.

"Because he said this place is like a burning hell," Ismail Agha said. "But I like this hell and with your permission I want to settle here."

"That's all right with me," the Muhtar said. "Since Arif Bey has seen fit to send you to this hell . . . I can give you a tent if you like."

"We've got our own tents."

"Then you can pitch them wherever you wish. And what have you done that Arif Bey should banish you? He's got a temper, you might call him mad, but he's not a bad man."

"A matter of birds," Ismail Agha said.

"What? Have you killed a bird?" the Muhtar laughed.

"No. I just told Arif Bey that no bird can find rest in another's nest."

"True enough," the Muhtar said. "But that's no reason for him to get angry and banish you."

"He offered me the Kendirliyan mansion and I refused. That's a nest from which the bird has been driven away, I told him . . ."

"Indeed? And then?"

"He said Armenian and I said bird . . ."

"Really?"

"We both stuck to our guns and he went mad with rage!"

"Yes, he gets those fits when he's contradicted," the Muhtar said, much amused. "That's how it is with beys, they don't like people who answer back. Are you a bey too?"

"No, not by a long shot."

"Tell me now, if I find a house for you here that belonged to an Armenian, wouldn't you live in it?"

"Birds . . ." Ismail Agha laughed.

"But you're a refugee, banished . . ."

"Birds, I tell you."

"I see," the Muhtar said. "Well, make do with tents for this night. As for tomorrow, God is great."

They set up their tents a little way above the village at the foot of the castle ruins. A lonely hut stood there, its garden planted with maize that still bore a few dried cobs. There was no water and the river, which flowed in a blaze of light along the plain below, was a good half hour's distance away.

"We'll move to a place near the waterside tomorrow," Ömer said.

"No, we're staying right here," Ismail Agha declared, "with that plain stretching far and wide before us and the river lying like a sea over the flat land . . . I'll go and bring some water."

He seized the goatskin gourds, sprinted down to the river and was soon back at a run up the rocky hill. It had taken him only fifteen minutes. Afterwards he sat down on a rock and fell to contemplating the blueing plain with the white clouds racing above and the darkling villages dotting it. The others were busy putting order in the tents and lighting a fire for their meal. Hashmet Bey had given them a sack of *tarhana* and also some dried meat.

Ismail Agha was roused from his reverie by the arrival of a group of women and children. You are most welcome to our village, they said, and one after the other they deposited pots and platters and pans in front of the tents. An appetising odour of food came to Ismail Agha's nostrils. More women turned up bearing meal-cloths and plates and spoons. The afternoon was drawing to a close and the sun had sunk away behind the

Anavarza crags when a large group of men approached, headed by the Muhtar and followed by youths carrying pinewood flasks. Ismail Agha rose to greet them and they all embraced him. The meal-cloths were spread on the ground in a wide circle and everyone sat down to eat, the women in one group the men in another.

For the next week or so, every evening, the villagers brought food to the newcomers. It was a tradition in these parts. Ismail Agha could not very well refuse. Also, when they saw him run down for water to the river, they shook with laughter. A couple of young girls snatched the goatskin gourds from his hands, quickly filled them at the river and brought them up to the tents. It was another custom in this Turcoman village. Carrying water was not a man's job.

The villagers had all heard the story of the bird and were making good-natured fun of this peculiar Kurd who refused the mansions and farms that were offered him. The Muhtar, Memet Efendi, had asked Arif Bey about the incident. "Damn me if I've ever come across such a fool Kurd," Arif Bey grumbled. "The fellow refuses the house of an Armenian because he says we've driven them out. He won't cultivate any land of theirs either."

"He performs the *namaz* prayers faithfully every day," Memet Effendi remarked.

"It's Hashmet Bey sent him to me, so I wanted to do the very best for him. But he didn't understand, the fool!" Arif Bey was getting angry again. "Let him drag out a miserable existence in that rocky burning place, let him die of heat there!"

"Like all of us," the Muhtar murmured.

One morning, Ismail Agha, looking down from the foot of the castle fort, noticed an unusual stir in the village. People hurried about carrying beams and boards and reeds. There was a sound of sawing and planing, the women brought water from the river and the men wielded spades and hammers. There was much shouting and laughter and singing. Someone was playing the *saz*, another the pipe, and now and again the young men fell to dancing the *halay*.

The next day Ismail Agha realised what all this activity was about. The villagers were building a house, a largish one, but like all the others in the village, its walls were of reeds and the roof of rushes. The house was completed in one week. It was built against the rock, between a large pomegranate tree and a well. All around it they planted a hedge of cactuses. Inside, the walls were daubed with earth of all colours, blue, green, red, mauve, orange, and it was Lame Ibrahim, the village artist, who painted them. Like a wizard he worked, this Lame Ibrahim, tracing flowers, birds, gazelles and human beings, the men half birds, the women half gazelles . . .

Early one morning soon after, the Muhtar, accompanied by the village notables, appeared before the tents. Ismail Agha, who was making the *namaz* behind a rock, saw them arrive, but did not interrupt his devotions. Zéro laid out felt mats and cushions for the visitors. They chose to stand and it was not long before Ismail Agha ended his prayers with the ritual salute to right and then to left. He rose, smiling, adjusted the mauve tassel of his fez and walked up to his visitors.

The Muhtar held out a key. "This is yours," he said. "May you prosper in your new house. It's not good enough for you, but it's the best we could manage."

Ismail Agha had not been without his suspicions about the house, yet his eyes filled with tears. One by one he embraced the Muhtar and the notables. "How will I ever thank you for this?" he exclaimed again and again.

That very day they moved into their new home. Ismail Agha ordered wooden divans from a carpenter in a neighbouring village and Zéro set up a loom under the pomegranate tree. She obtained wool from the Yörük nomads in the hills and the old women of the village provided her with natural dyes. Then for days on end she sat at her loom and in the space of a month and with the help of five or six young girls, she wove five richly-coloured *kilims*, the age-old designs flowing like sparkling water from her practised fingers onto the tight-stretched warp. The girls were happy, for Zéro paid them well and, what's more, they were learning new designs and weaving methods. As for Zéro she was picking up some Turkish from the girls. By the time they broke up the loom she was able to make herself more or less understood.

Now that the house was spread with *kilims* and the walls too, Zéro looked around for a good broody-hen. Is any home ever complete without chickens?

"Chickens can't live here," she was told.

"Why not?"

They pointed to the steep sharp crags above. "Because of the eagles . . . The minute they spot a hen, a duck, a goose, they swoop down and carry it away."

"But doesn't anyone in this village wield a gun?" Zéro asked, astonished.

"Yes, but it's no use shooting down one or two. Those eagles are ravenous. They even attack human beings."

"Once, the whole village fell upon them with sticks and clubs, and still we couldn't save the chickens."

"Why, they were almost tearing through the brush roofs to get at the chicks!"

"So we had to give up breeding chickens."

But Zéro would not give up. She sent Hassan to buy three broody-hens from a nearby village and sat them each over twenty-five eggs. After the chicks were hatched, she kept them in a barn with Salman on guard. The boy's wounds had quite healed by now and the hair was beginning to grow, stiff and blond on his head. He had put on flesh and grown taller in the space of a few weeks. It had been Péro who, on their arrival in the old pomegranate garden in the town, had cried out joyfully: "The boy's speaking! Come quickly, he's speaking."

"What's your name, my child?" Ismail Agha asked, but it was clear that the boy did not understand him. He just stared emptily, smiling a little, a sad bitter smile, the corners of his thin lips creasing like an old man's. Maybe he knows the Zaza tongue, Ismail Agha thought. He tried that, then Arabic, Persian, Sorani, even Syriac in case he might be from Mardin. It was no use.

Suddenly the boy burst out laughing. He laughed and laughed. "Sal . . . Sal . . . Sal . . ." he repeated, and something else that they could not gather.

"Why, his name's Salman!" Zéro exclaimed. "That's what he's telling you. He must know one of these languages. Is that so, Salman?"

The boy laughed still more. "Sal . . . Sal . . . Sal . . ."

"There," Zéro cried triumphantly. "I told you it's Salman."

And Salman it remained from that day on . . .

Salman was asleep inside and Zéro and the other women had gone out into the village, when the hens and chicks somehow escaped into the yard. In no time, the eagles had swooped down in a hissing mass and were snatching up the chicks. All was confusion as the mother hens fled to the shelter of the pomegranate tree and the cactus hedge, pursued by a horde of eagles jostling against each other, feathers flying, wings awry. Salman, wide awake now, almost drowned in a flurry of wings, had seized a stick and was hitting at the eagles. Then, desperately, he grabbed hold of a huge eagle and started struggling with it, pitching and plunging and uttering piercing cries. The villagers rushed up at the uproar, some drumming on cans to frighten the eagles away, others shooting or attacking them with sticks and stones. At last the birds retreated, but only to assemble in even greater numbers, wheeling endlessly above the house. Salman's face, his arms, his legs were streaming with blood, his clothes were torn to tatters, but he never let go of the eagle's neck. Struggling to free itself, the bird raised clouds of dust and dragged Salman all over the place. Two strong youths finally succeeded in loosening Salman's grasp on the bird's neck. The eagle fell away motionless, its eyes vitreous, its wings spraddled.

It took a good month for Salman's wounds to heal. As for Zéro, she was determined to try again next year. "Seven hens I'll set to brood this time," she vowed. "Salman killed one eagle this year. By next year he'll be able to kill them all . . ."

Summer came early that year. Suddenly the yellow heat of the Chukurova was upon them. The earth and rocks crackled, the river flowed in a steaming haze, a scintillating radiance made it impossible to open the eyes. From Akchasaz swamp at the foot of the Anavarza crags and from the rice paddies that formed a vast marsh near the village, clouds of mosquitoes infested the nights, bringing sickness and death. Nearly half the village suffered from malaria, and there had been quite a few deaths since the beginning of the hot weather. Ismail Agha and his family had also caught the fever and so had Ömer's family. Their teeth chattering, they shivered in the torrid heat as they had never done even when Van Lake froze so hard it could be crossed on horseback. One morning Ismail Agha hired a waggon and took them all to the town, all except Salman who had not been touched by the fever and was thriving from day to day. The only doctor in the town was Ahmet Bey. He had no quinine, no medicines at all, but he gave every patient an injection before sending them away. "That's all I can do for you," he would say despondently.

"The name of this disease is malaria," he told Ismail Agha after giving them an injection each. "There's no remedy for it here. The medicines for malaria haven't yet come to this country. All I can do is give you some advice. First, try and see to it that your people eat plenty of vegetables and fruit in the summer. And second, you must get mosquito-nets for yourselves. Have you ever seen a mosquito-net?"

"Never. I don't know what it is . . ."

"Well, this mosquito-net that you don't know, is what you'll sleep under all through the summer. D'you understand?"

Ismail Agha went straight to the market where he bought mosquito-nets not only for his family, but for Ömer's as well. And these were the first mosquito-nets to be seen in the village.

That summer was exceptionally hot even for the Chukurova. The sunlight hit the crags above the village, striking up blinding sparks that instantly turned to steam. The swamps, the vast blackthorn scrub, the rushes, everything crepitated in a shimmering heat haze. Not a bird flew in the burning sky. Bees, butterflies and insects had retreated into sheltered nooks, wings closed, sweating . . . In the distance the pale blue plain melted, greying, into a grey sky. A gauzy incandescent whiteness, the whiteness of tempered iron, floated tremblingly over the earth. Only the rice paddies and the swamps stood out freshly green, for the trees and shrubs and even the kermes and holm oaks that grew among the crags up on the hills were all black and seared. Men and beasts had to open their mouths wide to breathe. The stifling heat went on right into the evening. The swallows were the first to shoot out of their nests, then the cicadas uttered a few timid chirps and way down south, a few white clouds appeared over the Mediterranean. The south wind began to blow. Tenuous dust devils spiralled up and subsided almost at once. Swallows streaked by, tracing black lines in the white translucent sky and eagles surged from the crags to ride the wind, wings outstretched. The clouds swelled high, pile upon pile, very white now, the greyness of sky and plain veered to blue and, as the south wind freshened, the dust devils multiplied on the roads, taller now, like a dense glittering forest marching northwards to the blue ranges of the Taurus Mountains. The stridulation of the crickets reached a deafening pitch. The shadows lengthened to the east, less dark now. This was the hour when the malaria struck. Moaning, teeth chattering, its victims rolled in the dust and dung of their yards. Every living creature, even the trees, were yellow, convulsed in a life and death struggle. Ismail Agha would take Salman by the hand and walk up to the shade of the tall crags below the castle fort, where it was always cool even when the whole world was afire, where the wind blew clean and laden with the pungent scents of thyme and scorched earth and cardoons. There, he would spread his mother's deerskin and perform his *namaz* prayers, while Salman looked on, his eyes wide, unblinking, as though not to miss the slightest move made by this fine valiant father of his, as though to stamp his every gesture into the depths of his heart.

Salman was the only child in the village not to suffer from malaria. This was surely because he had been so well taken care of. Apart from the Muhtar's two sons, he was the only one to wear shoes. Ismail Agha never went to town without bringing back something for Salman. The freshest butter, the best virgin honey, the fattest meat were all for him. Sometimes, Salman waking up in the night would get up, snuggle into Ismail Agha's arms and fall asleep there, his nose buried in Ismail Agha's hair. And when at times Ismail Agha was seized by a fit of malaria, up there behind the crags, when that big man moaned and writhed among the rocks and thorns, his teeth rattling as though they would break, then Salman too would be taken sick just like him. Whimpering under his breath, trembling like a leaf, huddling in the hollow of a rock, his eyes huge, full of pain, he shared his father's agony, his body ached as though it had been pounded in a mortar, and as soon as he could summon the strength to get up he would clasp Ismail Agha's huge hand and hold it to his breast.

After only a few months, Salman was suddenly speaking Turkish so fluently, it was impossible to tell the difference from the other children. He had also learnt some Kurdish and would interpret for Zéro and the others if necessary. Ismail Agha was proud of the boy and would take him along wherever he went. Sometimes Salman would break into song in a language no one had ever heard or could understand, but now and again the name of Ismail Agha would recur in a lilting joyful melody and Ismail Agha would know the boy was singing of him. In his turn Ismail Agha would intone one of those ancient long-drawn-out Kurdish ballads, his warm deep voice raising echoes from the crags. And Salman would sit at his feet, quite still, staring at him with love and devotion.

It was the time when refugees from the Mesopotamian plain were streaming into the Chukurova. They lived in worn tattered tents that they set up in the shelter of rocks and trees or beside swamps and rushbeds, and every day they died in hundreds, decimated by epidemics and poisonous fevers. The survivors did not have the strength to bury them. Dogs and jackals, eagles and vultures devoured the putrefying corpses cast away in the fields and bushes. Those whom the fever did not kill died of hunger. On the fertile land of the Chukurova these survivors from the wars could not find a morsel of food to stave off starvation and sometimes fought tooth and nail with the local inhabitants for a handful of barley or wheat or a bowl of *ayran*.

Ismail Agha decided to do something about it. Taking Muhtar Memet Effendi along, he tackled the Turcoman Beys of the region. They were aware of what was going on, of course, but somehow Ismail Agha's moving account told in his warm East Anatolian accent was more persuasive than anything else and, soon, the Turcoman Beys were organising food and lodgings for the refugees, and though nothing could be done about malaria a great many were saved from starving to death. Despite Zéro's and Hassan's protests, Ismail Agha was dispensing money without stint and before long he had spent all they had got from the sale of the belt. He was now known throughout the region as Big Ismail Agha. Everyone had heard of him, everyone wanted to see that kind generous man. The story of Salman, how he never left his adopted father's side, the love that linked those two and also the quarrel over birds and Armenians was told and retold and embroidered upon until it became legend.

That winter was a hard one for the family. They were reduced to a pittance of dry bread. The neighbours guessed the situation, but could not make them accept any kind of help. Only one night, Muhtar Memet Effendi could bear it no longer. He appeared at their door with a cartload of *bulgur*, flour, chickpeas, dry beans and lentils and also a firkin of butter. He had the things carried inside, then hurried away without a word to anyone. Still, a mill will not go round with buckets of water carried to it. How long could Memet Effendi's provisions last them? There were moments when Ismail Agha felt a twinge of remorse at having given all he owned to the refugees. Then he would chide himself for the thought. I could never have gone on living with my pockets full of gold while people were dying of hunger around me, he would say to himself, recovering his serenity.

The icy north wind raging down from the Taurus Mountains was more exhausting than a shivering bout of malaria. Huge thistles, uprooted from the mauve crags, swirled through the air, filled the deserted alleys and open spaces between the houses, and were swept on to the river, which turned into a flowing bed of thistles. At night, the ground was covered with hoarfrost that crackled underfoot. And in this bitter cold the family were bereft even of firewood.

"Hassan," Ismail Agha said to his brother, "we must do something. We've run out of butter and there's hardly any flour left. How are we to get through the winter?"

"We can always borrow from the headman," Hassan said.

"But how are we going to pay him back?"

"We'll find some work come the summer."

"That won't do. But I've been thinking. The only thing we can do is to go stumping for Memik Agha."

"But we've never cleared land before," Hassan protested.

"We'll learn," Ismail Agha said. "No one's born to it."

"What will people say? It's not a job for us . . ."

"Why not?" Ismail Agha laughed. "It's as good as any other."

Memik Agha's big house was situated at the foot of the hill, beneath a tall rock down which water trickled and fell drop by drop into a pool. At the gate of the yard they were met by a servant wearing the brown handwoven *shalvar*-trousers of the mountains with knee-high embroidered stockings. On his feet were a pair of rawhide sandals.

"Why, Ismail Agha!" the man exclaimed with pleasure. Then he hesitated. "You want to see the Agha?" he asked. "I'll tell him you're here."

At that moment the wooden shutters of a window overlooking the yard were thrown open. "Well, son of a Kurd!" Memik Agha called out mockingly. "What brings you here?"

"My name is Ismail . . ." Ismail Agha's voice trembled.

"I know, I know, son of a Kurd. Now what d'you want?"

"We've come to ask for work," Ismail Agha said with an effort.

"What work?" Memik Agha's long face,with the thin lips as though slashed by a razor, the jutting cheekbones, pointed nose and slanting eyes, put one in mind of a jackal . . .

"We could do some stumping for you, my brother and I. If you need it . . ."

"Have you people ever done any stumping before?" Memik Agha sneered.

"We can do it."

"It's the most difficult task in the world. D'you know that?"
Ismail Agha smiled. "We know it."

"And d'you know what the pay is?"

"We know."

"Very well then, son of a Kurd. See that you're in front of my stable tomorrow before the morning prayer. The overseer will give you pickaxes and shovels." And he slammed the shutters back to their faces.

At home, Ismail Agha set about making sandals for himself and Hassan out of a length of rawhide he had bought from a neighbour. He had already finished one pair when he noticed Hassan crouching a little way off, his eyes fixed on him sombrely. "Why Hassan!" he exclaimed. "What are you staring at me like that for?"

Hassan knelt down before him and seized his hands. He was trembling. "Oh brother, dear brother, don't do this," he implored. "Don't go stumping for that miserable sneering man. Didn't you see how he meant to humiliate you, calling you son of a Kurd?"

"So what?"

"Please don't do this! Let me go alone. Not you, not the head of this family in whose house Abdalé Zeyniki knelt to sing, that he celebrated in his epics. We mustn't be disgraced before the whole of the Chukurova."

"What's there to be disgraced about here?" Ismail Agha laughed. "Why, if Abdalé Zeyniki were to hear that I'm stumping in the Chukurova and a little agha here has treated me like a lackey, he'd compose a song about it!"

"Don't please . . ."

"But I will! Aren't they human beings, those who do this for a living, year in, year out?"

"Yes, but they're poor . . ."

"And so are we, Hassan," Ismail Agha flashed. "So are we, poor . . ."

The next morning they were in front of Memik Agha's stable long before daylight. Hassan never opened his mouth, as downcast as though he had lost his whole family. He had always looked up to his much older brother as to a saint, a noble bey, surpassing all others, unapproachable . . . How could such a superior being go stumping like any ordinary mortal, and wearing rawhide sandals too . . .

There was no one about yet, so they sat side by side on an

ancient sculpted marble slab and, presently, the first sounds came from inside the stable. A few men stumbled out in their under-clothes, still half asleep, and went to relieve themselves behind a reed hut. More men drifted into the yard and squatted down before the stable door. From the big house, two women emerged holding a handle each of a large copper cauldron that steamed gently in the still morning air, exhaling the odour of *tarhana* soup and of garlic and red pepper fried in butter. They carried it into the stable and were followed by a manservant bearing a tall pile of *yufka*-bread. At that moment the overseer stuck his head out of the door. He had a wrinkled face, dark as a negro's, with long moustaches. His eyes gleamed as they rested on the two brothers sitting on the slabstone. "So you're the Kurdish fellows the Agha was telling me about?" he laughed. "So you've come to stump land like anyone else?"

Ismail Agha held Hassan's arm just as he was about to fling a stinging retort at the swarthy man. "So we are," he said haughtily. "Like anyone else, as you see."

"Well, come inside you-all and grub up," the man said. "It's a rough job, this stumping. Not every mother's son can do it. As for me, I don't spare the rod, not even to my own father, and I don't tolerate idle hands." He spoke in arrogant tones, clearly imitating Memik Agha. "Well, you can fall to. It's not everywhere you're offered such plentiful fare in these times of famine. Eat your fill, but work your fill too." He handed them a couple of dirty old wooden spoons. "Hurry up now! It doesn't do to dawdle at the board and, anyway, we must be in the blackthorn scrub before sun-up."

With the help of the two women, the Arab started ladling out the soup from the huge soot-blackened cauldron into three large tureens and the labourers busily wielded their spoons that knocked against each other.

The blackthorn scrub stretched, dark and forbidding, up to the distant blue rise of hills. The cut trees had been heaped in a tall neat pile and their uprooted stumps into another, and next to these was a great stack of oak timber. Memik Agha had bidden that not a trace of sapling should remain in his fields. "God has created nothing so harmful as a tree," he was fond of declaring. Acres of land had already been cleared and the earth was level and smooth as though passed through a sieve, starting from the old abandoned graveyard on the hillside to the river of which only a short bend was visible, but whose reflection hit the crest of a long file of willows.

"Listen!" The Arab took Ismail Agha's hand. His voice was less harsh now, but Hassan still resented that such a one should dare touch his big brother like that. Ah, he sighed, I'd show you what's what, you black dog, if we were back in the home country . . . "You don't look like a fellow who's done this work before," the overseer was saying. "So pay attention to what I'm telling you. First, you slash down the blackthorns with this sickle as close to the roots as possible and carry them to the pile there. Or you can carry the whole lot in the evening if you like. That's up to you. Then you take this pickaxe and start digging. And I mean digging, brother! Let me tell you, son of a Kurd, three years I've been on this job. I came here from the desert way east, a desert so dry a man craves for a drop of water, a green leaf, a blade of grass. And now, here I am, hacking down every tree in sight, so that in a few years this vast Chukurova plain will be nothing but another desert! Well, the Agha promoted me, he made me overseer after only six months. Mark my words, there are many who try their hand at this job and just as many ways of stumping, but the trick is not to leave a scrap of root in the earth. This blackthorn's more troublesome than the undying grass, let the slightest bit of root remain in the earth, however deep, it'll soon sprout tendrils and spread in no time. Another thing, don't dig into the ground like a well for the roots, you'll never make it that way, just track them carefully with your pickaxe till the last bit. It'll be easier. The rest depends on your skill and ingenuity. And keep in mind that I pay the highest wage to the man who's cleared the most in one day. See that chap there? The tall dark one . . . That's Zalimoglu Halil. He earns three times more than the other labourers. There's no stumper the likes of him in this Chukurova. Look at his hands! They're like the roots of the blackthorns and oaks that he stumps. Halil!" he called. "Come here a minute, will you, these fellows would like to meet you. I've been singing your praises . . ."

Still clutching his pickaxe Zalimoglu walked up to them. He was smiling and there radiated an impression of good cheer from his gnarled rough hands, his lean well-built body and his bright friendly eyes. "Well met, brothers," he greeted them. "May your new work be easy. May it bring you luck." He looked curiously first at Ismail Agha, then at Hassan, and laughed good-naturedly.

"Look, let me clear this bit of land here before you. Watch me. It'll be much easier once you've seen how it's done. You've never seen anybody stumping, have you?"

"No, never," Ismail Agha said almost apologetically.

Halil seized an axe and in no time he had hacked away a thick clump of blackthorns, cast them aside and was attacking the roots, his body stooped and gathered into a ball. It was unbelievable. "There!" he laughed as he straightened up, bathed in sweat. There was not a trace of a root before him. "And don't forget," he added. "Never hold the helve too tightly or you'll have blistered palms. You'll have them anyway, but still . . ."

"Thank you, brother," Ismail Agha said.

That day they worked almost without a break and were so exhausted they could hardly walk on the way back to the village. Their hands were already all swollen and blistered.

"Tomorrow, I'll bring you an ointment that I make for this," Zalimoglu told them. "You'll soon feel better and after a few days the skin will harden. You'll find it easier. Now, I know so well how it is, you're aching all over, you're so worn out you don't know where your head is, where your feet . . . Stumping's a difficult job. I wouldn't wish it on any of God's creatures. Pray God to deliver you from this quickly."

As soon as they came home, they threw themselves on their beds without a thought for food. But they could not sleep. Racked with pain, they turned and tossed until morning. Again before sun-up they made their way to Memik Agha's stable, heavy-eyed, swaying like drunken men and sat down on the ancient slabstone inscribed with strange signs.

The steaming cauldron of soup with the savoury odour of garlic was brought into the stable again. Ismail Agha and Hassan could hardly lift their spoons, their hands were so sore.

"It'll pass," Zalimoglu laughed. "Last night I boiled some herbs for you." He handed a bottle to Ismail Agha. "Spread plenty of this over your hands and bind them up this evening before you go to bed."

At first it seemed impossible they could ever hold a pickaxe or a shovel in their swollen, suppurating hands. But there was no help for it. At every stroke of the pickaxe, a lancinating pain shot into their very heart and made them want to vomit. But as their bodies warmed up, their palms grew numb and the sick feeling abated.

That evening, they returned to a household silent as the grave.

"What's the matter?" Ismail Agha asked.

"Nothing," Zéro said moodily.

"Nothing really," Ömer said. "Except that we've been talking things over and we've decided that I'd better go stumping instead of you."

Ismail Agha stopped short in the middle of the room. "I mean to go on stumping," he stated in ringing tones.

"But it's not right," Ömer protested. "For a bey like you to go stumping . . . Is it for this you studied all those years back in Van?"

Zéro intervened. "Be quiet, Ömer. It's no use. You'll only make him angrier."

Breathing hard, Ismail Agha went to sit by the hearth where Salman was crouching, his head hanging.

"Now now, Salman! You too?"

Salman looked up. His eyes were full of tears. "It's such a pity for you," he blurted out. "Such a pity . . ."

Ismail Agha took him in his arms. "Don't cry, son. I must do this work or we shall all go wanting. These days will pass. It'll be better when summer comes."

"Why don't we sell the *kilims*?" Zéro said. "Are they worth more to us than this child's tears? I can always weave some more, and better ones too, as soon as we're easier." But Ismail Agha gave her such a look that she froze to her place, regretting a thousand times having ever mentioned the *kilims*.

Cradling Salman gently in his arms, Ismail Agha began to talk to him very low, and before long the child burst out laughing. Ismail Agha laughed too and Zéro took courage. "Shall we eat now, Agha?" she asked.

"What are you waiting for?" Ismail Agha cried joyously. "And afterwards you'll help me bandage my hands. Our friend Zalimoglu, who's the best stumper hereabouts, has made us a salve. See, it's there in that bottle."

Zéro hurriedly unfolded her best embroidered *jijim* and placed the food on it. It consisted only of *bulgur* pilaff and a jug of *ayran*. Ismail Agha was anything but hungry. Still he forced himself to eat with a show of appetite so as not to give rise to more tension. That night he managed to get a little sleep.

On the third evening it was Memet Effendi who tried to talk Ismail Agha out of his resolution to work for Memik Agha, but it was no use. The Muhtar gave up and left in a huff.

As for the villagers, they did not know what to make of this man who had been rolling in gold on arriving in the village, killing sheep and lambs every so often, not only for his own household, but for all his neighbours as well, setting up looms in his yard and paying the village girls to weave the most beautiful *kilims* ever seen, each week bringing all kinds of clothes and a new pair of shoes from the town for his foster son, providing the sick with medicines, taking them to the doctor . . . And now look at him! Reduced to go stumping for Memik Agha!

"The man's crazy. Selling his wife's gold belt and then spending all the money on needy Kurdish immigrants!"

"That's what comes of being generous! They call you crazy," someone objected. "What can the man do except to go stumping? He doesn't own land or cattle and where can he find work in the dead of winter on this cursed Chukurova plain?"

"But a man who entertains beys and aghas in his house, who is respected by all! He shouldn't go stumping for that low-down Memik Agha . . ."

"Indeed not!"

"It's the feet suffer for what the stupid head does . . ."

"Yes, it's his poor family that's suffering."

"They don't dare show themselves in the village."

"Even the boy avoids the other children and creeps along under the cover of the cactus hedge up to the fortress."

"Salman, who never went without patent-leather shoes, who strutted around the village in city clothes . . ."

"God keep us from such a downfall!"

"Only God Almighty knows no ups and downs . . ."

"It was to be expected that these Kurds would end up like this."

"Giving themselves airs . . ."

"Hush now! They never gave themselves any airs at all. Don't tell such lies or your tongue will wither."

"If that crazy Ismail Agha hadn't given away his gold so freely to all and sundry, it would have lasted them for ages, and the whole village as well."

"Ah yes, and for all of us too . . ."

"To think we fool villagers made such a fuss of these people who don't even know Turkish! To think we built a house for them! Indeed, a palace!"

"And Lame Ibrahim who never bothered to decorate anyone's house, not even his own, painted the walls for these barbarian Kurds!"

"How he regrets it . . ."

"That's a lie!"

"Oh no!"

"Oh yes!"

"Ismail hasn't gone anywhere since he started stumping."

"Poor Ismail! And he so sociable, so cordial . . ."

"A bey, a pasha he was, Ismail, in his own country."

"God preserve us all from being cast into exile . . ."

"Well, but why didn't he move into that Armenian's mansion?"

"Yes, and why did he refuse to take the Armenian's land?"

"A Kurd in rawhide sandals defying the Adana Beys!"

"And now, every morning before daybreak, he's there in Memik Agha's stable, along with all those hillbilly stumpers . . ."

"With that Arab overseer always breathing down his neck . . ."

"Harder, harder, son of a Kurd, he shouts, it's not for nothing God gave you such a huge body . . ."

"Yes, that's how the Arab mocks him . . ."

"And when Memik Agha appears, Ismail leaps to his feet . . ."

"He stands there with his hands joined humbly on his belly . . ."

"Before that wretched Memik Agha!"

"And Memik Agha jeers at him! Well, son of a Kurd, how's life, how d'you like stumping . . ."

"What can poor Ismail answer . . . God grant you long life, Memik Agha, you've flown to our help in our exile, thanks to you my family has been saved from dying of hunger . . ."

"Zéro goes to fetch water under the cover of night."

"As though she's doing a shameful thing!"

"What's there to be ashamed of? Everyone works in this village."

"Even in the dog days of summer . . ."

"We made too much of these outlandish Kurds."

"Yes, we thought they were important people and were glad to have them settle in our village."

After a week, the brothers' hands had begun to heal under the bandages, but their bodies were still so sore that they tossed and turned in their beds till long after midnight. Zalimoglu did his best to make it easier for them. All through the day he diverted them with stories from his mountain village, making them laugh and forget the day's long labour, the ache and the pain, their tattered clothes and the fresh cuts and bruises. Lighthearted and gay as a child, he had yet the kindness and indulgence of a wise man. "Never you mind, Ismail Agha," he laughed. "This is the rule with stumping. He who wrecks another's nest will see his own nest ruined. We cut up the blackthorns, root and branch, we destroy their hearth. Well then, they put up a little resistance, they bite and scratch us in their turn, but after a while they are used to dying and we get used to killing them."

There was something that Ismail Agha could not understand. Why, with all the acres hereabouts that lay empty and untilled, with so many deserted Armenian farms, why did this Memik Agha persist in clearing land under such difficult conditions? One day he put the question to Zalimoglu.

"Blackthorn earth must be particularly fertile, I suppose," Zalimoglu said.

"It can't be worth that much trouble," Ismail Agha remarked. "There's surely something behind this."

Later on they learned that Memik Agha had appropriated a great deal of Armenian farmland. Should he be asked one day to account for it, he would pretend he had cleared it all from the blackthorn shrub. Labour was dirt-cheap and the mountain villagers were ready to work for a pittance. Besides, being of a stingy and calculating nature, he never gave his labourers any other lunch than plain boiled *bulgur* and thinly diluted *ayran*. In the morning the *tarhana* soup was good, with garlic and mint and red pepper and even a little butter. Somehow, Memik Agha had not thought of breaking with this old Turcoman custom. How the labourers could subsist on so meagre a diet Ismail Agha soon found out. The blackthorn shrub abounded with mushrooms, fat mushrooms as large as two hands. Zalimoglu was expert at telling the edible from the poisonous ones and the labourers ate only those he recommended.

Ismail Agha and Zalimoglu had soon grown to be as close as brothers. "Only a little while more," Zalimoglu confided to Ismail Agha. "Just a little, and then I'll be able to go home. I've a lot of money saved up with Memik Agha. There's also all the money I earned the five years I worked as a farm hand in Adana. Memik Agha's keeping it for me. If I work this year and maybe the next too, that'll be enough. I'll go home at last. It's years since I've seen my mother . . . I've got an old mother up there in the mountains . . . My dear, dear mother . . . And there's someone else waiting for me . . ." Bashful as a child he hung his head and his face lacerated by the thorns flushed with confusion.

Suddenly it was spring and by then Ismail Agha and Hassan had become expert stumpers. But Ömer had been unable to bear the work more than a few days. Taking his family and belongings, he had disappeared one night without a word to anyone.

With the anemones and poppies and burgeoning plants, spring brings bees to the Chukurova. Swarms of honeybees cluster on the branches and wheel round and round the rocks and hives in ragged clumps, while the wild bees, the yellow-jackets, wasps and bumblebees flash through the air, drops of gold, fulgent silver, steely blue, glistening green, drowning the world with their buzzing, deeply pulsing over the combs, tossed here and there in the sky, scattering in all directions and joining again, wave after wave.

The spring rains had made stumping easier. Zalimoglu sang gaily from morning to night, making them all want to dance and filling them with intoxicating joy. The family had accommodated itself to this new life. Stumping no longer seemed a shameful occupation. The villagers, for their part, had forgotten that these immigrants were not labourers from the mountains, and Memik Agha did not pester them any longer with the same mocking greeting every morning, eh, my Kurdish sons, have you got used to stumping yet . . . ? Things had settled into an uneventful routine. Ismail Agha was even able to buy Salman a pair of new red shoes from the town.

And then, one morning as they were working in the blackthorn shrub, Hashmet Bey's Jemshid came riding up. "Well!" he laughed as be embraced them. "What a job it's been finding you! It's a good thing I thought of Arif Bey. At first he couldn't remember where he had settled you. Then suddenly he gave a shout. The bird! Is it that crazy bird Hashmet Bey's looking for . . . ? He mentioned this village. So here I am! Now listen, Ismail Agha, Hashmet Bey wants to see you. He said you're to come straight away, without wasting a minute. He needs you badly. It's in narrow straits that a man shows his true colours. Everyone hereabouts knows that you're here stumping because you gave away all your money to the refugees."

"It's not worth talking about," Ismail Agha said calmly. He offered his tobacco case to Jemshid.

"Have some of mine rather," Jemshid said producing a case from his waistband. "It's Niyazi tobacco . . ."

"All right," Ismail Agha said. "We can set out tomorrow," he continued as he rolled himself a cigarette. "Except that I don't have a horse. I'm afraid I had to sell the horse Hashmet Bey gave me . . ."

"You'll ride mine, then, and I'll buy one the next town we get to."

"Very well," Ismail Agha said. "We have to work till nightfall here. Why don't you go to our house and rest? Or you can stay here if you like."

"Let me stay," Jemshid said. "I'll tether the horse so he can graze. Famous grass you have here, knee-deep!" he added with a glance at the thick blackthorn shrubs. He laughed. "God help you all."

Ismail Agha began stumping again. He was quick now, almost as quick as Zalimoglu. Without a break, he went on till evening. Small yellow flowers had bloomed on the blackthorns and, hanging on to nearly every bush, was a honeycomb as large as a tray. Ismail Agha was careful to remove the comb crawling with bees and carry it to a safer place further away before cutting down the bush.

The next morning they were up long before the morning prayer, as was their habit now.

"Brother," Ismail Agha said to Hassan, "I don't know when I'll be back. Hashmet Bey must have a good reason for sending for me. So the household's your trust now. Don't stop stumping. No job is shameful that earns you your daily bread. Always keep in with Zalimoglu. Remember, he's been a real brother to us. If you run into difficulties, he'll help you with all his heart."

"I'll do just as you say, my Agha," Hassan said, kissing his brother's hand.

"Be kind to Salman. He's suffered so much, the poor orphan. Don't scold him and if possible buy him a little something each time you go to town."

After drinking their mint-scented *tarhana* soup, they set off, Ismail Agha on horseback and Jemshid walking beside him. They entered the town by sundown. It was the town they had first come to in the Chukurova and they stayed in the same house with the wide garden shaded by vines that twined about the poplars and fig trees. Their host gave them a lavish welcome and begged them to be his guests for a few days, but he did not insist when told that Hashmet Bey was expecting them. He gave Jemshid his own horse.

"You can send it back any time," he said. "We don't ride so much here. Why don't you come again at vintage time, and Hashmet Bey too? He never used to miss the vintage in the old days . . . Well, Godspeed to you."

Hashmet Bey had a shock when he saw Ismail Agha. "Whatever's happened to you, my poor friend?" he cried. "Look at your hands! And your face, all mauled and scarred! And you, nothing but skin and bones. What's the matter? Quick, tell me!"

"I had to go stumping," Ismail Agha laughed, somewhat abashed. "Clearing land for an agha down in the Chukurova."

"Why ever's that?" Hashmet Bey exclaimed as he led Ismail Agha upstairs into the reception room. "Didn't that low-down Arif allot you one of those empty Armenian farms and mansions?"

Ismail Agha sank onto the sofa, accepted a cup of coffee and started to explain. He told of his mother's last injunction before her death and how it had led to the argument with Arif Bey about birds and Armenians, of his banishment to the village, of the needy refugees pouring down into the plain, which ended in Ismail Agha's having to seek work, of how the villagers, who had built a house for him when he first arrived, turned against him after he went stumping and, as he talked, Hashmet Bey's face cleared. "Good for you!" he laughed. "My good, noble son, my lion!"

They went on to talk about the state of the country, Enver Pasha, the French, the English, the Russians, until Hashmet Bey rose at last. "We'll talk about certain matters tomorrow," he said. "Now, have a good rest until dinner."

As soon as he had gone, Niyazi rushed in. "Welcome," he cried as he embraced Ismail Agha. "You're in luck, my friend. And what luck! See what a chance encounter on a bridge can do? If we hadn't met that day . . . It's by sniffing at each other animals get acquainted, and human beings by talking, isn't that so, my dear Ismail Agha? It's on the night of *Kadir* your mother gave you birth, that's for sure!"

"Wait a minute, wait! Come and sit here and give me one of your Yellow Maid cigarettes."

They rolled their cigarettes. Niyazi waved aside Ismail Agha's pocket lighter. "Let me light yours, Agha," he said and, producing his tinderbox he struck the flint. Sparks flew, the tinder caught fire, yielding that pleasant odour which Ismail Agha loved above all and had missed so long.

"This is what I call a good smoke," Niyazi said. "A cigarette shouldn't be lit any old way."

"Very true," Ismail Agha assented, his eyes closed as he breathed in the first smoke.

"D'you know why the Bey's asked for you?"

"No, why?" Ismail Agha said, intrigued.

"I'd better leave it to him to tell you, then. There's no knowing where you stand with these Beys. One day showering you with gifts and the next knocking you to pieces. Do you know that all the woodland in these parts belongs to Hashmet Bey? All the pines, cedars, junipers, firs, plane trees, every single tree . . . And the foaming mountain springs, the deer, the red trout, the squirrels, wolves, hyenas, jackals, bears, lynx, eagles, falcons, whatever the eye can see all over the Gavur Mountains and even the Taurus, the sky and clouds, everything . . . It's the Sultan himself bestowed them on Hashmet Bey's grandfather or his father . . . A reward for mustering up troops to stop the Arab incursions from the desert below. One of those desert invaders, Ibrahim Pasha, who had his eye on the Sultan's throne, had crossed the Chukurova and was almost at the gates of Istanbul when who d'you think stopped him? Our very own Hashmet Bey's grandfather! Or father, I don't quite know. Anyway a brave fierce Kurdish Bey. And then when Küchükalioglu rebelled and staked a claim over this Chukurova land, when Jadioglu, Kozanoglu and Chapanoglu declared that the mountains and citadels to the north, the whole of Anatolia, was theirs, again it was this Hashmet Bey's ancestor who defeated them. So of course the Sultan opened his purse to him! Hashmet Bey can have as much timber cut down as he wants. The timber is then loaded onto huge ships that anchor in Mersin port. Hashmet Bey never concerns himself with all this. His steward supervises everything and collects the money. But, the other day the fellow was murdered by some lumbermen on their raft. Nobody knows why. The lumbermen, you know, saw down the logs up on the mountain, bind them into rafts to float down the river to Adana. From there, the timber is toted on oxcarts to Mersin port. Yes indeed, Hashmet Bey's got a long arm, money flows in to him from all sides. Only, he can't keep his men for long. Not even the most unskilled worker will stay, not for a million. I thought I'd better let you know, so you should be on your guard."

"But . . . Is there any reason for this?"

"If you ask me, it's because everyone's afraid of him."

"Why?"

"He's got a fearful temper and, when roused, will draw his gun without any more ado . . . And he's such a good shot he'll get his man right in the centre of the forehead. He won't rest without shooting one or two men each year. That's why people fly for their lives after having worked for him a short time."

"Then how is it he hasn't killed you up to now?"

"I'm not in his service. Besides, I know his moods too well."

"I don't believe a word of all this, Niyazi."

"Suit yourself. But don't say I didn't warn you. Then there's the livestock business. All over these mountains from Antep to Marash, from Marash to Kozan, from Nemrut Citadel down to the Chukurova, the Yörük nomads and the villagers breed sheep and goats, horses and cattle for Hashmet Bey. Half and half, if the mother doesn't die . . ."

"What on earth does that mean, Niyazi?"

"Let me explain. Our Bey didn't invent this. It's an old custom, to the good of all the beys, of course, or where would they get all these riches, how would they build all these mansions for themselves?"

"Well, explain then."

"That's just what I'm doing! So you don't know about this business of half and half, eh?"

"How would I know?"

"Well, here's an earful for you, Ismail Agha. Hearken to the feats of our beys! Hear them from a widow's son who has never known father or grandfather. Don't get me wrong, I'm no bastard. My father went off to fight in some war or other when I was still in my mother's womb and he never was seen again, the poor bloke. Who knows in what desert he fell and became food for the ants . . . Ants are particularly fond of human eyes. Who knows how many thousands of eyes they ate there along with my father's . . . Ants love honey too, they will cluster in yellow millions over a pot of honey, haven't you ever seen this, gleaming like so many bees? And so it is with human eyes, they feast on the eyeballs, never touching any other part of the corpse . . . Where was I? Yes, I was telling about ants devouring the eyes of that father I've never known . . . All these desert ants have become Turkish. Maybe Kurdish too . . . Did Kurds go into the army then?"

"They didn't."

"Then all the ants of the desert are Turkish, since they've each got a bit of a Turkish eye in their belly. But tell me, you come from a cold climate, are there ants in the winter too, in the snow? Are they also partial to human eyeballs?"

"They are indeed!" Ismail Agha laughed.

"Oh dear," Niyazi said. "Then it was a real feast the ants had at Sarikamish with our ninety thousand dead. Think of it, millions of ants, long dark trains in the snow, swarming over a hundred and eighty thousand eyeballs, nibbling the eye sockets bare . . . Oh mother! What was I saying? I've lost the thread. I always do when I think of my father's eyes. Who knows, his eyes were like mine maybe . . . Every morning on waking, ever since I was a boy, my hand goes straight to my eyes. God, how happy I am to find them in their place! It's for fear my eyes would be devoured by ants that I deserted. But I know it, my eyes will be devoured by ants in the end. Just like my father's."

"Who told you this about your father's eyes?"

"Nobody."

"Then how d'you know that ants got at his corpse? Maybe he fell into a river."

"Hah, as though you'd find a river deep enough in the desert!"

"Why not? There's the Nile."

"My father didn't go that far."

"What about the Tigris? And the Euphrates?"

"Well, I don't know. I'm just afraid, that's all. Isn't it sickening to think of ants nibbling at a dead man's eyes?"

"Yes, it is," Ismail Agha assented.

"But what were we saying?" Niyazi asked again. He was sweating profusely. With his handkerchief, he dried his face and neck, but broke out into a sweat again almost at once. "There! You see? Whenever I see an ant, even just call ants to mind, I get all in a lather. Like this . . ."

"Never mind. Tell me about this business of half and half."

"Yes, yes, half and half. That's in the nature of beys and aghas. It's not *their* eyes the ants will feast upon! Or their sons' . . . Only the poor people are food for the ants. Yes, yes, half and half . . . Say you've got a mare, a young one, say three years old, and you give her into the care of a peasant and in the next six years she foals six times. Three of the foals are yours, and if they're fillies you'll have a right to half their foals too."

"And the mare?"

"She's yours. That's why it's half and half if the mother doesn't die. And so it's been all over these mountains for a hundred or more years, for nobody knows how long. And all those herds and herds of horses, the cattle, the sheep, the goats, Hashmet Bey sells to the military or to Istanbul and even to foreign countries. That's why this mansion here is full of gold underneath, as I told you, roomfuls of gold . . ."

On and on Niyazi talked without giving Ismail Agha a chance to open his mouth until darkness fell and Hashmet Bey entered the room ushering in a few guests whom he introduced to Ismail Agha, while casting Niyazi such a look that the latter vanished at once. Soon afterwards, dinner was brought in and an appetising odour filled the air as young girls laid out the platters, piping hot, on a wide tray.

When it was time to retire, Niyazi reappeared and offered to take Ismail Agha to his room. At the door, he leaned to his ear. "There's something I must tell you, Ismail Agha," he whispered. He was pale and trembling.

"What is it?"

"That man, murdered by the lumbermen . . ."

"I remember. Hashmet Bey's steward, wasn't he?"

"You believe they did it?"

"That's what you told me."

Suddenly, Niyazi turned away. "Perhaps it's as well," he mumbled. "Goodnight."

The next morning at breakfast, Hashmet Bey got down to business. "This stumping affair of yours has been a lucky thing for me," he began.

"How so?" Ismail Agha laughed.

"You've given it up, though, haven't you?"

"Only to come here."

"But if you had some other, more rewarding occupation . . ."

"I'd have come to you all the same," Ismail Agha answered quickly.

"Very well then, listen. I'm sick of having just anybody working for me. I need someone who's loyal and true."

"Of course."

"For years now I've been sending livestock to Adana, Mersin and Istanbul, and supplying the military at Dörtyol, in Adana. I've had many stewards, but from now on I want you to look after my business."

"What happened to the other stewards?" Ismail Agha asked abruptly.

Hashmet Bey was taken aback. Then he laughed. "They died," he answered. "People do die, you know."

Suddenly, Ismail Agha was struck with doubts. Could it be that Niyazi had spoken the truth? That this outwardly good-natured man had killed in a fit of temper? And not once but many times?

"Well, do you accept?" Hashmet Bey pursued. "Will you undertake to transport my livestock to Adana and Istanbul?"

"All right."

"We'll go fifty-fifty on the profits."

"Thank you, Bey."

"I furnish the army with horses and mules. You'll take care of that too."

"Very well."

"My Arabian steeds are brought over from Syria and Iraq. These and other purebreds from five studs in Urfa province are sold mostly to clients in Izmir. In all of these transactions we'll be partners."

Hashmet Bey went on to explain how all over the Taurus and Gavur Mountains the woodsmen worked for him. It was easy, this timber business, and in association with foreigners it went like clockwork and brought in a lot of money. From this, too, Ismail Agha would get a percentage.

"You can read and write, can't you?"

"Well, yes," Ismail Agha said modestly.

"To what extent?"

"I attended high school in Van."

"In that case, you can superintend the timber business too. And all the accounts and money matters will be in your hands."

Hashmet Bey then produced batches of papers. He stuffed them all into a leather bag which he handed over to Ismail Agha.

In the space of only a few months, Ismail Agha had the whole business under control and Hashmet Bey was well pleased with his new steward. Ismail Agha seemed to be everywhere at once, on the road taking livestock to Adana and Dörtyol and as far as Istanbul, up in the mountains supervising the lumberjacks, down in Mersin port regulating the work in the sawmills, in Urfa tackling the horse breeders. Hashmet Bey had given him strict injunctions. "On no account are you to bring me banknotes. Paper money's never entered this house and never will as long as I'm alive. When you collect payments, you're to turn the money into gold at once. And I advise you to do the same with your own earnings." Ismail Agha followed his advice. He entrusted the gold to Zéro.

Ismail Agha now spent very few days in the month with his family. His short visits were a joy to Salman, whom he showered with gifts of clothes and toys. The boy would don his new things at once and walk out into the village, new shoes, fez and all, stopping before each house, smiling, his eyes on the ground, until he had made the round of all the houses. Sometimes, Ismail Agha would take him riding pillion to Adana and Payas, and to the orange groves at Dörtyol.

Ismail Agha's life was spent among droves of sheep and russet bullocks and cattle and herds of horses, flowing endlessly through the Chukurova in the mud or the clouds of dust. "I would have been lost without you, Ismail brother," Hashmet Bey kept repeating. "You've saved me, bless you, Ismail brother."

Three years went by and the business flourished. During this time, the French occupied Antep and Adana and the mountains filled with partisans. Hashmet Bey and Ismail Agha supported the partisans, they supplied them with food and weapons and provided cover for the officers sent over from Ankara. Many of the partisans were men who had worked for Hashmet Bey and Ismail Agha, so it was easy to assign them to this or that officer. Then came the end of the sultanate and the republic was proclaimed. For Hashmet Bey and Ismail Agha things went better than ever.

But one day the unexpected happened. Hashmet Bey was killed by one of his bodyguards as he was performing his prayers. The murderer threw himself down a precipice and immediately afterwards the big mansion was burned down. Nobody ever found out how the fire started.

Ismail Agha was very much affected. By this time he had grown tired of spending most of the year on horseback. So he returned to the village, and his first concern was to build himself a house. He consulted with master-masons from Marash and Sivas, among them an Armenian whom he sent to Hashmet Bey's to inspect what was left of the mansion.

"It's quite impossible to build anything like that nowadays," the Armenian declared when he returned. "Neither money, nor stones will ever be enough, nor is there such a master builder to be found in all of Anatolia."

"Well, can't it be something like, though smaller?"

"Much smaller, yes," replied the Armenian master-mason.

Skilled craftsmen were brought in from all over the country and in less than a year the mansion was finished.

"Why ever did he go stumping?"

"To keep the wolf from the door."

"But didn't Memet Effendi give him *bulgur* and *tarhana* and butter?"

"Memet Effendi would have provided for him to the last."

"So why go and put up with Memik Agha's dirty mouth?"

"There's something fishy here."

"And now all this money, gold too, these herds and herds of sheep, horses, cattle . . ."

"Where does it all come from?"

"Didn't we see with our own eyes how he gave away all his fortune to the refugees?"

"So how come he's suddenly so rich?"

"What about the knoll of the Forsaken Graveyard . . ."

"The stumpers say he never rested with them during breaks."

"Yes, they say he always went to the knoll."

"What can there be on that knoll?"

"Ismail knows only too well what there is there!"

"All the way from Van he came with papers, scripts with the plan of the Forsaken Graveyard knoll."

"The plan an Armenian had given him back there."

"He was offered an Armenian house in the town, a real palace. Why did he refuse?"

"And all those Armenian farmlands? Why did he insist on leaving all and coming here, to this village?"

"Why did he squander all his money, why did he go stumping?"

"What was he doing, day in day out, on that knoll?"

"Digging, that's what! The knoll's full of pot-holes now."

"Just look at that Salman! Scabby Salman . . ."

"Sporting patent-leather shoes.'"

"And silk shirts.'"

"His pockets full of money . . ."

"Strutting about the village, his nose in the air . . ."

"As though he was the Peri King's son!"

"With never a word for the other village boys . . ."

"And all the children trying to curry favour with him . . ."

"Yes, because they're scared, the children, they're terrified of that scabby Salman."

"You know what he said?"

"But he never says a word to anyone . . ."

"He forgot himself this once. My father's dug up an iron chest from the Forsaken Graveyard, he said, a huge chest, all cram-full of gold coins."

"Just this one time he opened his mouth and look what he said!"

"Ah, who knows the things he'd tell if he did talk . . ."

Memet Effendi was first to go to the knoll on a moonless summer night, accompanied by his sons and workhands, all armed with picks and shovels. One by one the villagers followed suit and started digging with intense fury, bent on finding some gold-filled iron chest. For ten nights they dug without respite until the knoll was reduced to a stretch of pot-holed level earth. Wherever they dug they brought to light inscribed marble slabs and statues, heads of women with beautiful eyes, straight noses and elaborate coiffures, men with plaited hair wielding swords and shields, shooting arrows, playing the flute, and horses at a gallop, and bounding deer and greyhounds. The villagers smashed the human likenesses on the spot in frustrated anger, but the inscribed stones, the animal statues they offered to Ismail Agha, who never failed to give them a little something to make up for the gold they had not found. He himself made use of the inscribed slabs for the walls of his new mansion. The villagers went back to their fields, but suddenly after a month or so, seized with a fresh hope, they were at the knoll again, turning the ground upside down, mad with fury, smashing the marble statues that came up instead of the expected gold-filled chests. After a while they returned to the village, subdued, silent, until some new event in Ismail Agha's household, a gold belt at Zéro's waist, a gold watch and chain hanging from Salman's neck or a spirited horse rearing under Ismail Agha, set them going again, more frenziedly than ever.

When the mansion was finished, people came to visit it from the nearby towns and from as far as Adana, Antep and

Mersin, each bringing valuable presents. Even Arif Bey arrived, accompanied by four friends, to see the famous mansion of the man he had sent into exile. To all who came the villagers found a way of telling about the gold-filled iron chest in the knoll and many of the guests on returning home lost no time in tackling surrounding hummocks. Ismail Agha had made many friends during his years with Hashmet Bey and these sent presents from all over the country. Salman had his share, carved walnut boxes containing fruit from the various regions, grapes, figs, dried mulberries, fruit paste, apples, oranges. He would go out into the village to eat them in front of the other children without ever offering them a bite.

Ismail Agha had a large stable built near the house and stocked it with choice purebred horses from Urfa, Aleppo and Iskenderun. The grooms were Circassians from the Long Plateau. His business prospered and he grew richer from day to day, but the village was growing poorer and so were the neighbouring villages. Ismail Agha, a generous enterprising man, did his best to help. No one returned empty-handed from his house. He never forgot how the villagers had aided him in his days of need, how they had even built a house for him, nor did he forget the warm friendship of Zalimoglu during that difficult period of his life. He had asked Zalimoglu to leave off stumping and come and work with him, but Zalimoglu refused. "Sink or swim, I've come this far," he said. "After all these years of exile I'm going to take my savings from Memik Agha and return home at last." Time and again Ismail Agha invited him to the mansion, but Zalimoglu never came. It was as if he did not want to see Ismail Agha any more and in the end Ismail Agha took offence and never spoke his name again. He could not imagine what he had done to hurt Zalimoglu's feelings, especially as Zalimoglu still saw Hassan from time to time. Hassan was rarely at home now. He had acquired a beautiful felt shepherd's cloak with a sun design and was minding herds in the countryside. Each herd, sheep, goats, cattle, horses, had their own shepherd, but Hassan was head of them all. He had soon earned himself a reputation, for he could recognise at a glance the various flocks and even individual sheep and goats and bullocks. He never lost a single animal to the wolves that were rampant in these parts. There was something strange about Hassan. He had never liked Salman, and with time his aversion grew to the point that he longed to wring his neck. He might even have done so one night, but for the affection his brother bore this mad-eyed boy. Salman was putting on flesh and growing prouder every day. He looked down on everyone, gave himself airs as he strutted about sticking his chest out and ignoring the other children. Time and again Hassan had attempted to incite them against him. Get together, beat him black and blue, the snotty bastard, he egged them on. But the children were much too afraid of Salman.

One day an Arab arrived from Aleppo bringing a bay horse for Ismail Agha. "This is a present to you from your friend Onnik," he said and left without even stopping for a cup of coffee. The horse was very beautiful and for years Ismail Agha would ride no other. To Memed Effendi he confided the story of Onnik's escape from Van. It was soon the talk of the whole village.

The snow lay almost poplar-high that winter, when the news was brought to Ismail Agha by a shepherd. "I've seen your friend Onnik," the shepherd said. "In a cave among the rocks of Sor Valley. He was dying of hunger, too weak even to eat the milk and food I gave him. So I left him there with the food beside him and ran to you because I know Onnik's like a brother to you. The villagers have found out that there's an Armenian hiding in Sor Valley and they're after him, all armed . . ." So Onnik had not been able to shake off Bald Riza after all . . . ! Ismail Agha grabbed his rifle, gave another one to the shepherd, fastened on his snowshoes and set off at once. As they entered Sor Valley, they came across a group of villagers. "There's an Armenian hiding around here, Ismail Agha," they shouted. "We've come to kill him."

"He's sick, "Ismail Agha said. "You can't kill him."

"Why not? He'll die all the more easily."

"But this is Onnik. My friend . . ."

"He could be your father," Sofi said. "But we'd still have to kill him."

"It's a sin and you know it, in our religion, to kill a sick man."

"Who says he's sick?" Sofi countered. "He's sound as a roach."

"Have you seen him?"

"I'd have killed him already, if I had!"

"Well, you can't kill him before killing me first."

"If it comes to that, we'll kill you too, together with that unbeliever."

Ismail Agha and the shepherd made a dash for the cave. "Onnik, it's me," Ismail Agha cried, "your friend Ismail. Answer me."

A faint sound like a moan came from the depths of the cave. Onnik could hardly stand. His body had shrunk to the size of a child. "I haven't eaten for days. They're going to kill me. It's all over with me. Is Bald Riza out there?"

"No, he isn't. And I'm going to get you out of here . . ."

There were more than thirty men in front of the cave and Sofi was haranguing them, his beard trembling with excitement.

"Sofi," Ismail Agha thundered. "Shepherd Ali's coming out right this minute with my friend Onnik, carrying him because he's sick, dying. I'll be walking in front of them. If you kill Onnik you'll have to kill us too. I told the Bey I was coming here. He will know if I'm killed that my blood is on your head."

Sofi ran up to him. "Give me that Armenian. I must kill him to earn my place in Paradise. Just this one more and I'll have my score which will enable me to go to Paradise. Let me have him. I bought him from Bald Riza."

"He's a sick man and he's my friend. I won't let anyone kill him."

Sofi grabbed his hands. "Don't do this to me," he pleaded. "Your father was my friend. I've suffered so much to keep God's path . . . For months I've been searching high and low for my last Armenian, my one chance of Paradise. And here I've got him. Don't take him away from me. I'll have to kill you before I let you do this to me."

"Go ahead! Kill shepherd Ali too, and then go to Paradise!"

"I implore you, son of my friend. There's not another Armenian left in these parts, not one! If I knew I could find just one other, I'd spare Onnik to you. Besides, Onnik's a good man, worth ten Moslems, kind and generous and gentle-spoken, but what can I do? I must kill him to earn my Paradise."

Ismail Agha shook him off roughly. Sofi fell over in the snow, screaming curses and tearing at his face and beard. Ismail Agha turned back into the cave. "Here," he said, handing his cape to the shepherd. "Wrap him up in this and take him in your arms. I'll go out first and you'll follow pressing him close to my back."

As they emerged Sofi made a rush at them. "Stop," Ismail Agha shouted, his finger on the trigger, his gun pointed straight at Sofi. "Another step and you'll get a bullet in your head."

The villagers stood frozen in their tracks as Ismail Agha and the shepherd set out across the snow. Then, recovering from the shock, Sofi started after him, the others following. "Give him to me, oh Bey of Beys, Ismail! He's my providence, my place in Paradise. If I kill him . . ."

Ismail Agha never answered a word. Several times Sofi tried to take an aim at Onnik, but without success for Ismail Agha kept his gun trained on him all the way to the village.

Ismail Agha's mother met them at the door. "Why Onnik, my poor son," she exclaimed, "whatever have they done to you, those infidels? Come in quick, let me make you one of my balms and I'll soon have you on your feet again." She had some food brought in first, but Onnik's jaws were clamped tight, so she covered him with blankets and with her own hands she poured some warm milk, spoonful by spoonful down his throat. It was a full three days before he was sufficiently restored to tell his tale.

"Sofi was after me with some men. I gave them the slip. For two days I hid in a hollow on the banks of the lake. Then hunger drove me out. I went to Isviran village to Ibrahim the Sufi's house. So many times we'd visited there with my father, and once he'd offered to initiate us, to become his disciples. Well, he pretended not to know me! God's guest is always welcome, is all he said . . . I stayed there five days. Then, we learnt that Sofi and his men were in the village. It's too dangerous here for you, Ibrahim the Sufi told me. How can I protect God's guest from these bloodthirsty fiends? God's guest had better get away from here tonight . . . So that was it. Wherever I went after this, whatever village, whatever mountain, Sofi always found out, until he tracked me down in Sor Valley. If I hadn't seen Ali, the shepherd, and asked him to get you . . ."

Again and again Sofi came to Ismail Agha. Give me Onnik, he begged, he's my due, my claim to Paradise . . . With his men he kept a watch on the house day and night. But after a while Ismail Agha managed to smuggle Onnik out. Accompanied by half a dozen armed companions they reached the frontier. From there, Ismail Agha took Onnik into Iraq to a Yezidi chieftain who had been a friend of his father's.

It was surely this same Onnik who had sent him the thoroughbred all the way from Aleppo.

One morning a black Ford drew up at the gate to Ismail Agha's mansion, a beautiful car, brand-new, although covered with a thick layer of dust. The villagers crowded up to look at it. A large paunchy man with ox-like eyes alighted. He wore a summer suit of striped linen and gleaming white shoes. He had no tie and his shirt was open at the neck. Ismail Agha hurried down to greet him.

"Welcome, Bey! Welcome, Arif Saim Bey. This is a great honour."

"Have you seen me before, Ismail Agha?" Arif Saim Bey asked as he was ushered upstairs. "How did you know who I am?"

Ismail Agha was trembling with excitement. "Anyone would know you at a glance," he said. "Even the ignorant mountain shepherd would know you, our deliverer, our nation's most valiant son . . ."

After that Arif Saim Bey addressed him in Kurdish and went straight to the point.

"We are highly considered in Ankara. The Pasha trusts us. He loves us. So we must take advantage of this. And that's why I've come to you. I want you to buy the Panosyan farm from the Treasury in partnership with me. I'm going to the town to have the place put up for public auction right away. It's fifteen to twenty thousand *dönüms*, maybe more. Nobody will hear of this auction. And even if people do, I'll spread the word that I'm interested and nobody will dare to bid. Indeed, woe betide anyone who tries! You're to draw up the title deeds in your name. That's because I own a larger farm down south. The Pasha knows that, but he hasn't remarked on it. He didn't ask me how I'd bought it, with what money . . . I intend to buy farmland north of Kozan too. The Kozan treasury has put it up for sale. A friend of mine, Büküoglu, is going to buy it for me, a trusted friend who wouldn't give me away for all the money in the world, so the Pasha won't hear of it. He wouldn't say anything if he did, but it's always best to keep our mouths shut. As I said, you'll take out the title deeds yourself. And when the time comes, God make it late, God take our soul instead of his . . . Only he drinks day and night, the poor man, he won't last long at this rate, well, if something untoward happens to the Pasha, then you'll hand over half of the title deeds to me."

"As you wish, Bey."

"We hadn't met before, Ismail Agha, but I'd heard of you from my good friend Hashmet Bey. I know I can trust you. I'd trust you not only with half of a farm that belongs to me, but with my life, my wife, my whole family."

"Thank you, Bey."

"As a token of friendship I'm giving you this watch." From his waistcoat he produced a gold watch with a chain weighing perhaps two hundred and fifty grams, and hung it on Ismail Agha's neck.

"It's too much, Bey, really too much," Ismail Agha protested in confusion.

"All right, all right, listen to me now. How much are we going to give for this farm? But first, tell me, can you afford to buy? If not, I can pay your share."

"I've got enough, Bey."

"How much should we pay then? It's not as if the Treasury and the State are strangers to us. After all, the State is ours, no? What I mean is, they mustn't lose too much on the deal. A state farm is not to be bought for nothing."

"No, of course not."

"What I have in mind is three hundred liras. How's that?"

Ismail Agha hesitated. "It's too little," he said at last.

"True, but afterwards we'll need all the money we can spare. Of course the State will provide us with seed and machinery, but still . . . For the crops and all the produce we'll go fifty-fifty with you."

"Whatever you say, Bey."

"So you think three hundred's too little?"

"It's more than twenty thousand *dönüms*, this farm . . ."

"Five hundred?"

"That's still not enough."

"Oho!" Arif Saim Bey laughed. "You'll soon have us bankrupt at this rate. Are you acting for the State against me? Well, anyway, you're putting up the money. Say, seven hundred and fifty, then."

"Make it one thousand at least," Ismail Agha said diffidently.

"Very well," Arif Saim Bey assented. "But only to please you."

That is how the title deeds of this large farm passed on to Ismail Agha for the sum of only one thousand liras.

A close relationship developed between Ismail Agha and Arif Saim Bey after this. The Bey consulted him on all matters that concerned him, even the affairs of the National Assembly where he was one of the most influential members. Furthermore, he put many a lucrative business in Ismail Agha's way. Money flowed in without count now. But these last days, the first thing Arif Saim said when they met was: "There's something on your mind, my friend. You look worried . . ." Ismail Agha would deny it and hastily change the subject. But he did indeed feel burdened and oppressed. Maybe it was this farm . . . Maybe he regretted having betrayed his mother's last request not to build a nest over the spoiled nest of another bird . . . Maybe he apprehended some ill luck because of this.

At last Zéro could bear it no longer. "I know why you're like this," she burst out one day. "You won't admit it even to yourself but it's because we can't have a child, isn't it? And you blame it on me, don't you? But what can we do? We've got Salman, haven't we? Besides, there are doctors, midwives, hodjas, holy places we can visit . . ."

Furious at first, Ismail Agha was soon immensely relieved that his wife had brought the matter into the open. Husband and wife started visiting holy places and consulting holy men, but weeks and months passed and nothing happened. Ismail Agha gave oblations, vowed to make sacrifices, he spent nights on end praying, in vain . . .

One morning, very early, as the sun was just dawning, Arif Saim Bey's automobile stopped at the gate. Arif Saim Bey's face was black as thunder. He did not get out of the car, he did not even hold out his hand to Ismail Agha who had run down to greet him.

"Go tell your wife to get ready. At once. I'm taking you both to Adana."

"Won't you have a cup of coffee?"

"No, nothing."

All in a flurry of anxiety, Ismail Agha and Zéro were soon ready. They got into the back of the car. The Bey sat in front beside the chauffeur. He had kept the engine running and they were off at once. The road was so dusty that the wheels sunk into the dust up to the axle. It took more than five hours for them to reach Adana and all this time Arif Saim Bey never opened his mouth, nor did Ismail Agha have the chance to say a word. It was almost evening when the car pulled up in front of a large house on the street that ran along the Jeyhan River. The driver held the door open for Arif Saim Bey. "Follow me," he said as he got out and mounted the stairs. A plate on the door read: "Doctor Nusret, gynaecologist".

"Here, Doctor, is the friend I told you about," Arif Saim Bey said. "More than a friend, a brother, and he could not confide his trouble even to me! Examine them both thoroughly and tell us whether they can have children or not." He turned to Ismail Agha. "I'm very angry with you, Ismail Agha. Does a man keep secrets from his big brother?"

"Forgive me," Ismail Agha said.

The doctor took Zéro in first. He examined her for more than an hour, while Arif Saim Bey and Ismail Agha waited outside. Then it was Ismail Agha's turn and it took nearly as long.

"There's nothing wrong with either of them, Bey," the doctor said as he sank wearily into an armchair and lit a cigarette.

"Then why don't they have children?"

"They will," the doctor said. "Don't worry. This lady's in the prime of health . . ."

Zéro and Ismail Agha were different people after this. Their happiness knew no bounds. They felt like sharing it with the whole world. Ismail Agha had all kinds of sweet candy brought almost daily from Adana and distributed it to the village children and when he went up to the castle fort in the afternoon as was his custom he took the neighbouring children along as well as Salman and showed them as much love as he did Salman. All this bothered Salman. He felt something untoward was going on, something that try as he might he could not understand and it grieved him.

Then at last Zéro became pregnant and on an autumn day she gave birth to a boy. It was the occasion for unprecedented festivities in the village. A great feast was laid out. Sacrifices were offered, drummers, pipers, musicians and minstrels came from all over the countryside. Songs were improvised to celebrate the happy event and Ismail Agha rewarded all the musicians with lavish gifts and money.

A few days later a lieutenant of the gendarmerie arrived, bearing Arif Saim Bey's express injunctions from Ankara. "Let them not name the child before I come. I'm going to come soon and do so myself."

And about a week later the gleaming black Ford appeared in the village. Ismail Agha had some more sacrifices offered in honour of Arif Saim Bey. Everyone was again invited to a feast and the child was named Mustafa, after the country's liberator and first president of the republic.

5

MUSTAFA WAS GROWING up, taking his first toddling steps, uttering his first faltering words. Arif Saim Bey had sent a nacre-inlaid rosewood cradle at his birth and whenever he came to Adana from Ankara, however busy he might be, he never failed to visit the family and bring presents for Mustafa. He liked to converse with Ismail Agha on matters pertaining to the Chukurova and developments in the country and the rest of the world. Flattered by this friendship, Ismail Agha had become devoted to Arif Saim Bey.

For his newborn son Ismail Agha's adoration knew no bounds. He could hardly take his eyes off him. He even sang him to sleep in his cradle. When he had to leave, he turned back again and again to kiss and cuddle him, then reluctantly he jumped onto his horse and spurred it on out of the village at breakneck speed in order not to be tempted to turn back once again.

Nobody paid attention to Salman any more. It was as though he did not exist. This was not at all intentional, just that the family had eyes for no one but Mustafa. Salman never tried to put himself forward. He moved through the house like a shadow and more often than not he was up by the castle fort all day long. He had found a partridge chick and lavished all his love on it. He talked and played and slept with it, fed it on grasshoppers he caught on the mountain and the fledgling grew apace, its legs and bill reddening, its breast turning from grey to green. Never once since the first day had Salman cast so much as a glance at Mustafa or at the cradle. Some instinct impelled him to make himself scarce. Maybe too, it suited him to be ignored though at first to be suddenly neglected, bereft of the love and attention he had been used to, was like being cast into a vacuum. The pain kept him awake for many nights. He recalled the time he had been found almost dead and felt his present position was much worse. Driven by some crazy impulse, he would rise from his pallet and glide silently into the room where his parents were sleeping. He would draw near the cradle, stopping at a distance, tense, rigid, unable to take another step. Once or twice Zéro had surprised him there, but she had not troubled herself much about it.

One day, when Mustafa was a little older, Salman suddenly decided to get rid of his partridge. He left it up on the mountain, but the partridge followed him in short bursts of flight with the tenacity of a stray dog craving affection. The next day he clambered up to the rocky heights where eagles perched, put down the partridge and quickly made himself scarce. But when he came home it was already there waiting for him. Why did he want to get rid of this beautiful bird who had been his companion for so long, who had grown so attached to him? He could not say. All he knew was that he must be free of it. So this time he tied it to a thornbush at the foot of the sharp reddish crags below the castle fort. It was said that a horned rattlesnake lived there which could swallow a live kid at one go. Salman caught a great many grasshoppers, stripped them of head and wings and piled them in front of the partridge so it should not feel hungry until the rattlesnake came. All through that night he visualised the snake creeping up to the partridge, the desperate flutter of wings, the screeching, the partridge trapped, suspended from the bush as it attempted to escape, the long long snake slithering up, red tongue flickering, and gulping the partridge down. In the morning, at break of day, he hurried up to the crags. The partridge was still there, tied to the thornbush. It had eaten all the grasshoppers and was scraping away at the earth. Salman was filled with a mad rage. "Just wait!" he shouted as he cast about wildly for the snake. "It'll come, you'll see!"

Again, he caught a heap of grasshoppers, tore off their heads and wings with expert fingers and piled them up beside the partridge. The rattlesnake was sure to catch the scent. It would come this very night. And why not, when here was this juicy morsel all ready, waiting, fattened on the grasshoppers, flies and eggs that Salman provided. But that night when he went to bed, he could not help imagining the snake slithering up to the partridge, tongue flickering, coiling and uncoiling, nearer, nearer, its coral eyes gleaming in the night, the partridge floundering, feathers ruffled, straining at the string, struggling to escape, casting itself desperately from the ground to the bush, from the bush to the ground. In vain. The snake's mouth opens wider, it snaps at the partridge and slowly, its jowls bulging, it swallows it down, then glides off towards the fort, rattling away, replete, the partridge's legs sticking out of its jaws. Exhausted, Salman fell asleep and in his sleep partridges and snakes fought in a cloud that flowed above the river, while all night long the rattling of snakes sounded and feathers fluttered among swarms of green grasshoppers and again and again snakes swam up the river, each one with a half-swallowed partridge, red legs dangling, in its jaws.

"Stop," Salman said. "Stop, don't come this way or I'll wring your neck." He seized a long snake by the tail as it was sliding into the cleft of a rock. "Come," he cried, tugging away at the tail, "come." The snake rattled, it quivered, it sweated, its rattle mingled with the stridulation of the cicadas and echoed from the crags. It was stretched to snapping point. Salman could not breathe. Stop Salman! What are you doing, Salman? He let go of the snake and took to his heels, a thundering sky under his feet, a flowing something . . . From Yilankalé, the Serpents' Castle, the serpents emerged and fell after him along the dusty road, whirling in a huge dust devil, rattling loudly. Yilankalé is where the king of the serpents lives, the Shah Maran. He has the partridge in his mouth, red legs dangling . . . Under the Shah Maran's red tongue is a pair of frog's legs. Slowly he swallows the frog, then an eagle, then Mustafa . . . From the mouth of the coral-eyed serpent Mustafa's legs are hanging out, twitching. Roosters begin to crow. The stridulation of cicadas raises the echoes. And still the serpents come, rattling their tails, streaming down the rocks. Salman squeezes the Shah Maran's neck and Mustafa springs out of its belly . . . At the foot of the crags below the castle fort, Mustafa is tied to a bush, a red rope round his neck, the partridge in his arms. The rattle of the snake rings out suddenly above the stridulation of the cicadas, loud and strong . . . The snake approaches, sending the stones rolling down the crags, down down, closer and closer to Mustafa, who all unsuspecting is playing with the partridge. The snake coils itself around him, tighter and tighter. No one can save Mustafa now. Salman grabs the snake's tail and pulls, the snake lifts its head and looks back, sees Salman, spits at him with its poisonous tongue and Salman understands what it means, he lets go. Stop snake, stop . . . But the snake swallows Mustafa whole, partridge and all, and goes on its way, its belly swollen, huge . . .

Again, in breathless haste Salman made for the castle fort. The partridge was still there. He set it free and walked away. The partridge followed, tripping and flying after him. What shall I do, what shall I do, he muttered to himself in a strange language only he knew but could not name. Things that had happened long ago kept rising to his mind in snatches, dreamlike yet true as life. Some men were flinging him into a river. He sank, resurfaced, with a pack of hounds all around him. He was drowning when someone dragged him out. And ever and again that river and himself drowning, then finding himself on the shore, surrounded by white dogs, fangs bared, snarling. He was frightened. Zéro, Péro, Hassan . . . They were going to throw him into the river. Only his father, only Ismail Agha protected him, prevented them from harming him. But still, he was on tenterhooks always, terrified of everything, the night, eagles, spiders . . . Especially spiders, almost fainting whenever he saw one. He must get away from this village, far far away. But he turned and walked back home. Zéro was standing at the top of the stairs. He stopped short in front of her, in the grip of a furious rage.

It lasted fifteen or twenty days, this tying of the partridge as food for the rattlesnake, but an eternity it seemed to him. Then it went stale and he felt nothing at all when he came home one day after leaving the partridge tied up there beneath the castle. He slept like a top and in the morning he breakfasted leisurely on a roll with fresh butter from the churn and a bowl of warm sweetened milk. Then he made his way up to the castle calmly, without haste, confident that he would find the partridge exactly as he had left it.

And then, one evening he did not go back home. With the partridge in his arms, he crossed the river on the raft and took the road in the direction of Yilankalé Castle. It was swelteringly hot. The south wind had dropped. The air smelled of hot scorching dust. Sweating, he walked on, his feet in the dust as though stepping on red-hot irons. The sun sank in a cloud of dust, a red blazing mass, and an eerie silence enveloped the world.

Suddenly it was very dark. Villages, trees, Anavarza Castle, Yilankalé, all was effaced. Salman was afraid now. His fear grew apace. It was as if he was tumbling into a pitch-black precipice. He retched and lost consciousness. It was daylight when he came to. He was lying on the bank of a stream. The partridge was at his side. Turtles sunning themselves on the bank plopped back into the water. His first concern was to feed the partridge. As he was catching grasshoppers on the waterside, a black snake slithered past his feet and vanished among the burdocks. White wisps of smoke rose over a distant village. From a nearby field came the muffled voices of labourers starting to work. Soon the sun would be up and the deadly heat of the day would descend upon the plain. After quickly feeding his partridge Salman dug a water hole in the sandy shore and drank of the cold water until his belly swelled. Then he set out at once with the partridge in his arms. He had tied his shoes together by the laces and hung them over his neck. It was easier to walk barefoot, but how long could he stand it when the sun would have turned the dust of the road into red-hot embers?

At its noon height, the sun poured down like molten lead and the world around him was drenched in a milky whiteness. It was impossible to see more than a couple of yards ahead for the . sunlight was like the blackest night. He staggered on, the heat making his brain boil, until he reached Yilankalé. Then everything went black. Passers-by saw a boy with hair standing on end, screaming as he scrambled and fell, barefoot over the crags, a partridge in his arms.

He never knew how he returned to the village. Perhaps someone brought him back, perhaps he himself in a dream had groped his way along. He woke to the crowing of cocks. He was lying beneath the old pomegranate tree, racked with pain. With his shoes still hanging from his neck, he limped into the kitchen. Zéro and the other women were up and about. Someone handed him a fat roll with fresh butter and honey and a mug of warm milk. He asked for more. No one inquired where he had been, what he was doing. No one had even noticed his absence. From upstairs came the sound of voices and laughter. Ismail Agha was playing with Mustafa. Salman went up the stairs and entered the room. He passed back and forth in front of Ismail Agha who only lifted his head and smiled vaguely, then went on playing with Mustafa. Five times Salman came and went, his partridge at his heels. He ran up and down the stairs, the partridge sometimes flying ahead of him. He whirled round Ismail Agha and Mustafa, spinning, the partridge speeding after him. At last they looked up as he rushed past ever more quickly, the partridge fluttering on a level with his head, all in a wild frenzied game. Round and round, then away down the stairs, whirling, flying, and out into the yard, in a different game now, Salman hiding under the cactuses, among the branches of the pomegranate tree, in the crevices of the crags, waiting for the partridge to seek him out, standing erect in the middle of the yard, with the partridge wheeling about his head, grazing his ears, clambering onto his shoulder, slipping down inside his shirt to the ground and, hooop, up on his shoulder again. Running, whirling . . . His arms flung out wide, his eyes closed Salman sways from side to side and the partridge too, exactly like Salman, wings outspread, sways at his feet. Slowly they make for the pomegranate tree, then Salman breaks into a run and the partridge comes flying after. Salman laughs out loud, he is bathed in sweat, lost to the world, engrossed in his game. Suddenly, he lifts his head, he sees Mustafa and Ismail Agha watching from the balcony. Mustafa's eyes are wide open, awestruck. Ismail Agha is smiling, a slight, imperceptible smile. Salman stands arrested, drained, stark naked now, the sweat pouring down his face, his neck, his hair. The partridge is at his feet, also sweating, its feathers glistening, the tips of its drooping wings touching the dust.

Salman's eyes went to the castle and the mauve crags where eagles were hovering with outstretched wings, and returned to meet Ismail Agha's gaze. In that same moment he saw the cactus hedge, the cactus flowers, a butterfly panting on the dust of the yard, a comb of yellow-jackets hidden under a cactus stem, in that split of a second he saw many things he had never noticed before. A thin column of yellow ants creeping up the cactus stalk, a feather fluttering out of the chalkwhite sky, sheering this way and that, a cloud rising above the castle and drifting south to the Mediterranean, the pale blue plain below, fading into white, with dust devils swaying here and there as though nailed to it, unable to break away. And overlaying everything, Mustafa's huge proud eyes, fearful now, widening, shrinking. And Ismail Agha laughing, showing his strong white teeth, brimming with happiness, not the slightest trace on his face of sorrow, of all that he had gone through, his laughter limpid, untainted as always. Even a child must have a tinge of pain in its laughter, of despair, of confusion, of thoughts good or harmful. But Ismail Agha's laughter was pure joy, his face the picture of happiness. And Salman's eyes saw nothing else now. He bent down and picked up the partridge. His hand went to the partridge's neck. In an instant the bird's head remained in one hand, its body in the other. Dumbly he stared for a moment at the dead partridge, still quivering, its legs and wings jerking feebly. Then he laid it down gently and placed the head beside it. The partridge's beak sagged open, its eyes were veiling over. Mustafa's eyes, wide with horror, were riveted on the dead bird and Ismail Agha's laughter had frozen on his lips. Salman turned his back on them and slowly walked out of the yard and down to the riverside, a shivering joy, akin to fear, rising within him. He picked up a pebble and cast it into the water. From the heather on the opposite bank came the call of a bird he had never heard before. At last he walked off towards the Valley of Hawthorns. Half-hewn millstones of blue granite had been left lying at the foot of the mountain. Tiny, glasslike particles glittered along the veins of the granite stone. There was a hawthorn tree in the valley that was different from the other hawthorns. It was as large as an aged plane tree and its wide trunk was quite overgrown with branches and roots. From a distance it looked like a little hill in the valley. In the springtime it was all abloom with white flowers, casting a white radiance over the mauve crags and swaying gently like a billowing cloud. Bees of every kind were attracted to it in flashing clusters, sometimes hiding the flowers from view and filling the valley with a loud droning. The wind blew in waves into the valley carrying the many scents of the mountain, bitter plants, thyme, pennyroyal, rocks and earth. Though the place was a haunt of snakes, Salman liked to sleep there, stretched out on a flat rock and lulled by the warm scents and the droning of bees. This time he was asleep the minute his head touched the stone.

It was long past midnight when he woke to the insistent hooting of owls. The mountain throbbed, it was shaken to its very depths. Salman fled as though some fiery-eyed monster was after him. For Salman the world was a place of fear. Everyone, every creature in the world felt fear, even the bees and birds and butterflies . . . The grasshoppers and ants, even the eagles on high . . . As he was tearing apart the partridge's head, that very instant, they had come eye to eye. The partridge had veiled its eyes not to see death coming, but it had died too soon, and its eyes had remained half-veiled. As he thought of the partridge, his brain stopped working, his throat went dry, his body twitched and jerked just like that of the dying partridge. Then Mustafa's wide glassy gaze, Ismail Agha's frozen smile rose before his eyes and he was filled with a wild exuberant joy.

Mustafa was sitting in the sun on the balcony all by himself. Inside, Zéro was busy at her cookstove, stirring a steaming saucepan. Ismail Agha had left early in the morning on his horse, probably for the farm. He had been doing this very often lately, leaving before daybreak and riding all the length of the farm from the mountain to the river, never taking his eyes off the land. Now and again, he would get off the horse and scoop up a handful of earth from a mole burrow, poring lovingly over the rich black earth, fine as *bulgur*, then scatter it over the grass as though sowing grain. At such times he forgot everything, even Mustafa. He could have remained for days there on the perfectly flat land of the farm.

When Ismail Agha was absent Mustafa never took a step out of the house. He stayed on the balcony near the pots of sweet basil, playing with his toys, then with his nose, fingers and feet as a cat playing with its tail, until he got tired of playing and fell asleep. Salman pitied him then as he would a poor beggar boy. He wanted to go to him but did not dare, for he read an agonising dread in Mustafa's eyes.

But now Salman drew up and stopped beside the boy who was so engrossed in what he was doing that he did not notice him.

"Mustafa . . ." Salman said softly.

Mustafa looked up. He did not even give a start, but his eyes widened in a glassy stare. It was perhaps the first time Salman had spoken to him or even pronounced his name.

"Mustafa, shall we play together?"

Mustafa only stared blankly.

"I know some lovely games," Salman said. "Look." He did a handstand, then lowering his head onto the floorboards he began to spin.

There was no reaction from Mustafa. From inside Zéro saw that Salman was trying to play with her son. She was surprised. Why this sudden change? It frightened her. A strange feeling settled in her breast, an intimation of sorrow, of mourning.

Salman stopped spinning. Still on his head, his legs opened and shut like scissor blades. Then, bounding to his feet, he shinned up the balcony post and slid down again at top speed. He ran to the stairs, glided down the banisters and was soon back, laughing, astride a bright green hobby horse made of reeds, a rearing horse with wide open mouth and long pricked ears. It had a bridle too, a cord of silvered silk, and on its back two large silver-nielloed rings that had once belonged to a belt and through which a patch of gilded leather had been passed in guise of a saddle. Salman reined in before Mustafa. He stamped and reared and whinnied, he pranced and galloped up and down the balcony just like a real horse. He raced against imaginary riders on imaginary horses. He tried to make his horse descend the stairs. The horse bridled and reared, it sank down three times, but Salman whipped it on. Breathless, laughing uncontrollably, he rushed up the stairs, holding the horse and planted himself before Mustafa. His face was crimson. "Come," he said. "Come along . . ." He hoisted the child onto his back as though pillion-riding and off they went galloping along the balcony, up and down the stairs, the neighing of the horse ringing through the whole village. And now the balcony could not contain this herd of horses. They descended into the yard and started racing between the cactus hedge and the pomegranate tree. Soon the yard too was not wide enough, so they speeded down to the river, neighing, rearing, then stopped and Mustafa stood on the bank watching as the horse drank long and thirstily. Afterwards they scaled the rocks and there, beneath the castle Salman tethered the horse to a holly oak and brought over an armful of fresh grass from the hollow of a rock. He threw it before the horse and began making crunching and munching noises.

"Look, look! Look how it's eating!"

Mustafa sank onto a rock and watched intently. He made no sign of surprise or wonder. His face was waxen, filmed with sweat.

"Come, get up and let's go pick flowers now. I can find plenty of horses like this one for you." Salman vanished among the rocks. After a while he was back with a bunch of flowers, some only budding, others in full bloom. "Come! You too." Mustafa only stared as though spellbound. "Come on, together we can pick such a lot, come!" He pulled Mustafa to his feet and led him down towards the ravine. Overhead the mouth of the deep cave gaped darkly, soughing. At the end of a long reddish flat rock was a thornbush with bright blue flowers. "There!" Salman cried.

"Just look at those flowers, masses and masses of them . . . And those yellow ones too, go and pick some."

Mustafa slipped off between the rocks. Soon he was back with an armful of long-stemmed yellow flowers and a ray of joy and pride flitted across his strained face for the first time. At this, Salman fell to capering and laughing anew. He crowed like a cock and the crowing resonated and multiplied among the crags, he yowled like a jackal, howled like a wolf, rattled like a rattlesnake and was echoed by a thousand rattlesnakes. And then he began to sing. He sang the very song in the tongue which he himself did not understand, a dream song from a language of dreams, a song that he vaguely remembered having learned from a long-bearded man who also played the flute. And he saw again the tapering narrow knife, red, slashing, sparkling, swishing like rainfall, its redness flaring and fading, sprinkling down, crystalline . . . The smoke, a yellow stream, a swamp . . . A scream . . . And again the flashing crimson pinpoints . . . And rows of black black eyes closing in death . . . At the Mardin Gate, below the ramparts of Diyarbakir town white-cowled women are rocking from side to side, keening for their dead. Smoke lies over the plain. He sees again that speckled water-melon as tall as the children huddling beside it. They are beheading the flute player. Blood spurts forth, staining the headkerchiefs of the keening women. Some men drag a boy from under the dead. They look at him, pursing their lips and say something in a strange tongue. Darkness falls like a shroud over the land. Hoofbeats pound through the blackness raising the echoes, sounding even louder in the damp heavy night. The anguished neighing . . . Scorpions, big as a hand, glistening blackly on the walls, like burning amber. That severed head rolling down a rocky slope, still playing the flute as though sounding the first notes of creation . . . The keening resounding from the mountain beyond . . . Then total silence . . . The dank large bush . . . The weakness that drained even the fear of death out of you . . . The stench, the retching . . . Death among the odour of violets and fresh grass . . . Darkness. A voice . . . A face, smiling, a face from out of the past, forgotten . . . The fumes of an odorous ointment, laden with mountain scents . . . A light spreads out, dazzling . . .

Mustafa had put down his bunch of flowers and was watching the snails that crept over the rocks, leaving a silver trail behind them.

"Hey, d'you want me to pick you that purple flower? That one at the tip of that rock? Isn't it beautiful?"

Salman began clambering up the rocks. Mustafa gave a start, but quickly resumed his impassive air. His eyes, though, were riveted on Salman, who was slowing now.

Salman looked down and his head whirled. His eyes went black. His arms, too, were growing weak. Yet he would die rather than give up now when Mustafa was looking at him so admiringly. The rock wall was very smooth, but for a while he managed to shin up, keeping a hold on the small clefts on its face. At last, try as he might he could not advance another inch. Slowly, carefully, he began to back down. His heart was pounding, his strength draining. He stopped for a moment alongside a red mastic bush, his hands clamped into a largish crevasse, only just keeping himself steady. Again he looked down and met Mustafa's eyes. In the same moment he recalled how Haji Yusuf had scaled a rock wall much steeper, much higher than this one and had captured eaglets from their eyrie, three of them. After that it had been the dream of every boy in the village, even of Salman, to reach up to the eyrie just like Haji Yusuf. He caught a gleam of laughter in Mustafa's eyes and when he managed to come down at last he was quivering with rage, his face so distorted that the boy blanched. "What are you laughing at, damn you? Seen my parts in the raw? Why don't you try yourself, if it's so easy?" He dragged Mustafa to the foot of the crags. "Come on! Try going up yourself instead of laughing at me."

Without a word, Mustafa made a superhuman effort and started to climb the rock. He was already up the height of a man when he heard Salman shouting. "Come down! At once, or you'll fall. And if you fall, you'll die and that mother of yours will tear me to pieces with her bare hands . . ."

Slowly, Mustafa slid down the rock. His face was ashen.

"Come, let's go home now," Salman said. "We'll come again tomorrow and then I'll reach the top and bring down those flowers for you." He marched off and with difficulty, stumbling and falling, Mustafa tried to keep up with him.

Zéro had been worrying herself to death. "Where have you been all this time?" she asked.

"Up by the castle," Salman replied nonchalantly, with a touch of defiance. "We played there, Mustafa and I. We'll go again tomorrow, won't we, Mustafa? We'll play the horse game and the eagle game, won't we, Mustafa?"

Mustafa was silent.

"Won't we, Mustafa?"

The boy hung his head.

Salman grabbed his hand and squeezed it hard. "We'll go, Mustafa, won't we?"

"We'll go," Mustafa said dully.

"Hurray!" Salman shouted. He capered and somersaulted and stood on his head. "Hurray! We'll go out every day." He lifted Mustafa up and tossed him. "I'll make you a horse tomorrow out of a huge reed I've got, with ears pointed up so . . . You'll see . . . Tomorrow morning . . ."

That evening when Ismail Agha returned from the farm, the first thing Zéro did was to tell him what had happened.

"Indeed?" Ismail Agha said. "So Salman took his brother right up to the fortress to play, did he?"

"I'll take him out every day," Salman said fawningly. He looked hard at Mustafa. "We'll go, won't we, Mustafa."

"We'll go," Mustafa faltered.

After this, Salman never left Mustafa alone. Every day he took him to play beneath the castle ruins or down by the river or among Lame Ibrahim's beehives. He had finally succeeded in scaling the crags and picking the purple flowers for Mustafa. They still stood in a vase at home, quite dry now. Once they went to Adaja to pick narcissus among the crags. Adaja was a small rocky rise which stood out starkly on the flatness of the plain. When the wind blew, it carried the scent of narcissus far out along the road. They also went to the Valley of Hawthorns and picked and ate the fragrant fruit. Some days they remained for hours staring up at the eagles' eyries. They fashioned carts from chaste trees and horses from reeds, and when they were thirsty they dug out water holes on the river bank. But somehow Mustafa still maintained a stubborn silence while Salman dragged him here and there like a rag doll and made him do whatever he willed. As the days went by Mustafa grew more and more reticent. This did not escape Zéro's notice, but she hesitated to interfere or to speak to her husband about her doubts. Sometimes she caught a strange gleam in Salman's eyes as he looked at Mustafa. It filled her with dread, but still she said nothing to Ismail Agha.

Salman now held Mustafa in his thrall and gradually he began to torment the boy. He knew that Mustafa was disgusted by grasshoppers, snails and frogs. So he broke the shells of snails, tore off the heads and wings of large grasshoppers and skewered green frogs onto reeds that he had sharpened to a point. The boy would tremble and close his eyes to avoid the sight of the wounded snails, the lifeless heaps of grasshoppers and the impaled frogs panting their last, their eyes bulging even more. And all the while Salman whooped and whirled round and round the child in a kind of savage dance. Then he would light a big fire and throw into it the snails, grasshoppers and frogs and a nauseating smell would spread about the crags. Once Salman caught a very long black snake. Mustafa gave it one look and closed his eyes tightly. His fingers stiffened. Salman could not prise them open. "Coward, coward!" he yelled. "What's there to be frightened of? It's only a tiny little snake." He forced open Mustafa's hand. "Hold it now," he cried. "Hold this beautiful snake." The child trembled. "Hold it, you dirty coward! What kind of a son will you be to my father when you grow up? Hold it, come on hold it." Suddenly, Mustafa's eyes snapped open. He seized the snake with both hands and bolted down the hill. Salman shouted after him, but the child rushed on, unheeding, the snake's head and tail undulating on each side of him. He had almost reached the road when he tripped and fell. He lay there, breathing heavily, his eyes open in a fixed stare, his face chalk-white. The black snake lay alongside, quite still. Salman tried to make him sit up. "Coward," he hissed. "Coward . . . Damn you and all the cowards on earth . . ." He heaved Mustafa onto his back and carried him down to the river. "Don't die," he pleaded as he splashed water onto his face. "Please don't die, Mustafa. I won't ever make you touch a black snake again. My father will kill me if you die." Suddenly he was moaning, beating his sides, running this way and that, muttering to himself. At last he slumped down beside Mustafa. "Die then!" he cried. "I didn't kill you, did I? You died all by yourself. Your mother shouldn't have borne a weakling like you. Die!" He did not speak again, but remained by the boy's side, on tenterhooks, heart jumping at the slightest sign of change, at every twitch and tremor on his face.

The sun was sinking in the west and Mustafa still lay lifeless on the shingle. Salman had only one thought, to escape beyond those distant hills, to hide among their mauve shadows. How could he face his father if Mustafa died? Ismail would kill him on the spot and bury him beside Mustafa. He must run away. But before going he must tear this Mustafa to pieces. In a frenzy of passion he was imagining how he would sever limb from limb, when Mustafa opened his eyes. Salman went limp. "Mustafa," he murmured, "Mustafa . . ." Mustafa sat up and looked about him dazedly. His shadow fell over the water, lengthening, undulating. It caught his gaze and he remained like that as in a trance. He was roused by Salman, skipping, dancing, turning somersaults all around him. "You're alive," he kept saying. "You're not dead. Father won't kill me. I won't have to go away beyond those mountains where the ogres live . . ." Then he stopped short. "Mustafa," he said sharply, "get up now. Come here."

Mustafa took a few faltering steps towards him, his head drooping.

"Mustafa, you're not to tell your mother or our father that you died today, understand?"

Mustafa said nothing.

"If father hears of this, he'll kill me right away. D'you want me to die?"

Mustafa just stood there, his arms hanging, his eyes fixed on the ground.

"Look here, if you go and tell father about the black snake, then . . . See those crags? Behind them is a pit filled to the brim with rattlesnakes. I'll throw you in and the snakes will devour you even as you fall, even before you reach the bottom. They'll finish you, bones and all. You won't tell, will you?"

Mustafa did not change his stance. Not once did he lift his head and look at Salman.

"D'you see that cave?" Salman grabbed the boy by the chin and made him look up. "You see it?" He let go and Mustafa's head fell again. "That cave is full of bats, a thousand bats maybe, all dangling heads down. If you tell father about the black snake, about how you died, I'll tie you up inside that cave where nobody dares to go in and the bats will stick to your eyes and suck and suck . . . And then to your head, to your tummy, to your willy . . . They'll cling like leeches and drink up all your blood. Will you tell father?"

Mustafa's face was drained white. He swayed.

"You know that swamp, the one below Anavarza Castle? I'll drive you into it and the quicksands will drag you down slowly, very slowly, while the mosquitoes are devouring you and you'll die screaming. So. Will you tell or not?"

At last Mustafa spoke. "I won't tell," he quavered faintly.

Salman was transported with joy. He lifted Mustafa up in his arms and kissed him. Then they walked on, hand in hand, to where they had left the snake. It was still lying there, coiled. "It's dead," Salman stated as he picked it up by the tail. "Poor little snake. Come on, let's go, Mustafa." The snake came after them, its head knocking against the stones, its black body white with dust. Salman dragged it along never once turning to look at it.

As soon as they were home Mustafa took to his bed, shivering and burning with fever. They brought him some food, but he could not eat. Soon he became delirious, screaming about snakes and bats and rattles. Ismail Agha never moved from his side till daybreak and towards noon the doctor arrived from town in a car. He found nothing wrong with the boy, gave him some medicine from his bag and left.

For a while after this, Salman was careful with Mustafa, even affectionate sometimes and sincerely so. This began to make the boy relax and almost happy. Salman pretended he was a horse and let him ride piggyback. He fashioned toys for him, horses, carts, whistles and even little mills with paddles that wheeled in the water, and also barrows from the branches of chaste trees which they loaded with fragrant herbs to carry back home. They picked luscious honeyed blackberries and huge mushrooms, large as two hands. Mustafa still did not speak, he remained reserved, wary of Salman's doing things again with snakes, bats, lizards and scorpions.

"Come, let's go up to the castle," Salman suggested.

Mustafa hung back, but at the look Salman gave him he was soon trotting along docilely after him. And it all began again, the snakes, the frogs impaled alive on long reed stalks and also the breaking up of swallow's nests, tearing off the chicks' heads . . . Mustafa was getting inured to all this when one day Salman said: "Today we're going to go into that cave." They were standing under the castle fort beside a barberry shrub. "We'll go in and catch bats. Come on."

Mustafa did not stir.

"Hurry up, man," Salman shouted. "Must I drag you in?"

He seized Mustafa's hand and tugged him on. Sweating, their legs torn and bleeding, they reached the mouth of the cave. From here, the walls of the castle seemed to reach into the sky, far up, lost among the clouds. "Here we are, let's go in now . . ." Salman was afraid too. As for Mustafa, he was almost fainting. Suddenly Salman swept him up in his arms and began to carry him inside. Mustafa, struggling like one possessed, scratching and kicking, shook himself free and went rushing down the slope. He tripped and fell and rolled on like a ball, followed by Salman in desperate haste for he saw that the boy was heading straight for the precipice beyond. But before he could reach him, Mustafa crashed into a bramble bush. He was bleeding profusely, his eyes, his whole face invisible under the running blood. Seized with panic at the thought that the boy would go straight to Ismail Agha, just as he was, steeped in blood, Salman dragged him writhing and straining towards the crags determined on casting him down the precipice. But Mustafa sank his teeth into his wrist and the lancinating pain brought him to his senses. There were sounds coming from the road below. Salman hoisted the boy onto his back and carried him down to the river bank. He washed his face and hands and even his clothes and saw that Mustafa was not really hurt, just scratches here and there, but what a lot of blood he had lost . . .

"You won't tell anyone about this, will you?"

Mustafa looked sullen.

"It's death for you if you tell, and for me too . . ."

Mustafa shivered from top to toe.

The sun was setting as they came home.

"Where have you been?" Zéro exclaimed. "Darling, look at the state you're in!"

Mustafa was silent.

"We were picking berries," Salman said. "A barberry shrub . . . The thorns . . ."

"Oh my poor lamb! What will your father say? Wait . . ." And she set about applying ointments on his face. "You mustn't go gathering berries among the brambles again. When your father sees you like this, he'll never let you two go out at all."

Some days later Salman beckoned to Mustafa who was leaning on the wooden parapet of the balcony. "Come Mustafa," he urged in a low voice, "come, let's go to the river. I've found three eagle eggs and I'll show them to you."

Mustafa faced him blankly. He did not move from the parapet.

Some way away, Ismail Agha was inspecting a silver-nielloed

saddle he had just received from the Long Plateau. The pommel, the stirrups, the whole of the harness were also worked with silver. Zéro was spinning wool and the bodyguards were conversing in low tones under the staircase as they oiled their German carbines and filled their gold-embroidered bandoliers with cartridges from the heap in front of them.

"We shan't go into that cave again, never fear . . ."

Mustafa was silent.

"Look I've picked some medlars for you . . ."

The boy did not seem to hear.

"Come down, do! Let's go now." Salman's pleading was now charged with angry undertones. "So you won't come, eh?" he said sharply at last. Rushing up the stairs, he grabbed Mustafa's arm and pulled him roughly.

And then the unexpected happened. Tense as a bow, the boy hurled himself at Salman, hitting, biting, scratching, uttering piercing screams that could be heard all over the village. Ismail Agha sprang forward and seized Mustafa in his arms. The boy was still struggling and shrieking and trying to free himself.

"I've done nothing to him. Why should he . . ." Salman quailed. "I didn't . . . I just said, let's go to the river. And then he started hitting me . . ."

In the days that followed Salman attempted several times to make up to Mustafa, laughing off the incident or acting sorry, threatening or pleading, but Mustafa's reaction never changed. He always attacked Salman with bloodcurdling screams, so much so that in the end Ismail Agha had to intervene.

"Salman," he said sternly, "you must have done something very bad to this child. Don't ever come near him again or . . ."

Salman heard him in silence. He bowed his head and from then on it was as though he did not live in this house. He came and went like a shadow. In the village, too, he moved around so furtively that people soon forgot that he had ever existed.

Some years had passed, maybe four, maybe five, when one day Salman presented himself before Ismail Agha. His shoulders had broadened, he had grown a little taller and his moustache was sprouting. His eyes were two slits, hard, sly, sorrow-wounded. He wore black boots, polished bright, *shalvar*-trousers with silver embroidered pockets and seams, a striped shirt of pure silk and a jacket cut from some expensive blue-green English cloth that had come from Syria. At his waist he had bound a Tripoli sash with the fringes hanging down to his knees and into it was thrust an ivory-handled Nagant revolver.

Why, he's dressed just like me, Ismail Agha thought, down even to the Nagant revolver at his waist. He's only added a bright handkerchief in his pocket.

"What is it, my child?"

"I would like to have a German carbine. And also a horse for my own."

Ismail Agha laughed. "Aren't they all yours in this house?"

"Mine? Yes, but . . ." Salman smiled bitterly.

"Go to the stables and choose any horse you fancy. Go to the armoury and take the rifle you choose. And if there's nothing that satisfies you, then . . . Here, take this money and buy yourself horse and rifle just as you want."

"Thank you father," Salman said. He took the money his father was so gladly offering and left.

Ismail Agha looked after him fondly. Scenes from long ago passed through his mind, his meeting with Hashmet Bey, the time of stumping for Memik Agha, the death of his mother, Salman, a mere skin and bones, his head and hands swathed in white bandages . . . He smelled again the fragrance of the soothing balms rubbed onto Salman's wounds, redolent of the thousand and one forest scents . . . He could not understand why Zéro and the rest of the household had taken such a dislike for the lad, and to make up for that and also for having neglected him somewhat after the birth of Mustafa, he treated him with a warmth more akin to pity. Mustafa, he could not fathom at all. What efforts had Salman not made to draw close to him . . . But Mustafa had repulsed him at every turn and with growing animosity. Could it be that Salman had done something to him when the child had been three or four years old? This thought came to him now and then, though he did not dwell on it, but there were other thoughts that he could not drive away. Is it Salman who loves me more or is it Mustafa? Mustafa's love was instinctive, natural, his own flesh and blood, a thing of joy, flowing clear as a spring. With Salman it was quite different, an adoration, an infinite devotion. Salman's whole being was centred on him, whatever he did, his every move was for him. He lived and breathed only for him. Salman had no relatives, no roots, no god. Ismail Agha was everything to him, he felt him in every drop of his blood. Maybe this was real love, to have eyes for only one thing in the world, to breathe for that one thing only. Ismail Agha was the very breath of Salman. The lad had such a way of looking at him, secret, hidden even from himself, that the love in him gushed from his eyes, his hands, his hair, his whole body, even the ground on which he stood. Since the beginning Salman had been an exceptional source of happiness for Ismail Agha. No one, not his mother, not his wife, not his brothers, not even Mustafa, no one had been so close to him, no one's friendship or love had ever filled him with such tremulous pleasure . . . If anything were to happen to him, Salman would never survive, whereas Mustafa would take it naturally, like any son losing his father, he would grieve a little, and then he would forget, just like he himself had his own father. Maybe he would name one of his sons after him, never even thinking of him when he called that son by his name. The name, only an abstraction, would in the end belong entirely to his son.

The thought obsessed him. He must do something for Salman, endow him with some property or other. But how? Zéro would never forgive him. Still he had to find a way of showing Salman his affection and the special place he held in his heart.

Salman had selected a three-year-old bay horse, an English half-blood, one of the most beautiful horses in Ismail Agha's stable. He would ride away before dawn, a German carbine slung over his shoulder, his body girded with rows and rows of gold-filigreed bandoliers, and make for the new farm at the foot of the opposite mountain, returning a week or a fortnight later, bolt upright on the bay horse, looking neither to right nor to left, sometimes rushing through the village at full gallop.

"Father," he said one morning, just as Ismail Agha, his face serene and happy, was folding up his prayer rug after the *namaz*, "today if you'll give me leave, I'm going to rid the village of that eagle curse."

"What have the eagles done then?"

"Can't you see? There are no chickens at all in the village. And no birds or partridges left up in the hills either. I'm going to wipe those eagles out, root and branch."

"Very well. But how are you going to set about it?"

"Leave that to me, father. Just give me your permission."

"Warn the villagers first. We mustn't frighten the children."

Salman then went to Zéro. He kissed her hand. "From now on,

Mother Zéro," he told her, "you can raise chickens, geese, turkeys and pheasants too, if you like. No eagle will ever come to this village again."

"How's that?"

"I'm going to shoot them down, one and all."

"Well, good for you. Let me buy some brood hens then and a hundred eggs and set them to hatch right away. Show us what you can do."

Salman laughed gleefully. Nobody had ever seen him in such an animated mood. He went down to the storeroom and emerged at once carrying a huge cage crammed with starlings.

From the balcony Ismail Agha, Zéro, Mustafa and the bodyguards all watched as he made for the pomegranate tree, weighed down sideways by his heavy load, and clambered up onto the crags behind it. There, he took a starling out of the cage and tied it to the topmost branch with a string a fathom long. The other starlings he tied to the pointed crags, to the hollyhocks and thistles that grew among the rocks and to the thatched roof of the trellis in the yard. Then he settled in a secluded nook, his rifle at the ready, with all around him starlings bobbing up and down as they attempted to fly away.

The villagers soon got wind of the affair. They gathered to watch the battle of Salman and the eagles.

And so they waited, Salman, Ismail Agha, his bodyguards, each one a crack shot who could hit a coin cast high up in the air, they waited silently for the eagles to come and pounce upon the birds. It was long past noon and still they waited. Only once a group of eagles was seen circling high up east of the craggy mountain peak, but they turned away without even attempting to draw near. What was the matter with those eagles? It was as if they were making fun of Salman. Why, up to now, if a chick so much as ventured into the yard, the eagles, catching the scent, would be upon it at one fell swoop and up into the sky in the twinkling of an eye.

It was only in the afternoon, as the south wind started to blow that the eagles reappeared in ones and twos, gliding slowly, heads tilted sideways as though scanning the village below.

Salman, his finger on the trigger, was trying to keep calm, not to panic. This was the first, the greatest trial in his life. For years he had watched the eagles, he was wise to all their ways. He knew they could be down in an instant before one had time to see them and up again with their prey, and that was what he feared most, to miss them as they swooped down over the starlings. He had tried his hand countless times these last days up on the hills. Not one eagle had he missed. But what if his hand were to shake now . . .

And so he waited, his body taut as a bow, unable to repress the trembling inside of him, his agitation heightening whenever he glanced at his father leaning on the balcony railing, where a dozen men from the village had joined him. Others came and went up and down the stairs. But Ismail Agha's eyes were fixed on him, steady, unwavering, with who knows what love, what fervour, eager, wondering . . . Will my son kill those eagles . . .

"Allah," Salman prayed, "don't let me be shamed before my father. Kill me rather. Send down your eagles, please Allah . . ."

The eagles seemed to be looking for something in the village. Heads cocked, wings stretched taut, they rode the wind as though floating on still waters, moving effortlessly along the sky. Salman watched, tense, his heart leaping at the slightest change, the blood draining from his limbs as once or twice they dropped a little lower. And so he waited till nightfall, till the last few eagles barely discernible in the darkening sky, had gone away. He was stiff all over, the finger on the trigger numb, his head in a stupor, his eyes glazed. At last, he wrenched himself from the rock, untied the birds and put them back into the cage, which he took down to the storeroom again. Then, without stopping to eat or drink, he mounted his horse and rode off into the plain.

He was back in the morning, his saddlebag crammed with plucked chickens and chicks. From the storeroom he took out the starlings and tied them to the same places as the day before, scattering a few chicks before them. Then he sat down to wait, his rifle on the ready. Ismail Agha came again with Mustafa and stood on the balcony beside the sweet basil. Salman's spirits lifted. So his father had faith in him still . . . "Come on you muckers," he muttered. "What more d'you want? I've even plucked birds and chicks for you . . . Please, Allah, send me those eagles, please, just three, and I'll sacrifice a huge ram for you. I'll do anything for you, anything . . . You send eagles by the dozen when I'm all by myself on that godforsaken mountain and I don't miss a shot, then why, oh why, Allah, not even one today?"

This morning the eagles appeared earlier than the day before. It was not yet noon when they started circling in the sky right above Salman and his hopes rose. Ismail Agha was on the balcony and the villagers had gathered around again. But this day too not one eagle attempted to attack the starlings. And though one of them did come down as low as the height of two poplars, though Salman could have shot it down unerringly, his courage failed him and the eagle slowly rose up again and as the day came to a close not a single eagle was left in the sky.

On the third morning Salman was at his post again after a wakeful anguished night. If this day too the eagles did not come, if they made no attempt to get at the decoys, it would be all up with him, he would be disgraced in front of everyone. The only thing left for him would be to shoulder his rifle, mount his horse and take himself away for ever. But not to see his father again, not to have proved his valour, his love . . . Why, he could not breathe, he could not live away from his father! Just a few days without seeing him were enough to fill him with unbearable longing. What would it be like not to see him for months, years, a whole lifetime? Salman's mind boggled at the thought.

The sun was quarter high and hot already when he saw two eagles rise up from the crags. His heart leaped. He knew them, those eagles, coppery red, their eyes ringed with gold, the most rapacious of their kind. *Jingirs* the villagers called them. Five more appeared, then more and more. They've caught the scent, Salman jubilated. These *jingirs* could spot a tiny sparrow or chick from however high in the sky and be down on their prey like a bolt of lightning.

"The *jingirs*, the *jingirs*," the villagers cried joyfully.

On they came, the red eagles from behind a white cloud that was stuck over the sharp pointed peak of the mountain. Slowly they circled above the village, searching the ground. Very soon the circle tightened. They were right above Salman. He was confident now. His eyes, sharp as a falcon's, did not miss their slightest motion, the way they scanned the crags, heads bent sideways, the slight trembling of wings as they sighted the decoys and made ready to plunge, hesitated, trembled again, lower now, nearer . . . It would not be long before one of them, drawing itself tightly into a ball, glided down with a long swishing sound, then seizing a starling . . . He had even selected that bird. It was there in the west facing eastward, its angled wings quivering. He was ready, his finger on the trigger. The eagle stopped, suspended, its wings vibrating ever more quickly. Suddenly it rounded itself into a ball, its red back flashed lightning-like as it dived. It was almost on the pomegranate tree when Salman pressed the trigger, his hand steady now, cool, unafraid. The eagle swirled in the air, a reddish mass, one wing hanging, then dropped limply over the rocks above the pomegranate.

The *jingirs* were coming in ever greater numbers. Even as they bunched up and pounced, Salman pressed the trigger and hit them before they were half-way down. His aim was unerring, not one shot was wasted. And now some large, broad-winged eagles materialised above. It was much easier to shoot those big birds. Salman did not even bother to take a proper aim, he just lifted the muzzle and fired and the bird, losing speed, came staggering down, head limp, wings awry, legs still quivering. Some of them, wounded but not killed outright, acted ever so strangely. The last one that he hit while still high in the air, first began to spin round and round, all in a flutter, closed its wings, soared up swiftly, then sagged and lost height, swaying, pulled up again, wings wide open, gliding this way and that, nodding its head in a kind of funny dance and at last, wings flapping like a butterfly, it came to land not far from Salman near one of the plucked chickens. It stared at it in amazement, craning its neck as though sniffing it, then hobbled away, stumbled over the sharp rocks and remained sprawling there until it sprang up one last time, whirling round and round.

Dead and dying eagles lay strewn all about the village. The children had caught some of the wounded ones and, tying strings around their necks, were playing a merry game as though with the best of toys, forgetting even their fear of Salman. Old people, rheumatics, the sick, hastened to gather the birds which they dressed and set to boil in large laundry cauldrons, for it was widely believed that the fat of the eagle is a panacea for all ills. Quarrels broke out, the children wanting to play with the birds while the villagers wanted to boil as many as they could lay hands on. They need not have worried, for Salman, basking in his victory, did not give up until not one eagle was left in the sky over the village. He would go on tomorrow and the next day until he had exterminated them all, until they had departed from the crags never to return.

At sundown Salman rose, wiping his clothes. A pleasant odour of thyme rose to his nostrils. He had very little ammunition left.

Gathering the empty cartridges, he filled them into the hunter's pouch tied to his waist and made for the mansion.

Some of the villagers had left to perform the evening *namaz* prayer, but others were still there with Ismail Agha, waiting for Salman. As for Mustafa at the first burst of the rifle, when the first eagle fell dead from the sky, he had been seized with a fit of trembling. His face ashen he escaped into one of the closets and hid among the stacked downy pillows and quilts.

Salman approached, put down his rifle and bowed before Ismail Agha. Then, kissing his hand, "Father," he said in a voice strangling with emotion, "may your enemy's life be that long."

"Thank you, my child, my brave Salman," Ismail Agha said. "I knew you'd turn out to be a man."

"Indeed, Ismail Agha, I congratulate you," Memet Effendi said. "You couldn't come across such a good shot in Fevzi Pasha's army even. Not even in the whole of Kurdistan, Georgia, Arabia or among the Franks either. Your son is a real hero."

The other villagers all concurred, while Salman stood before them, erect, stiff as a dagger thrust into the ground. "Father," he said, and now his eyes were strange, like the eyes of a bird of prey, "father it's not for nothing that I've been practising day and night all these years. Not just to kill a few miserable birds . . . I've got something to ask of you." He stopped and hung his head.

"Say it, my child." Ismail Agha's voice was gentle, brimming with love.

"We have many enemies on this plain, aghas and beys, and bandits up in the mountains . . ."

"Well son, what of it?"

"I want to be your bodyguard from now on, to keep watch over you day in day out." He glanced at his father's regular guards standing on the staircase, their rifles on the ready. "These comrades will also watch. They are brave men, they would give their lives for you. But I must be with them, guarding my father."

Slowly Ismail Agha reached over and kissed Salman's brow. "I knew my son would turn out to be a lion of a man. So it's my son who will guard me, how marvellous." He caressed Salman's hair, his shoulders, his back, all his love was in his hands.

Zéro stood by smiling contentedly. No one noticed that Mustafa was nowhere to be seen.

"My friends," Ismail Agha addressed the company, "tomorrow

you'll all be my guests. I'm going to offer *kurbans* for my brave son, to ward off the evil eye."

"Good for you," Memet Effendi approved. "Such a brave son, he deserves it."

"Indeed he deserves it," the others agreed.

Early the next morning, sheep and goats were brought over from the flocks, slaughtered and distributed to every house in the village. The men were invited to a big banquet at the mansion. Salman never left Ismail Agha's side, beside himself with joy. And that evening he took his rifle and went to stand guard beside the pomegranate tree, as he had been planning to for years. There he waited his hand on the trigger, his eyes wide open, never dropping off for one second. At daybreak, before retiring to his room, he went to wake Ismail Agha. "Father," he said, "I'm going to take some sleep now. Wake me up if you intend to go out. From now on you're not going anywhere without me."

It was a month or so after this that a loud commotion arose from the houses beneath the crags. Salman was asleep. They woke him up. "The eagles," they cried, "the eagles are attacking us. They're everywhere in the sky and coming on and on . . ." Salman dressed quickly and went outside. It was drizzling. From the peak of the mountain opposite, eagles were flying towards the village, wing to wing, wheeling lower and lower over the Narrow Pass. Salman realised at once what was happening. He strapped on his cartridge-belts, seized his rifle and set off in the direction of the Narrow Pass, followed by a crowd of villagers, young and old.

Widow Fatmali's daughter, Hüsné, one of the prettiest girls in the village, was seventeen years old and betrothed to Duran, now away doing his military service. Long Osman came up to her one day as she was gathering lentils with a group of women on Memet Efendi's land.

"Come Hüsné," he said quietly, without haste, "we're going."

Hüsné stared at him without a word.

"Going where, Osman?" Fatmali asked.

"I've come to take Hüsné away, Mother Fatmali," Osman said. "She's my intended, not Duran's." He waited awhile, then, "Come along Hüsné," he repeated and stepped up to her. At this, Hüsné turned and fled. Osman caught up with her as she was about to jump into the river. She fought him tooth and nail, but Osman was a large man and the slim frail girl gave way at last. Osman lifted her onto his back and clambered up into the mountain, the girl screaming and biting him whenever she came to. Scaling the craggy summit they passed through a wood of gum trees and came to a long wide cave with a floor of flintstone. Osman had fitted up this cave like a house, with bedding, food and drink. He set the girl on the bed, quickly ripped off her clothes and lay down, naked, beside her. At the contact of the man's hot flesh, Hüsné became quite rigid. All Osman's frenzied efforts to loosen her limbs were in vain. After a while he felt her body slacken and just as he was prising her legs open he realised that she was dead. At that moment he went completely mad. Seizing his dagger, he slashed at her nipples, then her pubis, her nose, her eyes . . . He went on tearing at her body till evening came. When the gendarmes found him, he was sitting beside a shapeless heap of flesh that had been Hüsné's body.

Osman was held one week at the district police station, then taken to town and brought before the public prosecutor who released him after a couple of days. At the sight of Osman back in the village, scot free, Fatmali rushed to the Kaymakam, the court magistrates, the councilmen. For days she cast about the town knocking on every door, to no avail. Memet Effendi and Ismail Agha also tackled the magistrates about this incomprehensible miscarriage of justice, but on their return to the village they had not a word of explanation to say to anyone. At the news of Hüsné's fate, Duran ran away from the army, taking a Mauser rifle with him. He came upon Osman in front of the village mosque. Osman was unarmed and took to his heels. For some reason, Duran did not fire. His face grim, unrelenting, obstinate, he pursued Osman who was running for his life, trying to enter one of the houses but finding every door shut against him. Screaming, he blundered on until he found himself driven back before the mosque. And there at last, Duran fired. He fired three times before Osman fell. Then, standing over him, he fired two more shots into Osman's eyes. He kept on shooting, reloading his rifle with charge after charge. When he had no more ammunition he jammed the rifle over his shoulder, seized the dead man by one foot and dragged him away to Fatmali's house. "What can we do, mother, what can we do against fate . . . ?" he said and turned away still dragging the corpse. The whole village followed him as he made for the Narrow Pass. There he stopped and flung Osman down a large deep pit. The corpse fell over a clump of thistles at the bottom of the pit and remained there, its mouth open to the sky.

Duran turned to the crowd. "Let no one try to take this corpse out of here, neither his mother, his father, no one. No one's to take him out and bury him. If anyone so much as touches him, I'll wreck his house over his head. I swear it. It will remain here like the carrion of a dog until his bones rot."

He broke through the silent crowd and disappeared up into the mountain.

When he came to the Narrow Pass, Salman looked for a place to sit and settled down on a rock. An unending train of eagles and buzzards was streaming down from the mountain into the pit with strange wild cries. Osman's clothes had been torn off in an instant and his bloody naked body exposed to the attacks of the birds of prey. All eyes were on Salman. Would he kill the birds, aiming unerringly like that last time? But Salman did not move. As in a dream, he sat there, his forehead leaning against the cold iron of his rifle, on he sat while the birds rose and fell over the pit, a jostling screeching mass of wings. He waited till nightfall, then he got up and joining the crowd of villagers, they all made their way laughing and chatting towards their homes.

6

DURING THE SPRING months the river swells into a turbid mass, flooding fields and villages and depositing layers of yellow silt for miles around. Then suddenly it subsides. The water becomes so limpid that the fish and even the pebbles at the bottom can be seen clearly. Flowers abound on the plain, big green flies flash hither and thither, bees of every kind appear and shimmering-winged beetles, clouds of butter-flies, blue, orange, green, dart up and down in waves over meadow and marshland, birds flock in from the four corners of the earth, cranes, ducks, bustards, swans, flamingos, birds in their thousands, some no one can name or recognise. The hoopoes with their proud crests are the beauty of the plain. Long-legged storks pace the fields, swaying, undisturbed. Starlings, changing their glistening white-speckled feathers in the spring, make a brief appearance. The scent of flowers, of new grass, of water-heather fill the mountain and the plain.

Mustafa was awake and dressed before sunrise. Stealthily, he glided into the hall and crept out through a back window which could not be seen from where Salman and the other bodyguards were stationed. This window with its wooden shutters had never been used since the house was built and Mustafa was delighted to have discovered it.

Bird Memet was waiting for him beneath the cactuses in the old grain pit now overgrown with nettles, mallow, burdock and squirting cucumbers. Mustafa whistled. He had only just learned how to whistle and he did so at every turn. Memet emerged from the pit, numb all over. "Look," he said. "He's there." Salman's dark figure was pacing up and down at the foot of the crags.

"He hasn't seen me," Mustafa said. "I came through the back window. No one saw me. Come, let's go to Wiggler."

Wiggler Yusuf was hiding by the river bank. He showed himself when Memet imitated the call of a bird. "Hurry up," he whispered. "I've been waiting here for ages."

They cut back through the village, creeping fearfully past the graveyard, and came to some tall cliffs at another bend of the river.

"The others should have been here already," Wiggler complained.

"Well, let's get started anyway," Memet said.

They jumped down the cliff and started to walk along the shingle, but first Mustafa took off the shiny shoes that he had received only a couple of days ago from Adana, and with his socks hung them out of sight on a tamarisk bush. Like the others he went on barefoot, wading through the water at times. Shoals of tiny fish darted up sniffing at their feet, then dashed off timorously. On the opposite bank, water-birds were asleep, necks drawn in, perched on one long leg. Far away over the plain, three eagles were wheeling, tracing wide circles in the distant sky. They came to a thicket of chaste trees alive with the loud buzzing of bees and there they dug out the spade, shovel and pickaxe they had left buried in the sand. "Nobody's found them," Yusuf exulted. "Now we can get to work. The cliffs here are full of holes where those birds nest."

The kingfisher is a deep blue bird with timid velvety black eyes. Its head, a darker shade of blue, stretches out into a pointed bill and it is the prettiest, the most graceful of all birds. No child can touch its soft blue plumage or gaze into its warm eyes without his heart leaping and a thrill passing through his body, a kind of warm soft blueness. Heather-scented blue breezes blow about his head. His dreams are blue. A blue day dawns, blue sunbeams illumine the mountainside and the bed of the stream, striking up blue sparks from the swiftly darting fish. The rain falls blue, a drizzling blue haze, blue clouds unfurl in the sky. And the morning star, huge, coruscating, stains sky and earth a brilliant blue.

Mustafa had held a kingfisher once for an instant, but it had slipped from his hands, vanishing across the water in a flash of blue. From that moment he had lived in a kind of blue daydream. It was he who had persuaded the other children to join him in digging for kingfishers where they nested deep in the cliffs.

It was Salman who had caught that kingfisher and given it to him. He had cradled the palpitating bird in his hands, gazing spellbound into the soft shimmering black eyes, the kingfisher's trepidation communicating itself to him, its heart beating against his palms ever more quickly, the blue feathers ruffled, clammy, and suddenly it had shaken itself free, a blue streak over the water, weaving blue circles about the crags across the river. It seemed to Mustafa, whenever he looked at those crags rising like an islet on the opposite bank, that they were capped with blue clouds out of which bluebirds kept dropping over the water turning it to a silvery blue all ashimmer with the beat of thousands of wings. And the other boys also saw the blue clouds and the bluebirds with their flashing wings. And this spring the golden corn put forth blue ears, the fields glistened bluely all over the Chukurova.

"See that hole?" Bird Memet said. "Looks like there's a large nest in there. I'll start digging and when I'm in deep enough you can stop the mouth with your hands. There should be quite a few birds in there."

"It's always one only," Mustafa said.

"Must be two," Wiggler objected. "They live in pairs, these birds."

"They can't be caught," Mustafa sighed. "You dig and dig and just when you're getting near the nest, the bird flushes out and away."

"Well, mind you catch it this time." Bird Memed, wielding the pickaxe and sweating profusely, was nearing the nest at last. "Ready now! Put your hands here. Quick!"

Suddenly, a bluebird whirred out of the hole, soft in Mustafa's hands for an instant, and shot away, leaving three blue feathers floating gently in the air.

"I nearly caught it this time," Mustafa panted.

"You missed it again," Bird Memet twitted him.

"It was the loveliest one I've ever seen," Wiggler Yusuf sighed.

They dug a water hole in the shingle and drank of the clear icy water. Then they sat down leaning against the cliff.

"We'll never catch those birds this way," Wiggler Yusuf said. "We must find something, a net to spread at the mouth of the hole, a cage, some kind of snare . . ."

Just then the sun rose and the shadow of the castle fell across the river, dark and cool, reaching out to the level stretch of tangled tamarisks, water-heather and brambles.

Soon the other boys arrived from the village, talking at the top of their voices.

"Shsh! Quiet," Mustafa admonished them. "You'll frighten the birds away."

"Did you bag one?"

Bird Memet pointed to the burrow in the cliff. "It was huge," he said proudly. "And such a blue!" He whistled regretfully.

"And soft," Mustafa said. "Warm . . ." He licked his lips.

"Battal's mother is weaving nets for him," Poyraz announced. "Five in all."

"We want to catch them with our hands, not with nets," Wiggler said defiantly.

"Ohhooo," Mustafa scoffed. "Anyone can catch them with nets, boy!"

"What we're going to do," Battal said, "is to fix nets to the bird holes. When a bird comes out it'll get entangled in the net."

"But that's cruel," Bird Memet protested. "It's sinful."

"Not more than spoiling their nests," Battal countered. "D'you know how long it takes for a bird to make a nest like that?"

"What of it?" Wiggler objected. "It'll dig another hole. These birds love to dig nests."

"How d'you know?"

"My father told me. My father knows everything."

"Of course he does," Mustafa flashed. "His father's a smith. Is there anything a smith doesn't know? Which one of you here has a smith for a father?"

"No one," Bird Memet triumphed.

The others stared, nonplussed.

"Well," Battal said at last, "you can just sit and watch us catch those blue birds, ten, twenty, more even in one day."

"You can't," Bird Memet said. "Hunting birds with nets is forbidden here."

"Who's forbidden it?"

"I have," Bird Memet said, striking his chest.

"Then I'll set up my nets further down the river."

"We've forbidden it!" Mustafa shouted. "Want to fight?"

"Who wants to fight you, you little savage?" Poyraz retorted. "You're savages, you and your father and all your family."

"Savage yourself," Bird Memet flung at him. "We all know how your father goes cringing up to Mustafa's father, wagging his tail. Just for a few paltry coins . . ."

"What's it to me? I don't wag any tails."

"But your father does. He's your father, isn't he?"

Suddenly, a puny little boy, scraggy-necked, huge-eyed, who had not said a word up to now, shot out from behind Poyraz and hurled himself at Mustafa. This was Nuri. Mustafa, taken by surprise, fell to the ground, but was soon giving as good as he got. Then Bird Memet charged at Battal and Poyraz. Wiggler, for his part, just stood by, watching.

"I'm not interfering," he laughed. "Memet will thrash the daylights out of you both." And to Mustafa: "Don't louse up the poor bugger, let him go."

Mustafa straightened up, blinking in perplexity. Nuri was lying under him. No sooner did Mustafa let go of him than he leapt up and charged at Yusuf this time. Yusuf gave him one look and shoved him aside. The boy fell over the shingle, one foot in the water. Mad with rage he shot up and clamped his teeth into Yusuf's hand. Yusuf howled with pain. In an instant he was at Nuri's throat, squeezing for all he was worth. Strangling sounds came from Nuri, his eyes bulged, his arms sagged to his sides. Mustafa grabbed Yusuf and tore him away from Nuri who sank to the ground in a lifeless heap. Memet, who had driven Battal and Poyraz on the defensive against the cliff wall, desisted and ran up.

"Have you killed him?" he cried.

"He asked for it," Yusuf said angrily. "The little whipper-snapper . . ."

"If he dies the government will throw you into jail," Battal said.

"Let him die," Yusuf said obstinately. "Mustafa's father will get me out of jail. Didn't you all call Mustafa a savage?"

"No, we didn't really . . ." Poyraz protested.

"Oh-ho! How's that for a whopper! Allah can strike you blind for lying like that."

"Well, Nuri is dying, so there! And we never called that Kurd a savage."

"You did!"

"We didn't!"

Suddenly Nuri sprung up and sank his teeth into Yusuf's wrist again. Yusuf flung him back onto the pebbles. But Nuri would not give up. He was making ready to charge when Yusuf glimpsed Salman standing some way off under a clump of tamarisks, watching them.

"Boys. Hisht, hisht," he hissed pointing at Salman.

The children shrank back against the cliff wall, all in a huddle, their eyes riveted on Salman. His rifle was slung over his shoulder, his binoculars hung down his chest and his gun and dagger were at his waist as usual.

"He's after us again," Bird Memet said.

"He's come to kill Mustafa," Nuri said.

"He means to kill us all," Poyraz sighed. "All the children in the village. He's got that look in his eyes as if he wants to kill us and eat us too."

"He won't kill me," Nuri said.

"How d'you know?" Battal asked.

"My mum said so. It's Mustafa he wants to kill, then Memet, then Minstrel Ali . . ."

"Why should Salman want to kill Minstrel Ali?" Poyraz objected. "He doesn't mix with us. All he does is sing."

"Well, that's why!" Nuri said triumphantly. "It makes Salman cry when he sings. Mum says Salman will kill Minstrel Ali first."

"It's you he'll kill first."

"Why me?"

"Because your neck's thin as a rail," Poyraz said.

"Because your ears are huge," Battal said. "Like two ladles."

"Because your eyes bulge like a frog's," Bird Memet said. "Of course Salman will kill you."

Nuri snuggled up to Mustafa who had made himself smaller and smaller and looked at him piteously. "He's going to kill me," he moaned. "Before you, before anyone it's me he'll kill."

Keeping close to each other, the boys started to sidle along the foot of the cliff.

"Let's hide in that hollow," Bird Memet suggested. "Among those tamarisks and brambles."

They waited in the hollow for a while, holding their breath, and it was past noon when they emerged. The coast seemed clear and then suddenly they stopped short. Salman was sitting in a cavity on the cliff face, his eyes half closed, sunning himself. For a moment they stared at him, mesmerised, then took to their heels.

* * *

Every day more and more children had begun to join in the kingfisher hunt. They were up before dawn, making for the cliffs along the river by devious ways, finding each other by bird calls and whistles and quickly setting to work. They tried everything, traps and snares, cages and nets. There were hundreds of bird holes in the cliffs and many a time they saw the kingfishers shoot out across the river, over the level plain, like streaks of blue lightning, alight for one brief moment, then vanish. Their hands were torn and swollen with digging and with weaving nets, but they never caught a single bird.

And so their yearning for those blue birds grew apace, haunting their days and their nights. In their dreams – and it was the same dream for one and all – a cloud of blue birds rose from the river bank in a flutter of wings, whirled in the sky and coasted the cliff, their wings skimming the water, then spread out over the plain. And suddenly guns exploded, thousands, the cloud of birds was torn apart, flung this way and that, severed heads, mangled wings, mutilated bodies floating aimlessly, blue spots in the air. Then birds and river and plain, all was wiped away and Salman loomed into view, accompanied by deep booming sounds from the Valley of Hawthorns. His long dark shadow drove the children into the crags as he fired at them, shot after shot. Mustafa was hit by a hundred bullets maybe. Each time he was hurled high into the air and fell back splayed like a frog. The children, shouting and pleading, scrambled away, surrounded by a roiling horde of dogs, jackals, foxes and martens. Trees and bushes were alive with screeching swallow fledglings, mouths agape, eyes bulging. The whole mountain throbbed, and swarms of bees carried the scent of hawthorns far into the plain. Mustafa, steeped in blood was running blindly. Then his head was on the surface of the river, now floating, now sinking . . .

The children would assemble at the foot of the cliff and tell each other their dreams, and Salman was always there, near the clump of tamarisks, watching. Those children who had not dreamed concocted dreams that were exactly like those of the other children. It was Salman always, Salman standing above a pit filled with thousands of dead kingfishers over which lay the corpses of children, Salman wielding his dagger, his arm working like a shuttle, slashing away, most of all at Bird Memet and Mustafa. Blood spurted from the bodies of the children, splashing the swallow fledglings, the hawthorns, the bees, the crags . . . Splashing them all blue. Birds filled the sky shedding blue blood, the sky shattered and showered down, a rain of blue.

The courtyard gate opened and in walked Salman carrying a large cage full of kingfishers, shimmering blue. Ismail Agha and Mustafa were on the balcony. Salman looked up, smiled hesitantly, then came slowly up the stairs and held out the cage to Mustafa.

"I caught these for you, Mustafa," he said with pride, flushing to the roots of his hair.

Mustafa took the cage with a thrill of joy. His heart quickened. But only for a moment. Then a wave of anger swept over him. He turned this way and that, holding the heavy cage with difficulty, looked defiantly at Salman, bent down, opened the door of the cage, seized one of the birds and cast it up into the air. The kingfisher fluttered up and down for an instant, then straightened its course and headed for the river. Swiftly, one by one, Mustafa took the birds out and set them free. Then seizing the cage, he went to Salman. "Take it," he said.

The cage dropped from Salman's hand. His face was ashen. His eyes fixed on Mustafa were so full of hatred that Ismail Agha felt a shock and for the first time a twinge of fear. Mustafa fled into the house, crying, and hid in the closet among the stacked bedding. With a cold look at Ismail Agha, as if to say, you've seen for yourself, Salman turned away.

"He's only a small child, Salman, you mustn't mind what he does," Ismail Agha called after him as he went down the stairs and out of the courtyard.

After this, Mustafa was more afraid than ever. For days, he crouched in a dark corner of a room spread with *kilims* and did nothing but gaze at the bright colours of the *kilims* or play with the bees that buzzed up and down the sunbeams filtering through the blinds. It was only when his father returned from the farm that he allowed himself to be drawn out. He had grown used to being alone, retreating into a world of colours, buzzing bees and dancing sunbeams, forgetting everything, the blue birds, the other boys, but not Salman. And more specially Salman's doings with the bay filly, how he entered the stable, seized the filly by her haunches and, shedding his *shalvar* and pants, held his thing to her and gently, closing his eyes, rubbed himself to her. And the filly liked it, even pressed herself against him. And when Salman had done, she parted her legs and urinated and a strange kind of smell drifted to Mustafa's nostrils. Mustafa had never told anyone about Salman and the bay filly, but the secret weighed upon him more and more.

The first time Mustafa left the house, he went straight to Bird Memet. His friend greeted him with a mixture of fear and relief. They faced each other silently, then of one accord ran to the river bank where they found the pickaxe and spade hidden in the briars just as they had left them. At once they set about delving into the bird holes and unearthing kingfishers that slipped through their hands, blue streaks of lightning, barely glimpsed, but leaving a trail of blue in their wake, tainting the flowing water, the river bank, the shingle, the tamarisks and brambles and willows a brilliant blue.

The day was drawing to a close and they had worked their way far down the river hunting for kingfishers, when they realised that there had been no sign of Salman all this time. Deep inside they felt a kind of something missing.

"He hasn't come," Mustafa said regretfully.

"Why ever not?" Memet wondered.

"Maybe he thinks I'm still in that room."

"He can't," Memet said. "Because he's made it his business to keep an eye on you."

The next morning before cockcrow they hurried down to the river and started digging away again for all they were worth. This went on for a few days. Then one morning Mustafa slumped down on a rise behind the willows and remained there, his chin resting on his knees. Spade and pickaxe were left unused in the briars. Day dawned and the sun hit the battlements of the castle ruin. Muffled cartbells sounded from the road that led to the town. Anavarza Castle in the distance was swathed in smoke. A cloud of orange butterflies streamed past, billowing and zigzagging over the river, leaving an orange glow on the water. Another cloud, mauve this time, floated along over the water. Kingfishers flitted in and out of their holes in the cliff side. The sun grew stronger, striking up luminous reflections that rippled over the shore, the trees and the plain. Dust hovered above the distant roads and long straight trails of smoke trembled over the village.

The boys sat on, silent and tense, their eyes on the alert, not missing the slightest stirring of bird or insect or even the budding of a flower. A yellow spider was patiently busy weaving its web between the branches of a chaste tree. Further down, quite low in the sky, a red eagle hovered with outstretched wings, breasting the wind that was not felt down by the river. Wild pigeons and swallows flitted by, but the eagle never changed its stance. Ants lay around their holes, inert in the sun, barely feeling the air with their antennae. Tiny beetles, green, red, blue, were plastered on a thorny bush and sparkled with a thousand pinpoints of light. Booming sounds came from deep down under the earth and mingled with the murmur of the water. Big flies buzzed low over the shore. The oxen had begun to come down to the river.

The boys did not stir till nightfall. They came again the next day at the first crack of dawn and waited silently in the same place. On the third day, what should they see but Wiggler sitting there, his chin on his knees staring into the distance. Soon Battal appeared and Poyraz and next Nuri and Talip. That day the rest of the village children drifted in, in twos and threes and sat on the tussock in perfect silence till nightfall. Again and again, the next few days they came and remained there from dawn to sunset, not talking or asking anything of each other, as though turned to stone. Looking at them from afar, it would seem as though this was an ancient secret ritual and breaking the stillness a sacrilege.

One morning, Mustafa raised his head slowly from his knees. He looked at the children one by one, then lowered his head. When he looked up again all eyes were fixed on him, questioning.

Mustafa rose. "He won't come," he announced.

The children sprang to their feet. "He's not coming! He's not coming!" they cried, and suddenly they were away, prancing down the shore with whoops of joy.

Mustafa and Bird Memet looked at each other irresolutely, then at the tamarisks where Salman should have been standing.

"He won't come," Bird Memet said.

Mustafa drew near him. "Listen," he said, "but first swear that you won't tell anyone."

"I swear it," Memet said.

"Swear!" Mustafa repeated.

"May my two eyes drop down in front of me . . ."

"Swear!"

"May I be bitten by a venomous rattlesnake."

"Swear."

"May I see myself dead . . ."

"Come this way then so no one can see us talking." Mustafa drew Memet down past a gorse-lined incline and stopped behind a clump of reeds. "Now listen carefully. And if you tell any-one Salman will kill me, and you too." And he recounted to his friend all he knew about Salman and the bay filly, not missing the smallest detail. He was out of breath and all in a sweat when he finished. The two boys stared at each other, then of one accord dashed off into the village.

It was after noon, the time when Salman rose from sleep. The boys waited under cover of the cactuses until he appeared and went to wash his face in the courtyard. Then they heard him urinate in the outhouse near the pomegranate tree and after that he made for the stable. They hurried up stealthily and, peering through the chinks in the brush wall, they saw Salman cares-sing the rump of the bay filly while he let his *shalvar* drop to his feet.

"Mustafa," Memet whispered without taking his eye from the cranny.

"What?"

"The boys . . . They're all here . . ."

Mustafa looked up. Well nigh all the village children were at the brush wall, eyes clamped to the crevices, holding their breaths. His blood ran cold. "He'll kill us," he moaned. "He'll kill us all." Who could have told the other boys, how could they have given each other the word, how could they have known the exact minute when Salman would go to the bay filly? "Memet, did you tell anyone?"

"How could I? I didn't see anyone after you . . ."

Salman was slowing down. He went all tense, closed his eyes, then drew his penis from the filly. It still stood out, quite rigid. Blinking, he looked about him, then pulled on his *shalvar* and tied the cord. He must have caught wind of something, for he was peering suspiciously about the stable.

"He's smelled a rat," Memet said. "Quick, let's get away before he sees us."

Creeping through the cactus hedge, they slipped into the

courtyard of Memet's house and crouched there, listening, but no sound came from the stable.

"He hasn't seen anyone," Memet said.

"Oh, he must have," Mustafa said.

"But wouldn't he have raised hell, wouldn't he have killed us all?"

"He'll keep mum until it suits him. We mustn't go near that stable again. Let's swear not to or bad things will come of it. Salman won't take this lying down. It'll be terrible for those who've spied on him . . ."

"What a splendid rifle he has," Memet observed.

"My father gave it to him."

"Of course! After all he's your father's son too, from an older wife. When your people were on the road coming from that other country, your father killed Salman's mother and threw her into a well and then he married your mother."

"Who told you that?"

"Why, everyone knows it! Didn't you know?"

"What I know is that my father found him on the roadside under a bush. And my grandmother . . . I had a grandmother then, she was ever so good they say . . . So when my mother said, he's dying, my grandmother saved his life with her ointments and medicines. If it wasn't for my grandmother, the others would have left Salman there to die in the bushes. I wish they had . . . He wouldn't be here now ready to use that rifle and kill all the children."

"Like he killed the eagles. He'll kill us all. Your father too . . ."

"He'll kill everyone except my father," Mustafa said. "He's got no one else in the whole world."

"And he's his son after all," Bird Memet said with a meaning look at Mustafa.

"He's not his son!" Mustafa shouted, springing to his feet. "He's not!"

"But the whole village knows it is so. He's your very own brother."

Mustafa's face changed, his lips trembled. "Memet," he said, his eyes questioning, "is Salman really my brother?"

"My father said so. Your father told him and it's your mother who told the whole village. Everyone knows it is so."

"But I didn't know," Mustafa said plaintively. Then all of a sudden his mood changed. With whoops of joy, he started skipping and prancing, turning somersaults, standing on his head, laughing for all he was worth. "We're safe!" he cried, flinging his arms out wide.

Memet was mystified. "Safe from what?"

"From being killed? Salman won't kill me, or you, or my father."

"How's that?"

"Because he's my brother, and my father's his very own father. And you're my friend. Would a man kill his own brother?"

Memet pondered. It was a difficult question.

"What's there to think about here? Would a man ever kill his brother?"

Bird Memet, his lips pursed, wavered.

"Would a man ever kill his father?" Mustafa insisted.

Memet twiddled his fingers.

"Would he kill his brother's friend?"

At this Memet lifted his head and gave Mustafa a long look. "No, he wouldn't," he said at last. In a frenzy of relief the two boys ran towards the village square. There, in front of the mosque, not caring who was looking, Mustafa struck up a merry song with strange words, maybe Salman's mysterious tongue, and the two boys began to wheel round each other like two *köçeks*, at times miming the flight of some great bird, with steps and motions remembered from the dances of the gypsies who came every year at the onset of spring and again in the autumn and set up their tents on the edge of the village, fanning out into the mountainside. They worked silver plate and trinkets, and made braziers, trivets and hatchets that they sold to the villagers. There was one very old man among them, just skin and bones, who would go from door to door, and dance like a *köçek*, accepting whatever was given him. Dressed in a purple-striped red silk robe that draggled in a tangled dirty fringe down his spindly legs, he performed a different kind of dance before each house, accompanying himself sometimes with a pipe, at others with a fiddle or a *cura*.

He also carried a small drum on his back, but this was for big occasions in the village square when, stirred at the sight of the gathering crowd, he would dance to the beat of his drum, bending down, leaping up, whirling with a nimbleness that belied his age, the veins in his black wizened neck swelling, his curly white hair dripping with sweat, the fringes of his robe flapping wildly, then suddenly softening the beat of the drum as though caressing a loved one, he would stop and pass his fez around and the villagers would throw into it money, beads, pieces of copper or glass, anything they could spare.

Very often, the children would follow the old gypsy from door to door, mimicking his every gesture. And so it was perhaps one of his dances that Mustafa and Memet were stepping to, singing at the top of their voices in a language they did not know. A curious crowd was gathering, watching with astonishment their wild motions. They noticed nothing, now slowing down, singing very softly, next wheeling as though caught in a whirlwind, keeping to the rhythm of their song, creating movements of pure beauty. When for some reason they paused, sweating even to the tips of their hair, they stared at each other, then burst out laughing. Those who had gathered to watch found themselves laughing too, the sight of those two boys splitting their sides was infectious. More and more people drew up and joined in the general merriment.

Bird Memet was the first to see the crowd. "Mustafa, look," he said. Mustafa took one look and streaked off. Memet rushed after him. Gazing back as they were scaling the crags, they saw that the villagers, men women and children, were still laughing and singing and capering in a kind of merry dance.

"What happened?" Mustafa asked as though awaking from a trance.

"What happened?" Memet echoed.

Then suddenly: "We're saved," they cried.

"Salman won't kill you," Mustafa said.

"He won't kill you either . . ."

They raced back down the crags into the village and the first boy they came across was Talip. They grabbed hold of him. Scared by the look on their faces Talip struggled to escape. "But I haven't done anything," he cried.

"Yes you have," Mustafa said and dealt him a kick.

"You know you have," Memet said and flung the boy down.

"But I haven't . . . What have I done?" Talip howled.

"Why did you watch our Salman Agha when he was doing things to the bay filly, you sly wretch?" Memet said kicking away with all his might.

"But we were all there!" Talip yelped. "It wasn't only me!"

"Well, we're going to fix the others too," Memet said.

After giving Talip a good spanking, they let him be. On the warpath, they next pounced on Battal and beat him up soundly. Little Nuri was coming towards them holding a string with three bumblebees tied to it. "Look," he cried proudly. They snatched the bees away from him, threw them into the air, string and all, and dealt him a few blows. Next they attacked Poyraz, Minstrel Ali and Wiggler Yusuf, and soon all the village boys had joined in the fray, forming two camps. Still fighting tooth and nail, they found themselves on the river bank, pelting stones at each other, stopping awhile to rest on the rocks and to wash the blood off their hands and faces, then beginning again with renewed frenzy.

This went on till well past noon when Sergeant Halil, happening to drive that way, reined in at the sight of the brawling boys. After watching for a moment, he jumped from the cart, gripped his whip and plunged into the melee, bringing the whip down without mercy on heads and backs and legs. It was not long before the boys began to flee. Mustafa and Memet were the first to escape. They rushed down to the river and sank onto the shingle under a clump of tamarisks. After a while they were joined by the rest of their team who sat down beside them in a row, without speaking. Then the boys of the opposite team drew up, Veli at their head, and settled not far off under another clump of tamarisks, all silent and still as stones. The water rippled gently over the pebbles and white butterflies flitted above an eddying bend in the river further down. The boys never moved, never once looked at each other. Kingfishers darted over their heads, fulgurant blue streaks in the air. No one but Mustafa so much as gave them a glance. The sun was sinking slowly, drowning the river in a silvery radiance.

Suddenly, Mustafa spoke up: "Don't let's fight any more. We're all dead beat."

"Yes," Veli smiled, "but what a fight it was!"

"We never fought like that before," Memet said.

And in no time the boys were all friends once more. No one mentioned the fight again. It was as if these were not the same boys who had been gouging each other's eyes out a short while ago.

"We're saved," Mustafa said. "Salman won't ever kill us now."

Veli's eyes brightened. "Really truly?" he asked.

"Salman is Mustafa's own true brother, isn't that so Mustafa?"

"My very own," Mustafa asserted with a show of pride.

"Mustafa's people didn't find him on the wayside. Ismail Agha had another wife before Mustafa's mother and she gave birth to Salman. And then Mustafa's father killed Salman's mother, isn't that so, Mustafa?"

Mustafa sighed. "Yes, and it's because he killed his mother that Salman became so bitter and cross and wanting to kill people. Poor Salman . . ."

"But we're saved now," Memet said quickly. "Salman will never kill his brother Mustafa."

"He will though," Veli asserted jumping to his feet. "Didn't you see what he was doing to the bay filly?"

"He won't, so there!" Mustafa flashed, ready to start fighting again. "Which grown man in the village doesn't do the same with his mares?"

"I saw Veli's father once," Nuri spoke up. "On the river bank, the mare leaning against the cliff and he, with his thing up like a stallion, mounting the mare . . . Just like Salman. And he an imam too! And reciting prayers too as he mounted the mare. I was hiding in a clump of fennel just a little way away."

Veli burst out laughing. "I saw them too," he said. "I was behind another bush when my father was mounting the mare. I went and told mother, hush, she said, for heaven's sake don't tell anyone. What can your poor father do if I'm ill? He must do it with the mare . . ."

"Everyone's father does things to their mare," Nuri said. "My father said that a man who doesn't mate with his mare isn't a real man. The thing is, they all do it secretly."

"Not so very secretly!" Talip scoffed.

"Anyway, he's not killing anyone," Memet shouted. "Why should he? Would a man kill his father?"

"He wouldn't," Veli said.

"And Ismail Agha is Salman's father. Why would Salman kill his father?"

There was a long silence. The boys were thinking, chins cupped in their hands.

"But Salman will kill Mustafa," Nuri cried suddenly. "I saw it."

"Saw what, you fathead?"

"Salman's eyes. I saw them killing Mustafa. That's how he looked, killing . . ."

Howling, Mustafa flung himself at Nuri and would have strangled him if Memed, Yusuf and the others had not grabbed hold of him. "He won't kill me, he won't." Beside himself, trembling of all his limbs, Mustafa struggled to shake himself free. "He won't kill me."

"Stop, Mustafa, stop!" Veli said. "He won't kill you."

"Of course not," Poyraz said. "Why should he?"

"Would a man kill his little brother?" Talip said.

"I was joking, Mustafa," Nuri said penitently. "Would a man ever kill his little brother?"

"See, Mustafa?" Memet said. "Nuri was just joking. Why should Salman kill you?"

Slowly Mustafa's rage died down. He sank onto the shingle.

"And Salman won't kill me either," Memet said. "And if you ask why, it's because I'm Mustafa's friend. A man doesn't kill his brother's neighbour, his friend, his blood brother. You know we licked each other's blood, Mustafa and I. That makes us blood brothers. Would a man kill his own brother's blood brother?"

"No indeed," they all cried joyfully.

After that they fell silent, rapt in thought, scratching the sand with sticks, and remained like that till nightfall, not even once looking at each other, afraid even to talk, to move, to rise to their feet.

A covey of birds chirruping loudly passed overhead and roused them from their torpor. A small red-winged eagle was chasing them and the birds fled in a frantic flurry, now making for the crags, now swooping back across the river with the eagle in hot pursuit. On their feet now, the boys watched eagerly to see if the red-winged eagle would succeed in catching a bird. At each lunge of the eagle, instead of breaking apart and scattering away, the birds drew together ever more tightly, until they were a compact mass, very black, whirling over the water at the height of a poplar tree, sheering this way and that. Suddenly, a shrill squeak, a mad turmoil, and the red eagle was off, making for the mountain, a small bird clutched in its talons. In that very instant the covey of birds, as if exploding, dispersed in the sky, each going a different way.

"It's getting dark," Veli observed.

"Let's go," Memet said.

Mustafa was standing a little way off on a green patch of moss among the pebbles, still looking after the eagle as it vanished among the bare mauve crags.

Memet nudged him. "We're going," he said.

Mustafa turned and his eyes passed sadly over the boys, one by one. "He's going to kill us," he sighed.

"He will then," Memet said.

"He'll kill us all," Veli said.

Nuri clapped his hands and began skipping all around the boys, saying things no one understood. He looked at Mustafa. "So he will kill us then," he cried.

"It's dark already," Veli shouted and took to his heels. In a few minutes Mustafa and Memet were also running and had left him far behind.

7

"THEY NEVER COME back, those who go to work in the Chukurova," old Anshaja said. "Don't go, my child," she entreated her grandson Halil. "It's not as if we're starving here. Allah always provides one way or another."

Halil was standing under the plane tree beside the ancient watering trough. He smiled.

"Your grandfather went to the Chukurova and disappeared without leaving a trace, not even a grave. Your father went and was carried away by the poisonous ague. Your uncles returned, but crippled with toiling in the rice paddies or maimed by wielding sickle and disk-plough. Just like those who went to the Yemen wars and never returned, so it is for those who go to the Chukurova. Don't go, my child. You're all we have left now."

Anshaja was sitting cross-legged, her blue *dolama* spread about her. She struck the ground with her fist. "May he never see Paradise whoever invented this Chukurova. Who knows how many years it'll be before you come back, if you do come back . . ."

"I will," Halil said. "Before three years are past, I'll be back with money enough to buy a team of oxen, a cow, a horse, a drill plough, and enough to get married, too. Don't you fret yourself, granny dear."

"May your granny be your slave. You'll come back, God willing, but will you find me here? Me with one foot already in the grave . . ."

"Indeed I'll be back and so will you be here, granny," Halil said stoutly. "Why, you're a thousand times stronger than any girl of twenty!"

Halil kept smiling as he talked to his skin-and-bones grandmother. Döndülü, his mother stood on the threshold of their house, spinning wool on the beautifully engraved spindle that he had fashioned for her. Suddenly she stopped the spindle and lifted her head. "You'll go, my son," she said, resigned, worldly-wise. "Though there may be no return, you have to go. That's the fate written for us folk of the mountains. Though no one may have returned, was there a man who did not go to the Yemen, is there one who does not go to the Chukurova?"

Halil leaning against the trunk of the plane tree, smiled. They were to set out on the next morning, eleven young men who had all lost their fathers, nine of them in the wars and the others in the Chukurova. Halil's father was one of those who had gone to the Chukurova and never returned. For some time now the young men had been making ready, but had kept putting off the date of departure. They had never seen the Chukurova and they were afraid, for they had heard much about that hellish plain, its mosquitoes, the scorching heat, the poisonous waters, the cruel aghas and beys, the sickness and the death . . . Yet come what may, go they must, for those who did return would have earned enough to buy oxen, a harrow or a plough, a cow, a few goats, and even to provide a dowry for their betrothed and set up a lavish wedding feast to boot. They would also bring presents of clothing for all the household. Some there were who refused to go. These for the most part struggled on in direst poverty to the end of their lives. A man who had not earned some money in the Chukurova was held so low that no one would ever give him a daughter to wife.

For a year now, as the time to leave drew nearer, Halil had been haunted by the thought of that dreaded plain, its mosquitoes which tore at a man like ravenous wolves, its blood-warm undrinkable waters, the scorching sun that bored into a man's head like a nail, the seven-armed monsters lurking behind the clouds, the killing toil . . . That Chukurova plain where no one will give you a mug of water, where man is an enemy to man, where the parched earth cracks open in the summer, turns into a flooded expanse in the winter, where the casual labourer is looked upon with scorn, where the mountain people are held to be not human, more like animals, not to be spoken to, only to be made to work day in day out, and if they die their bodies to be cast into a ditch, like dogs, without even an imam to say a prayer over them. In that land the dry river beds, the ditches, the roadsides were strewn with the white bones of the mountain people and fragments of their bloody flesh dangled from the fangs of stray dogs. They fell sick and died, writhing in agony in barns and open fields, in the mud and dung and straw, on the scorched cracked earth, exposed to the stinging sun, tongues hanging, parched with thirst, abandoned by all. And those who did come back had nothing human left about them, crippled, consumptive, or bearing inside them the malaria that would plague them to the end of their lives, tremorous hands, incoherent speech, necks thin as sticks. Only one in a thousand would return unscathed, but even this one would be endlessly tortured by an overpowering fear of death.

Though it had become a tradition bred of necessity for the mountain people to go to that baneful land and work in the rice paddies, as cotton pickers or as day labourers, it was still very hard for them to leave their homes. How to find a way not to go? Halil wandered about the village hoping against hope, but except for his grandmother he met only with blank eyes. He raged inwardly at everyone, at this kind of life, even at his mother and Ipekché. "The Chukurova means death," he commented to one and sundry, and they only replied, "alas, yes the Chukurova's very dangerous." "Yet we're going in a few months, eleven of us . . ." Looking searchingly into their eyes for something, some trace of pity . . . In vain. "May you fare well then, God bless you," was all they said.

"Some go away and never return, some return and find their loved one gone . . ."

"Death can strike anywhere."

Limp with fear, he would confer with his friends and put off departure for another week.

"This time it's settled. Let everyone get ready."

So with their bundles over their shoulders, they would set out, but, coming to the road that led into the valley, they would stop and sit, heads hanging, faces twitching in thought, on the gnarled roots of a plane tree under which a clear spring bubbled forth. Suddenly, they would break into mumbled incoherent talk and turn back, making for their homes at a running pace. "Next week, next week . . ." was all they said to the villagers who looked on with indulgence, for this was the case with most young men leaving for the Chukurova the first time.

Tonight Halil had a tryst with Ipekché at their usual meeting place in the small cedar grove where the trees rose high heavenward, and he was all in a fever of anticipation. A warm gentle rain was falling and the grove smelled pleasantly of flowers, resin and rotting wood. Halil sounded his own special whistle and from a little further off Ipekché answered with a cough. They came together and perhaps for the first time they kissed. Leaning against the wide trunk of a cedar tree, they held hands, oblivious of the rain that filtered through the thickset branches. A few fireflies glowed redly in the pitch-dark night.

"I'll wait for you," Ipekché said, "ten years, fifteen years, until I die . . ."

"I'll work hard," Halil said. "In less than two years, I'll be back."

"It's raining," Ipekché said. "I hope it rains in the Chukurova too. That means the crops will be good there."

"It'll be a year of plenty, this year. I'm going to buy a woollen jacket for granny. She's always so cold . . . I hope your father will keep his word and won't ask for more money for your dowry when he sees I've earned a lot."

"You will always be beside me. Never doubt that," Ipekché said.

"When I'm back, I'll clear a field down there in the valley. We'll uproot the trees together. Or maybe I'll hire a couple of men to help us . . ."

They talked on like this until well past midnight. A turtle-dove cooed from the depths of the wood and a brook was purling gently nearby.

The fireflies multiplied, twinkling around the tree trunks.

Ipekché snuggled against him, so warm . . . At last they made their way back hand in hand. The village was in darkness except for a faint light from the window of Ipekché's house.

"Until tomorrow," Halil said.

"Tomorrow . . ."

After days of shuffling about the village and nights of struggling against nightmares, Halil and his companions found themselves once more sitting under the plane tree on the road to the Chukurova. No one spoke. They did not look at each other.

"Are we all ready?" Halil asked. The question was like a stone cast in their midst. They started as though roused from sleep.

"We're ready," one of them replied feebly.

"Right then, let's get going," Halil said. He rose and made for the valley. The others flung their bundles over their shoulders and followed.

* * *

With Halil leading, they pressed on ever more quickly and as the day was drawing to a close they were at the ancient walnut tree it would normally have taken a couple of days to reach. It was as if a man-eating monster was after them. Not once did they look back. But all the way Halil was hearing his grandmother's voice. "Halil! Halil! How can you go and leave me here like this at my age? How, how?" Her cries rang in his ears, echoed from the crags. "Halil, Halil! What shall I do without you? How will you feel when you return and find me gone . . . Halil, Halil!"

Ipekché too he kept hearing. He saw her in the dark rainy night, fireflies glinting and dancing all around her, clinging to her clothes, gilding them. "Halil! Halil! Do you have to go? What if you don't find me when you return, oh Halil, Halil . . ." Ipekché was flying after him, scattering fireflies in the darkness of the night.

And one day at the peep of dawn they came to a hill over-looking the Chukurova. It was raining and a mist shrouded the plain. They sat down under a mastic tree waiting for the rain to let up, and ate the last of their provisions. The mist was slowly lifting and the dawning sun brightened the stream that meandered in a thousand twists and turns around the villages. Smoke rose tremblingly into the sky from the houses. The clouds unfurled and slowly retreated beyond the surrounding moun-tains, leaving the sky washed clean, a limpid blue. The Chukurova spread before them like a blue bowl with rapid streams and smoking villages. Sitting there, under the mastic tree, the young men felt their fears melting away. Their hearts gladdened.

"This is the Chukurova," Halil said.

"Are you sure?"

"What other plain can be as wide as this?"

"There must be many like it in Anatolia . . ."

"But this one is so blue . . . Plains are never blue. See those white clouds massed way there? Well, that's where the Mediter-ranean Sea is and that's why the Chukurova plain is blue. The blue of the sea is reflected over the earth."

"Have you ever seen the sea?"

"No," Halil said, "but Sergeant Ibrahim says it is so. He fought the rebel Arabs on the shores of the sea for seven years. He said the sea is like the blue sky come down on earth."

"Why don't we ask that man who seems to be travelling from the plain?"

"Hey there, wayfarer!"

The man stopped.

"Is that the Chukurova down there?"

The man laughed. "Go on lads, don't play with me! I'm more dead than alive as it is . . . On the road these three days . . ."

"No, no truly," Halil protested. "We just want to be sure."

"Of course it's the Chukurova," the man said. "As if there can be another place like it . . ." And he went his way, bent double under the bulging sack he was carrying.

Suddenly infused with a new life, their weariness forgotten, they walked on singing gaily and gained the plain before noon. That night, in a little village they had never heard of, they slept on beds of corn stalks set for them up on a *chardak*. The villagers offered them hot soup, *bulgur* pilaff with butter, green onions and *ayran* to drink. They had never in their lives had a meal that tasted better and when they woke up the next morning they were surprised to find there had been no mosquitoes at all.

"Who knows," Halil said. "Maybe it's not the season yet."

They climbed down from the *chardak* and went to a pump that stood under a mulberry in a patch of muddy earth mixed with straw and dung trod down by men and animals. A row of tall poplars stretched from there to the outskirts of the village, their leaves shivering in the gentle breeze. They washed their faces at the pump and dried themselves with kerchiefs embroidered for them by mothers, sisters or betrothed.

A few peasants were gathering under a plane tree nearby. It was beginning to be very hot now. The village houses were built of reeds daubed with dung and roofed with sun-bleached rushes. Hens strutted about followed by their brood and a few dogs wandered in between the houses, ribs panting, tongues lolling. A small turbid brook flowed sluggishly through the village. In the distance, the Anavarza crags could be seen and above them, like specks in the sky, some eagles, immobile, breasting the high wind.

An aged man detached himself from the group under the plane tree. "Hey, you mountaineers," he called, "come here." And as the approached: "Have you come to work?"

"So we have," Halil said.

"Can you reap?"

"Certainly."

"How much do you want per day?"

Halil smiled. "You know best . . ."

"So we do," the other villagers approved.

"Just give us whatever the wage is this year. You wouldn't cheat us . . ."

"Never! Whatever's just, you'll get from us."

"You'll work for me first," the old man said. "My crop's plentiful this year, thank God. And early too. The stalks are bending under the spikes already. We can start in two days' time."

"All right," Halil agreed.

"You'll stay at my place of course."

The field to be harvested was perfectly flat, with not a single stone, not even a pebble. The black-spiked wheat, shimmering softly, undulated in rustling waves from one end of the field to the other like a sunlit sea. All in a row, they started reaping and the rhythmic swish of sickles sounded through the plain. A covey of startled birds shot out of the wheat and the chirr of three francolins calling in unison was heard from afar. The sun had not dawned and the dew that fell like rain in the night had not yet dried. The dawn breeze blew gently, refreshing the young men, filling them with joy as they wielded their razor-sharp sickles.

In the next three days, fired with zeal, they cleared so much wheat that the owner could not believe his eyes. "Allah, Allah! Bless me!" he cried. "You've been the saving of me this year. I'm going to add twenty-five kurush each to your wages."

And the young men pressed on, singing gaily as they swung their sickles that flashed brightly in the sun. Behind them they left neat sheaves of thick-eared wheat from which emanated a pungent sunny odour that caught at their throats.

Many households had already moved into the highlands for the summer and their crops stood unharvested in the fields, waiting for the labourers from the mountains. So when they had finished reaping the old man's field, they passed on to another one, and then to a third. And just about this time mosquitoes appeared. They came in such thick throngs that people were stung not only in the night, but in the heat of the day as well.

The reaping went on for a month. And next came the threshing. The cut sheaves had to be carried to the threshing floor whether on their backs or by horse-drawn sledges, and this took another twenty days.

Afterwards, the work with flails or threshers began. All over the Chukurova malaria was rampant and people trembled as though caught in an earthquake. But, wax up the devil's ears,

Halil and his companions had been spared up to now. They had kept all together and had taken care not to get engaged in separate fields. They dreaded being parted. Their initial joy at the first sight of the Chukurova had gradually died away and the immemorial fear of the mountaineers had taken root in them again, growing apace, making them cling to each other ever more closely with every passing day.

July went by and in the first days of August they took on a new, strange kind of job, that of guarding the rice paddies. Thousands of *dönüms* of land had been sown with rice from Anavarza to below Kadirli and on to Kozan and beyond the Jeyhan River to Osmaniyé, Toprakkalé and right down to Mersin. Each paddy field measured five thousand to ten thousand *dönüms*. Added to all this were the vast Akchasaz and Tirmil swamps, as well as several smaller ones, so that the Chukurova was turned into one huge swampland. Halil and his friends had to keep watch over these paddies. Armed with Mauser rifles, they waited from dusk to dawn, vigilant, never sleeping a wink, sitting on *chardaks* that were built every three or four metres or so on the edge of the paddies. As soon as night fell the wild boars that roamed in droves made straight for the freshly spiked rice, trampling the stalks into the mud, not only destroying the crop, but rendering the field utterly useless for future crops. Hundreds of rifle shots burst from the *chardaks*, whistling through the hot Chukurova nights, but still the wild boars found a way of penetrating into the fields, either slipping in under a *chardak* whose watchman had fallen asleep or charging through, leaving a few of their number dead, and disappearing into the depths of the paddies, so that as soon as it was light a drive would be organised. The carcasses of dead boars would be piled into a pit over which a cloud of green flies rose and fell, and from which emanated an unbelievable stench of putrefying flesh. And swarming all about the pit, night and day, were hordes of foxes, jackals, hyenas, wolves and dogs that attacked each other, snarling, kicking up the dust, fighting tooth and nail.

Halil and his companions were in a row of *chardaks* next to each other and they gave the boars no quarter. Not one boar had evaded their vigilance up to now, but the heat, the mosquitoes and especially the repulsive stench was almost more than they could bear. There was no help for it, however, for the pay was good. The owner of the paddies appreciated the mountain people and realised that they had their own efficient ways of fighting the ravages of the wild boars. Drumming on tin cans to frighten them off had been their idea. And now the clanging of tin cans sounded in the night even louder than the burst of rifles.

It was not long before eagles began to wheel above the carcasses that piled up higher every day. About this time Halil and his friends had their first attack of malaria. They rolled on the ground, convulsed, moaning, shivering as though in freezing winter, or in turn burning as though cast into a smith's furnace. The fits of fever would come upon them without warning, in the evening or in the heat of the day or early in the morning and those who had not yet been attacked would gaze in helpless dread at their companions, writhing in agonising pain as if the flesh was being torn from their bones.

"I'm leaving," Halil would groan. "I won't stay, not if they give me the whole of the Chukurova . . ."

"It'll be the death of us, this Chukurova," the others would say.

"It's torture."

"No human being can last long here!"

"Just let me get over this attack," Halil would repeat, "just let me get some strength back and see if I remain here another minute."

One day the paddy owner turned up holding a bottle in his hand. "Well, my lucky lad," he said, "your mother must have borne you on the night of *Kadir*. Have you ever heard of a thing called quinine?"

"Never, Agha," Halil said.

"Well then, this quinine I'm giving you here is a medicine and the sovereign remedy for malaria, the only remedy."

"God bless you, Agha," they cried, filled with joy.

The agha explained to them how they were to take the quinine and in a few days Halil was well again. For some of the others the attacks became less frequent, but with the rest the drug had simply no effect at all.

"Well Halil?" his comrades asked. "You're all right now. When are you setting out then?"

"How can I go, my friends?" Halil replied his eyes fixed on the paddies that swished and undulated far into the distance. "How, when I've still not earned enough . . . Besides, Allah who brings affliction brings the remedy too, as you see . . ."

Some days later the quinine was used up and Halil had a fresh attack. "I'm going," he cried out in pain. "I'm not staying here to end up as food for jackals and vultures, like the carcasses of those wild boars. I'm leaving, my friends, as soon as I can walk."

A fortnight later, the Agha turned up with another bottle. "Well lads," he asked, "was the quinine helpful?"

"It brought us back to life," Halil said eagerly. "But when it was finished the fever started again."

"It's because you mustn't stop taking the damn thing."

"Just bring us the quinine, Agha," Halil said, a smile on his yellow face, "and we'll be all right. But this smell is more than we can bear."

"It's strange," the Agha said, "because each year the eagles and vultures devour the carcasses in a jiffy."

"But we've killed so many! Though all the eagles, vultures, jackals and dogs of the country have been at it for days, they still can't finish them off."

"They will," the Agha said. "Very soon, and there'll be no smell or eagles left around here." He spurred his horse and rode off.

Soon Halil was his old self again, laughing and singing, but the others did not recover so quickly. The widow Döné's son, Aslan was the first to give up.

"I'm leaving, Halil," he said. "Another day here and I'll die. Anyone coming with me?"

No one made a move, so he went alone to the paddy clerk's shack, drew his pay and took to the mountain road.

The heat became more and more oppressive, the nights were clammy, unbearable with the putrid smell of marshland and the stench from the carcasses in the pit. Ravenous beasts and birds of prey, fighting over the bloody carrion, filled the night with their wild cries, adding to the blast of rifles and the clangour of tin cans. Halil and his companions had stood the fever and the mosquitoes, but this ear-splitting noise, amplified as it resounded from the opposite mountain, and the overpowering stench began to be too much for them. One by one they left, vowing never to return.

At times Halil stopped his nose and breathed through his mouth, but the greasy nauseous smell stuck in his throat and permeated his whole body from head to foot. The trees, the grass, the rice paddies with their golden undulating spikes that stretched far into the distance, the blood-warm water, all smelled of it. The whole sky, the stars, the dawn breeze, everything smelled. Halil would crush flowers and grass against his nose, thrust his head under the water, run to the top of the nearby hill, climb up the tallest poplar, walk as far north as he could, but there was no getting rid of the smell. It seemed to him that he never would be rid of it for the rest of his life, that it would follow him to his own village and all over the Taurus Mountains.

All along the dusty road bordered by brambles that skirted the paddy, Halil could see watchmen fleeing with their rifles. "Run, man, run," they shouted, as they hurried past. "How can you stand this smell? It'll be the death of you . . ."

New men came to take the place of the fugitives. Only for a few days, a couple of weeks at the most, and they too fled along the dusty road as though death itself was stalking them.

"Run, man, run! God, what a smell . . ."

But Halil stood firm. How could he leave? He must earn money, a lot of money, and quickly, so he could go back in time to see his grandmother, before anything happened to Ipekché.

Autumn came. More labourers arrived from the mountains, women too, whole families. They came for the rice harvest. Halil had grown thin as a rake, but this did not stop him. He took his watchman's pay and threw himself into the harvest. This was not so well paid, but it was still good money and he held on, in spite of the bouts of malaria that were weakening him so much. Next the threshing began in giant machines, but this proved too hard for Halil. He gave up after three days and made for Adana where he spent the winter working for a landowner who was laying out a citrus grove. All through the winter, come wind come weather, Halil dug holes over an area of several *dönüms* in readiness for the spring planting of oranges, lemons and tangerines. This was hard work too, but that winter he did not suffer a single attack of malaria. At night, he slept in a stable smelling of hay and fresh dung. As spring came on, the stench of the rice paddies was quite forgotten and for the first time he thought of Ipekché, of his grandmother begging him not to go, of his mother endlessly spinning away. For as long as he could remember, he had never seen her without her spindle. She knitted stockings which she sold to the beys of Marash. Some said that she had a tidy sum hidden away, but she had never given anyone a hint of it. That spring he thought of Ipekché so often that he was ashamed and tried hard to drive her from his mind. The orange gardens, the agha he worked for were all right, but he was the only labourer from the mountains and he had not seen a single man from his home village or thereabouts. The labourers here all came from down south, from the desert or from Urfa and Haran plain, the land of the gazelles. They were good men, all of them, but he could not understand their language. They had come with their families and spoke only Kurdish or Arabic.

Halil worked here for a year and a half. Then one day he sat down and counted his money which he kept in a solidly sewn pouch attached under his armpit. Too little, he thought, not enough for what I want to do, I must stay a little longer in the Chukurova. So he put the money back into the pouch, first wrapping it up in a piece of oilcloth, and tied it under his armpit again. It was quite safe there. No one could take it without killing him first. He had also got into the habit of lying down on his right side where the pouch was tied and not even in his deepest sleep would he change his position.

After this, every couple of days, he counted and recounted his money, pondering, calculating, and at last he took his leave of the agha, quite decided to make for home, although the agha was pleased with his work, and pressed him to stay on.

One morning he came to Jeyhan River. He was tired. Setting down the bulging jute sack he carried on his back, he sank onto the sandy bank to wait for the cableway raft that would ferry him to the opposite shore. He looked at the far mountains, but could not make out snow-capped Mount Düldül. Maybe it was hidden by smoke or by that castle topping a rise of steep crags. A few more men joined him to board the raft. They were all mountain people on their way back home.

"My name's Halil," he introduced himself.

"And mine's Dursun," the tallest of them said. He had a small dark face with thick eyebrows.

The others too gave their names. All of them except Dursun had caught the malaria.

"I'm not going back home this year," Dursun declared. "I haven't made enough money yet. I need a lot because I'm going to buy not only a pair of oxen, but also a horse and a greyhound with curly fur hanging from its ears and down its legs. I'll harness my horse with a Circassian saddle and bit and bridle worked with silver, and ride it up and down the village. And I'll go hare hunting on my horse with my greyhound. A gun too, I'll have to buy, a German carbine. They won't give you a girl to wife in my village if you don't own a German carbine. My uncle has a daughter, a real beauty. She's the one for me. Five years she's been waiting, and she'd wait another five, ten even . . . She loves me. I need a lot of money, so that when I'm back home I'll never have to return to this hell of a Chukurova, never . . ."

While he was talking Halil had slipped behind a bush and had quickly counted his money again. He was preoccupied, unsettled suddenly.

"Tell me," he said as he emerged from behind the bush, "where do you plan to work this winter?"

"Oh-ho! That's a good one," Dursun scoffed. "As if there's any lack of work in the Chukurova!"

"Yes, but what kind of work?"

"Stumping, for one. Over there across the river . . . Not so difficult and you get good money for it. There's an agha there they call Memik Agha. He seems hard and forbidding, but he's fair about money . . ."

The other labourers hung their heads silently and traced figures in the sand with little sticks.

"Why don't you come with me, my friend?" Dursun urged. "Come and do some stumping for Memik Agha."

The raft was moored to the opposite shore, but there was still no sign of the ferryman. A strong wind churned up the sand on the river bank.

"You'll see," Dursun went on enthusiastically, "you'll see what a man he is, this Memik Agha. A fellow villager who'd worked three months there took me to him, and the first thing Memik Agha said to me was, have you any money on you, and I said, yes I have. Then give it to me, he said, it won't do to have money about you when you're on the road or working. So I gave him all the money I had . . . With fear in my heart . . . And then he said, the day you leave come and get your money. If I happen to die the amount is marked here. He produced a black notebook, counted the money and, licking the point of his pencil, he wrote down the sum. Safe and sound, Dursun, my lad, he said. Now have a coffee with me before you start work . . . And when the time came, I went to the Agha and said, I'm leaving, Agha, and he got up and kissed me and gave me my savings and what I'd earned from stumping, and on top of that he took five green liras from his pocket, this, he said, is a bonus because you worked so well. I won't let you go before you have one last coffee with me. So I drank my coffee and kissed his hand. And he kissed me once more and said, come again Dursun my son, my door is always open to you and there's work for you any time. So I'm on my way to Memik Agha now to stump some more. Or maybe he'll give me another job, maybe he'll ask me to tend his horse, and that's a good thing, in our religion the horse is a sacred creature. Maybe he'll give me a German carbine, be my bodyguard, Dursun, he'll say, I put such trust in you . . ."

Meanwhile the raft had drawn up to the pier.

"Hurry up," the ferryman called.

They all trooped onto the raft and the ferryman began to draw the wire cable attached to the iron pulley and as the pulley wheeled the raft advanced to the opposite shore.

Leaving the raft they all walked to the foot of the old castle. There, Dursun stopped. "Well friends, this is where we part," he said. "I'm off to Memik Agha's place."

"God speed to you," the others said and they went their way while Dursun hurried off towards the village. Suddenly he heard Halil calling after him. "Wait, mate, I'm coming with you."

"Good for you, mate," Dursun cried joyfully as Halil approached. "You'll see what a kind fatherly man he is, Memik Agha . . ."

They walked on quickly and were soon in the village where they made straight for Memik Agha's house. Leaving their sacks in the stables, they went up the stairs.

Memik Agha was in his room and a look of satisfaction flitted across his face on seeing Dursun.

"Sit right here," he said. "Have a coffee with me."

They squatted down on the wooden threshold and waited, silent and stiff as stones. Memik Agha was looking out of the window. A very young girl came up bearing a tray with red-striped handle-less cups. The strong odour of coffee preceded her.

Turning away from the window Memik Agha addressed Halil. "Have you any money?"

Halil smiled. "Yes, my Agha," he said trustingly.

"Give it to me."

Halil was prepared, the money ready in his hand. "Here you are, Agha."

Memik Agha counted the money and counted again several times.

"Dursun," he said. "Take this fellow to the Arab tomorrow

and let him start work immediately. What's your name, man?"

"Halil . . ."

"Well, good luck to you, Halil."

"There!'" Dursun cried as they went down the stairs. "What did I tell you? Did you ever see a kinder man in the whole of this Chukurova?"

"Never," Halil rejoined. "He's a great agha. And he offered us coffee in his own room too!"

Halil could not sleep that night, so excited was he, so full of the wildest dreams for the future. He would root up that stretch of land below Asarkaya, tear away those thousand-year-old cedars and pines and plane trees and sow wheat, and that silty, fertile earth would yield such a crop a tiger could not penetrate. And afterwards he would build a house beside the village fountain, under the large plane tree, like the house of that agha in Adana, all of shining glass. He would buy a heavy plough and a pair of horses instead of oxen, strong *katana* breeds . . . Ipekché would live in clover like the wives of the Adana aghas. His mother would have a coat with a fur collar like the mothers of the Adana aghas. That land below Asarkaya was very large, but maybe with the help of five hands he could clear it in a matter of three years. Labour was cheap up there in the mountains. Maybe he could even plant oranges on the south-facing slope of the valley protected from the wind. And then, who knows . . . A tractor maybe . . . By that time there would be more of these machines and they would be cheaper. Halil had seen many things all these months in the Chukurova. He had learned a lot. So he gave free rein to his imagination and in his boundless enthusiasm it was as if he could transport the whole of the Chukurova to his village, earth and stone, grass and flowers, trucks, cars, factories, everything. I must be very careful, he told himself, watch my step, calculate my every move to the split of a hair, so that I may reach my goal.

In the morning he went with Dursun to the Arab overseer.

"So this is Halil," the Arab said. "The Agha told me about you, said you're a rich man. Well," he continued with a sour look, "I don't know about rich or poor. What I need is a man who'll work hard."

"I can work," Halil said modestly, his eyes fixed on the ground.

"What kind of work would that be? Look at the state you're in! Nothing but skin and bones . . ."

"I can work," Halil repeated, his voice trembling. "It's only the malaria fever got me down . . ."

"Everyone gets the malaria here, you mountain people worse than all!" the Arab growled. "You must eat a lot to make up for it. The food's free here. All right then, start away."

A cauldron of steaming *tarhana* soup, smelling sourly of garlic fried in butter, was brought in and poured into copper tureens and the labourers began plying their wooden spoons.

After a while the Arab leant over to Halil's ear. "You've got a healthy appetite, I see, rich brother! This *tarhana* soup is an old Turcoman recipe, quickens the blood. Eat your fill, for stumping is like no other work, it wants skill, endurance, force . . ."

They were in the fields before daybreak. The blackthorns stretched darkly far out to the edge of Anavarza. The labourers set to work at once with pickaxes, scythes and sickles.

The Arab gave Halil one of each. "*Ya Allah, ya bismillah, ya Kibriya* . . . Go ahead, Halil," he said. "But first say a prayer, like me."

Halil smiled. "I'm not going to work the first few days. I just want to watch for a while." He looked pleadingly at the Arab.

"As you like," the Arab said, taken aback. "But I'll strike off your pay, you know that?"

"I know."

"And also deduct for your food."

"All right."

Dursun and the other labourers were already at work. First they hewed down the blackthorns, ten to fifteen bushes each, then they dug out the roots. Halil counted the men, there were twenty-seven of them all lined up in a more or less straight row and they advanced very slowly. After thoroughly extirpating the roots, they heaped them up as they went, making two mounds, one of the roots and one of the cut blackthorns. Halil wandered about, noting the way the men used their hands, how they wielded their pickaxes and sickles, closely inspecting their every move, sweating and panting along with them and cursing with them at the occasional rebellious clump of blackthorn that had rooted too deeply into the earth.

And so every morning before daybreak Halil went out with the stumpers. He did not work, just watched, but in the evening he felt even wearier than the others and hardly had he eaten than he dropped onto the hay and fell asleep at once.

A week later, when they came to the blackthorn scrub, Halil was the first to start working. He was very slow, though, and managed to uproot only five bushes the first day. This did not escape the Arab's eye, but he made no comment. The second day Halil pulled out seven bushes and went on at that rate for the next ten days. The Arab waited, still saying nothing. A fortnight later the number of blackthorns rose to eleven. And by the end of the month he was stumping even better than Beardless Shahin who came from distant Sivas town. He worked tooth and nail, arms, legs, all his body in a whirl and the others were amazed and jealous, too, at the swiftness of this newcomer, emaciated as he was by the malaria fever.

"Ah youth!" Beardless Shahin sighed. "It's being young does it, youth it is that stirs his blood like that . . ."

Halil smiled at him. Beardless Shahin was the best of the lot, steady, skilful, confident, never leaving the smallest scrap of root in the earth. He had a huge head, huge hands and very long arms. His eyes were deep-set under reddish shaggy brows. His voice rang out bell-like, but he rarely spoke, keeping to himself, staring at his hands more often than not, hands that resembled the roots of the blackthorns, dark and gnarled and calloused. It was the same with all the stumpers, but more so with Beardless Shahin, and soon Halil's hands began to be like his. When Beardless Shahin walked it was as though a block of clay was moving, riddled with clefts and cracks and about to fritter away.

"Ah youth . . . We too were young once, like this young Halil . . . and what did we do with our youth? We wasted it miserably, toiling in other people's fields. Look at us now! Will Halil be any better? We earn barely enough to eat our fill. And that's how it'll be with Halil . . ."

There was something under his tongue, something he wanted to tell Halil, but somehow he couldn't get it out and only repeated, ah youth, whenever he looked at him.

One morning Halil did not go to work, but made his way to Memik Agha's house.

"Why Halil!" Memik Agha exclaimed. "Come in, come and sit over here. Zalimoglu Halil they call you, don't they?"

Halil was surprised. Wherever could this man have learnt his name? No one outside his village knew it. He hadn't even told Dursun.

"Send up a cup of coffee," Memik Agha called down the

stairs, then turned to Halil. "You haven't gone to work today, Zalimoglu, is there something you want of me?"

"It's like this, Agha," Halil said. "I work hard, I do the work of four and yet I get the same wages as the others. Is that fair?"

"True," Memik Agha said. "What d'you want me to do then?"

"You know best, Agha." Halil rose and joined his hands respectfully.

Memik Agha was pleased. "Sit down," he said. "We must think this over. I wouldn't want a good stumper like you to be cheated out of his right."

"I know you don't. I trust you . . ."

"Well what shall we do?"

"Let's settle for a fixed sum. We know how many acres a stumper can average a day. Arab Effendi knows it all. Beardless Shahin too doesn't get his due. He roots up as much as four or five men a day. Is it fair for him to be paid a daily wage like the others?"

"No, it isn't," Memik Agha admitted.

Her heels clicking on the stairs, the same girl as before brought up the coffee. Halil rose and took the cup from the tray. The coffee was steaming hot. The Agha held out his tobacco case.

"Help yourself, Zalimoglu," he said.

Halil blushed. "We like to see others smoking," he declined, holding a hand to his heart.

Memik Agha set the case down in front of him on the *kilim*. "Right then, we'll do as you say. I'll pay you per *dönüm*. How many *dönüms* each year . . . We'll settle accounts every *Kurban Bairam*."

"Thank you, my Agha."

"Tell Shahin that he'll be paid the same way from now on. The others too if they wish. I'll talk to the Arab to decide on the price per *dönüm*."

"Thank you, my good kind Agha."

Halil rose and withdrew without turning his back on the Agha until he came to the staircase.

That day, he wandered about the village all by himself. Down by the river he watched the play of the fish darting here and there in the water. Then he went on to the water-melon gardens to chat with the watchman who was also from the mountains. He had come to the Chukurova only this year and after talking a little with Halil, he broke into a song, his eyes closed. He had a high thin voice. His mouth and nose were covered with sores. Now and again he broke off and turned to Halil. "I'm going to die, Halil," he said. "This malaria, this curse, will make short shrift of me."

"No, it won't."

"It'll kill me."

"Of course not."

"Will I ever see my mountains again, the purple violets, the silvery pines, the cool springs, the scent of marjoram . . . Will I ever get back beyond snow-capped Düldül Mountain?"

"You will!" Halil so wanted the other to believe this that he almost shouted. "You will!"

"I'm pining away for the old homeland."

"So are we all . . ."

"You too?"

Halil laughed. "I'm dying with longing."

The young man laughed too. "Well, so am I, dying. Every night I dream I'm flying to beyond Düldül Mountain on the back of an eagle and the eagle puts me down under the plane tree in the middle of our village where a spring gushes out among the marjoram. The spring smells of violets and I drink of the violet-scented water. I drink and drink, and hey presto all these sores are cured. My belly's no longer bloated like this . . . And then . . ." He closed his eyes and broke into a song again, then drifted off, away from the sun-impacted, flaming river.

Halil got up too and went up to the old castle ruins. Grass-hoppers sprang about his feet as he went. From up under the castle, he could make out Mount Düldül, far in the distance, beyond the pale blue, smoke-swathed range of hills. Its sharp pointed peak glowed in the sunlight. Halil sat down on a stone. All around him bees of all kinds and colours buzzed to and fro. Flights of swallows came and went between where he sat and Mount Düldül. Soon he was lost in a trance, oblivious of the flashing swallows, deaf to the buzzing of bees, the call of the partridges from the castle and of the francolin from the chaste trees that fringed the river down below. His eyes were fixed on snow-capped Düldül Mountain where it rose high beyond the pale range of hills, ever-changing Düldül, different under rain or sun, west- or south-blowing winds, never the same from one moment of the day to the other, colours, shape, height and width, shadowy valleys ever changing, but ever lovely, ever graceful, deep blue, then waning into grey, shimmering in a coppery glow, then swaying like a slender cloud, barely perceptible against the sky, or etched out darkly, now bathed in a dazzling light, shining bright, now whirling in the thousand and one colours of the dawn, sparkling star-like, shedding its rays over the whole world, lighting up the pale blue tiered hills around it, wafting in the dawn breezes, freshly green, violet-scented.

He remained there, singing softly, until the sun set and darkness hid the mountain from view. When he rose, he felt laved clean inside, ready to fly with happiness.

After this, Halil worked without stint. Many a time, he was up long before dawn, at midnight even, and with the jug of water and bundle of food he had prepared the evening before, he was out in the fields and rooting up the blackthorns with furious speed. Not a trace now of the malaria-ridden Halil of the first days. Here now was a giant waging a mighty battle against the blackthorns. His clothes were in rags, the skin showing bare through his shirt. Even his boots hung in strips. His arms, legs and face had been lacerated by the thorns, his whole body was a mass of sores and bruises. One nostril had been torn off as well as the lobe of his left ear and also his right eyebrow. He had persuaded Beardless Shahin to go along with him and the two of them were fearsome apparitions to anyone who came upon them in the dusk. The other stumpers, the villagers marvelled at this sight, but they bore them no ill will. Not a word was said against them. Who knows what troubles they have, the poor things, they said, or would anyone work himself into this state, nothing human left about him, just for a little money?

"This year at the *Kurban Bairam*," Halil said to Beardless Shahin whenever they stopped for a breather, "I'm going to ask Memik Agha for my money and I'm going to buy a horse, a good horse from the Mercimek stud farm, with a Turcoman saddle and silver-worked bridle. Then, with a German carbine slung over my shoulder, I'll make straight for the other side of Düldül Mountain. There, I'll clear that flatland at the foot of the Asarkaya crags and till the earth into such a field as you've never seen the like. That silty soil will yield forty, even fifty to one, it can never be swept away by rain and floods. And I'll build a real mansion right beside the spring behind the tall plane trees, and surround it with a fence so as to have a garden which I'll plant with flowers and fruit trees I'll have brought all the way from

Adana. If you like, you can come too and settle in our village, with all your family . . ."

"I will," Beardless Shahin said. "Just let me put some order into my affairs at home and round out my savings here . . ."

There were still quite a few months to go before the *Bairam*. Beardless Shahin and Halil had already cleared a patch of land big enough for a farm. The brown blackthorns yielded yellow circular flat-seeded fruit that had a strange tartish taste. All along the vast blackthorn field, white spider webs were stretched taut across the bushes. They swung in the breeze, heavy with trapped flies, insects and bees. It grieved Halil to have to destroy these webs, each one as large as a sheet, to see the spiders retreating into a corner of the web and watching with sad eyes their beautiful handiwork ruined.

Quite a lot of bird nests and honeycombs too were lodged in the bushes. Halil would not touch the bushes that harboured chicks or eggs, at least not until the winter, so that the wide fields were dotted with these nest-filled bushes, solitary mounds with birds fluttering over them. As for the honeycombs, he toted them down to the riverside, painstakingly, his face and hands all swollen with the sting of bees, setting them carefully down on the blackberry bushes by the river. These bushes buzzed with angry bees that stung anyone passing by. But still Halil continued to bring them there, comb after comb, some of them large as a tray, with the bees swarming along.

"Halil, Halil! What's keeping you, Halil? How many years since you went away . . ."

Echoes sounding and resounding from the Valley of Hawthorns . . . Francolins calling from the sun-drenched yellow plain . . . All around him, men with skins blistered by the sun and scratched by the thorns.

"Halil, Halil!"

Some days, just as the east began to pale, he would go up to the old castle ruin and from there would watch Mount Düldül slowly emerging out of a luminous haze, the sun suddenly striking its summit, flaming gold one instant, then flowing like a shooting star swiftly across the clear dawn sky. Filled with delirious joy, Halil would rush off to attack the blackthorns even more quickly than before.

"Halil, Halil! Where are you, Halil? Was this what we pledged each other, oh Halil?"

And still Halil never let up, never slackened with Beardless Shahin always at his side, bewitched, doing whatever Halil told him. They moved at the same rhythm, their gestures alike, even their faces beginning to look alike. Shahin too began to hear a call now, coming from far away, from the distant steppes of Anatolia.

"Shahin, Shahin! Where are you, where, oh where? Go, cranes, go, fly to there, to beyond the mountains . . ."

At last, *Kurban Bairam* came and for the first time Halil and Shahin stopped working and appeared among their fellow men. First, they joined the congregation in the mosque for the early morning *Bairam namaz*. People stared and muttered at the sight of these haggard, tattered creatures. Next they went to Memik Agha.

"May your *Bairam* be blessed, Agha," they said as they kissed his hand.

Memik Agha offered them coffee which they sipped noisily.

"You've worked really hard," the Agha complimented them. "Like ten men. We've added up your earnings with the Arab and we found you're quite rich." He looked at Halil. "D'you also want that money you gave me to keep?"

"Keep it for me a little longer," Halil said after a quick thought. "I'll ask you for it in a few days, when I leave for home."

Memik Agha was jubilant. This was a sure sign that Halil would stay on this year too.

After taking their pay, Halil and Shahin made for the town on foot. They slept in a *han* and ate at Kurdish Ibrahim's restaurant, kebab flavoured with *sumac* and washed down with turnip juice, the same, morning, noon and evening. Then they returned to the village and the next day at the peep of dawn they went up to the old castle ruin and sat there all day on the wild thyme, staring at Mount Düldül. They did not speak. Only once, as dusk fell and the mountain faded away, Halil said: "Just there beyond that mountain . . . There it is, my village . . . My mother . . . My granny . . . All there, beyond that mountain."

The next day they wandered about the village, then sat down in the Valley of Hawthorns, counting and recounting their money.

"What d'you say, Shahin, if we don't go back this year? We'll have saved this much again if we go next year."

Beardless Shahin was silent.

"My granny was fit and fine when I left," Halil pursued. "And mother hale as ever. Nothing can happen to them. As for Ipekché, she'd wait for me a thousand years. Let's not go back this year,

Shahin brother, so that next year we can take back a really good sum. What d'you say?"

And without giving Shahin a chance to reply, he made for the village at a running pace, Shahin barely keeping up with him, and stopped only at the foot of the Agha's stairs to wait for Shahin. Memik Agha was sitting on the sofa. Without a word, his head hanging, Halil handed over his money, then dashed down the stairs. Shahin followed his every move.

"This year we're going to make a lot of money," Halil said.

"More than last year," Shahin concurred.

"Come along now, let's have a good sleep."

"All right," Shahin said.

The next day before sunrise, before the dawn breeze began to blow, while the morning star still sparkled brightly above the Gavur Mountains, they were in the blackthorn field, working with renewed vigour. Their speed increased day by day. Behind them they left a rich fertile soil that would yield forty or even fifty to one. They cleared the land not only of blackthorns, but also of brambles and trees, reeds and rushes. The bushes teemed with birds and bees and ants and hard-cased beetles which glistened, blue, and green, orange and yellow, and large, finely filigreed, mauve and orange butterflies. There were cardoons too that housed thousands of ladybirds. And whenever he came upon such a nest, Halil would be transported with joy. "See this, Shahin?" he said as he caressed them with his eyes. "Everything I ask for will come true! Did you ever see so many of these lucky insects, Allah's own harbingers of good fortune?" He bent down, selected one of the larger ladybirds and watched as it crept through the black hairs and blisters and earth-filled furrows of his hand. "Fly away, fly away, pretty little insect," he urged. "If you fly now, everything I wish for will come true." His eyes fixed anxiously on the shiny black-specked red ladybird, his lips trembling, he repeated like an incantation "Fly, dainty little insect, fly away, do . . ." The ladybird struggled through the hairs, then up and down the fingers and, just as Halil, his heart in his mouth, was beginning to despair, it stopped at the tip of his thumb, the right position Halil knew from long experience, lifted its wings, ready to take flight, and suddenly, to Halil's delight, soared into the air. Halil would repeat this with another ladybird, and then another, and after the third ladybird had flown away, he would heave a sigh of relief. "Come, Shahin brother," he would say, "let's rest a little under that oak tree." And he would drift into a reverie with thousands of black-specked red ladybirds flitting to and fro, glittering in the sunlight.

Even the way they ate, these two, was strange. They would carry their share of the *bulgur* pilaff and *ayran*, brought over in cauldrons, to some secluded spot and gobble it down in a trice, returning to work almost without a break. The other labourers looked at them as at some jinn-struck beings, not human any more, beyond redemption.

Come the autumn, the blackthorns shed their leaves, their flat fruit, large as coat buttons, yellow in the summer, turned dark brown like the thistly branches and the whole vast scrubwood took on a sinister aspect. Halil too began to change, slowing down gradually until he was working at the same pace as the others, and Beardless Shahin soon followed suit. As his listlessness increased, he intoned an endless threnody that went on and on as he worked. Now and then he stopped short and stood very still as though giving ear to some sound only he could hear.

"Halil, Halil! Why don't you come back, Halil? Don't you pine for the mountains of home, so sweetly scented, oh Halil?"

The flowering mountains, the violets knee-deep, the narcissus, the hyacinths . . . The dog rose and orchis . . . The blue-flowering marjoram by the springs. The cranes flying in, the Seven Stars, The Balance, the myriad stars in the sky . . .

"Halil! Enough, Halil, enough! Come back . . ."

He could hear the creep of an insect on the soil, the pitpat of grasshoppers, the gliding of a snake, the flight of a bee. Suddenly, he would turn back along the village path and climb up to the castle ruins. He would remain there, sitting on a stone, his face in his hands, lost in a trance until the sky above Mount Düldül was studded with stars.

"Halil, Halil! The purple violets no longer grow knee-deep, no longer fragrant, the springs are running dry, overgrown with moss . . ."

Come the autumn, men begin to arrive from beyond Mount Düldül, from beyond the mauve, coppery, vaporous, sharp-crested mountain.

"A man with oval eyes . . . From the other side of the mountain, from Doruk village . . . His name is Ali. A strong reaper . . . Tall, with tapering fingers, thin face, sharp nose . . . A twisted smile. He wears embroidered stockings and always ties an embroidered kerchief at his neck. He walks with long strides, a greyhound at his heels. He never goes anywhere without his greyhound. Have you seen him, brother?"

"No I haven't seen Ali . . ."

"He smells of hay, of fresh water and rain, of green-eared wheat, of *madimak*, of the coat of the fallow deer . . ."

"No, I haven't seen Ali."

"His house is only ten paces from ours, he owns a long flute, makes his own plough, gets down to the Chukurova on log rafts, seven days and seven nights under the stars. Ali came here, to this village, he asked after me, me Halil . . . Didn't you hear about it?"

"No, I didn't brother."

It was raining. Barefoot under the downpour, Halil and Shahin sloshed through mud and streaming water. Lightning flashed above the crags and the castle, illuminating for an instant the darkly flowing river, rending the skies, bringing Düldül Mountain nearer in a flood of light, filigreeing the night with thousands of streaks of light, then plunging back into the darkness.

Stumping in the rain is a formidable task. The other stumpers would hurry back to the village as fast as they could when it started to rain. But these two, Halil and Shahin, struck away harder then ever at the deep roots of the blackthorns, steeped in mud, only their eyes and teeth gleaming through.

You, brother, you've come on foot all the way down from the mountains, your pack on your back, drenched under the rain . . . Is it from the other side of Düldül Mountain that you hail? Did you happen to pass through Doruk village, did you see old Anshaja, did you ask after my mother, did you stop under the spreading plane tree, did you hear about Ipekché whose hair is like gold, glistening in the sunlight, did she say, remember me to that no-good fellow, did old Ahmet's rooster crow, have the turbid torrents abated? How did you weather that terrible rain?

The man was silent. He had stopped on the road and was looking at the sky where churning clouds rumbled, torn with streaks of lightning. The flashes came one after the other without a break, crisscrossing and clustering into balls of light that irradiated the whole firmament from end to end. Halil and Shahin were flooded with light one instant, then buried in darkness the next. The long widespread webs that hung all over the blackthorn scrub were pierced by the driving rain and the spiders had retreated into a corner of their destroyed homes, quite still, their eyes huge, their long legs taut. Thunderbolts cleaved through the sky, peal after peal, and struck the rocky mountain, whose crest was illuminated as though in broad daylight.

Brother, hey brother! You come from beyond the hills. Did you pass through Doruk village? Did you see him, tall like you, his face like yours, with laughing eyes and smiling lips under the same drooping moustache, his white teeth gleaming from way off, just like yours . . . He brought back a pair of oxen from the Chukurova, a German carbine and an Arab colt and paid three hundred liras as dowry to his bride's family. Such a fellow who's said to have led the dance at the Peri King's wedding three days and three nights, and had all the peri folk doting on him . . . Have you seen him, wayfarer? Do you bring me tidings from him? He looked just like you . . .

They worked by night now, in the moonlight. During the day, they roamed about the village and up and down the roads that led into the hills, looking for passers-by who might have some news from home, but not one person did they meet who could tell them anything about Doruk village or snow-capped Düldül Mountain, nor about Kazova in the sanjak of Sivas. After a while they lost all hope and returned to work, dejected and sorrowful and for a month or two they hardly lifted their heads from the blackthorns, forgetting even to eat and drink.

Then one day they suddenly left their work and fell to scouring the countryside again, hoping against hope for news from even the flying bird, the buzzing bee.

Would my own mother know me if she saw me now? My grandmother, would she say, this is Halil? And Ipekché, would she discern my own smell and throw her arms around my neck, crying Halil, this is Halil, Halil . . .

It was the eve of the *Kurban Bairam*. In front of Memik Agha's house were three sheep, their backs smeared with red, purple and green paint, and two goats with coloured ribbons tied to their necks, all ready for the sacrifice on the morrow. They were zestfully munching the grass that had been put in front of them.

"Tomorrow's *Bairam* day," Halil said.

"Your people will be watching out for you . . ."

"This time we must go," Halil said. And he rushed up the stairs to Memik Agha, who was there smiling as usual.

"Two coffees," Memik Agha called downstairs and drew out of

his pocket two wads of money. "Here you are," he said, and added scoldingly: "Last year you spent much too much money in town. Mind you don't do this again. This is money you've earned with blood and sweat. You mustn't squander it away."

The coffees arrived. Halil and Shahin had perched themselves on the edge of the settee. They took the cups with trembling hands.

"Why, my lads," Memik Agha laughed, "this year you've cleared land enough for a huge farm! Just the two of you, you've made as much money as all the other stumpers put together. Well, Allah give you the strength for more. Going to the town again?"

"That's right," Halil said.

"Well, Godspeed to you," Memik Agha said, smiling benignly. They backed out as usual and turned only on reaching the stairs. In town they went first to a barber. Halil simply could not recognise himself in the barber's mirror. It was as though he was looking at a stranger. Only the eyes were the eyes of Halil. He could not take his eyes off the eyes in the mirror, as though searching for something there.

Smelling of cologne, they entered the kebab shop and ordered double servings of kebab liberally sprinkled with *sumac* and accompanied by a large platter of radishes, green peppers and parsley. They ate slowly, savouring each morsel and drinking turnip juice. Then leaving the greasy-fumed shop, they made for the market place where they sat in a coffee-house and drank several glasses of very sweet tea. Tall plane trees shaded the coffee-house and below it ran a little stream over which were situated the latrines. Timorously they went in and once inside Halil was seized with a fit of laughter. Shahin burst out laughing too and they crouched and relieved themselves in the most pleasant way imaginable, the rippling flowing water carrying off excrement and urine. Halil vowed that the first thing he would do on returning to the village was to build just such a latrine, even before the mansion he dreamed of.

Yes, he would go straight to Memik Agha from here. Listen Agha, he would say, I can't stay another moment, let me have the money I gave you in trust, I'm going back home . . . Now right away? Right away, Agha . . . And does Shahin want his money too? . . . Yes, he's coming along with me to our village . . .

He straightened up, filled with joy. "Come on, Shahin, quick," he said. "We must go to the Agha now, straight away."

How they left the town, which way they took, how they crossed the river and how they found themselves at the foot of the Agha's stairs, they never knew. They halted there, only for a moment, then Halil went up, still trembling with joy.

Memik Agha greeted them even more benignly than before. "Come Halil, come my lion, my brave son, worth a thousand stumpers, come and sit beside me and have a coffee. And you too, Shahin, the brave companion of my Halil, you sit on this side. Two coffees," he shouted, rattling the thirty-three-beaded *tespih* in his hand. Then he threw his tobacco case in front of Halil. "Roll yourself one."

"We love those who smoke," Halil said diffidently.

"And you?"

"Thank you kindly," Shahin refused, his hand on his heart.

There was a long silence. Memik Agha did not speak and the others sat on, very straight, their hands spread out stiffly on their knees, waiting respectfully.

Suddenly the Agha boomed out: "Give me your money, before you forget it in your pockets and have it stolen by some good-for-nothing. I was going to forget and what if I had, what if someone had stolen that money you earned with blood and sweat, what would you do then?"

"Agha . . ." Halil began.

"Come, come!" the Agha thundered. He sensed something untoward in the air. "That's enough of wandering about with all that money on you! What if someone had got wind of it? God forbid!"

Somehow Halil's money was out of his pouch and in Memik Agha's outstretched hand. "But Agha," he stammered, "this year . . ."

Memik Agha laughed. "You're still very young, Halil," he said. "What's the hurry?"

Halil hung his head. His scarred pocked face blushed scarlet. Sweat beaded his brow.

Shahin's money had also somehow found its way to the Agha who was counting it now and shaking his head. "What a lot you've spent," he exclaimed. "Money that you've earned so hard! It's a shame to scatter it to the winds like this, a real shame! Next year I shan't let you have so much when you go to town."

Two steaming coffees arrived. Again they took the cups with

trembling hands and drank meekly. Once outside, they sat side by side on the ancient inscribed marble slabstone, silently, staring up at the old castle above which hovered a bird of prey, wings outstretched, as though nailed to the sky.

"We must ask him for our money," Halil said as though speaking to himself. "Who knows how they're faring way back home . . . ?"

"Who knows . . . ?" Shahin said. "But why did you give him your money, why didn't you ask for the rest?"

"I was ashamed," Halil sighed. "There's something about that man, makes you do what he wants. Your hands are somehow tied before him."

"Let's ask again. It's our money, isn't it? In trust . . ."

"Yes, in trust . . ."

They fell silent and remained there for a long time, still as stones, their eyes fixed on the bird of prey hovering above. Once in a while their gaze shifted to Memik Agha's mansion or to the river that glittered along the flat plain below. The sun was sinking fast and from the mansion they could hear the Agha's booming voice.

"We must go home today," Halil said forlornly. "I can't bear this any longer. I wish I never went in for this stumping business. If only I'd gone straight back home after the rice harvest . . ."

"Ah, if only . . ." Shahin murmured.

"But then I wouldn't have been able to buy a horse or a German carbine. I wouldn't have had money enough to give Ipekché's father. I wouldn't have been able to build myself a beautiful house there, by the spring under the tall plane trees, nor to cultivate that large fertile land at Asarkaya and grow a crop a tiger couldn't penetrate. Nor could I have brought back a cotton-padded jacket for my granny, a blue Chukurova wrap-around for my mother, silver bracelets for Ipekché . . ."

He spoke softly like an old-time storyteller.

"If only someone would pass this way right now, someone from our village . . . He would give us news from home, that they're all safe and sound, that Ipekché's waiting for me . . ."

"Why, then we'd run up those stairs, Memik Agha, we'd say, give us our money. And off we'd fly to the other side of Düldül Mountain . . . To your village . . ."

"Our village," Halil corrected him. Then his face fell. He looked stricken to the core. "But what if when I get home . . ."

His voice broke. He could not bring himself to say it. The words stuck in his throat. "What if I find my granny dead?" he blurted out. "Of what use will it be, all this money I've earned? What if my mother is dead? She was sick anyway when I left . . . What if Ipekché's gone and got married? She had that strange look on her face when we parted, as though to say, all right, go away, but how long d'you think I can wait for you . . . ? Ah then, of what use working myself to shreds, leaving a bit of my flesh on every blackthorn bush . . ."

"True, a girl cannot wait for ever," Shahin sighed.

"She must have called to me on her deathbed, my granny . . . Halil, Halil, why are you tarrying, Halil . . . ? I was going to bring her some good white cloth for her shroud. How she must have reproached me, Halil, Halil, they're burying me without a shroud, Halil!"

"We can't go back to the village like this," Shahin said. "Without having some news of what's been going on there . . ."

"No, we can't," Halil agreed. "But how shall we explain to the other stumpers that we've changed our minds?"

"Oh-ho," Shahin exclaimed, "what a thing to worry about! We'll say Memik Agha begged and begged us to stay another year, that it would be of great help to him, so we couldn't possibly refuse after eating his bread all these years."

"And anyway," Halil said, "isn't it the same with the other stumpers? Don't they all throw away pickaxe and all, intent on going home at every *Bairam*?"

"And aren't they back at work on the morrow of the *Bairam*?"

"Who are they to say anything to us!"

So they fell at the blackthorn scrub again, hewing and uprooting at a still greater speed, stopping from time to time to go up to the old castle ruins and gaze at Mount Düldül, swathed in mists beyond the range of blue hills.

And then the *Bairam* came again. They went to town and ate *sumac*-flavoured kebab. Willy-nilly they entrusted their accumulating pay to Memik Agha, sat hesitating on the ancient inscribed marble slabstone, then afraid to go back to the village, threw themselves at the blackthorns with the strength of old-time titans. And so a few more years went by in this way.

Wayfarer, where do you hail from? You have the eyes, the look of someone from the other side of the mountain, you walk like our mountain people, your *shalvar*-trousers are of homespun cloth dyed with walnut shells. Maybe it was your granny who dyed it . . . Where are you going to, wayfarer, on the road on the eve of the *Kurban Bairam*? Do you know Doruk village?

Time and again Halil would rush down to the road as soon as he spied someone coming and stand there expectantly until the passer-by had gone his way. Then he would return to the blackthorns, Beardless Shahin at his heels.

"Look, Shahin, look!" His voice trembled. Shading his eyes with his hand, he pointed to the road. "Shahin, look!" he repeated, his voice buoyant now. "That man there is from beyond the mountain, from our homeland."

"How d'you know?" Halil had waylaid dozens of people like this, only to have his hopes dashed time after time.

"From the way he walks," Halil replied, choking with excitement. "No one like that has come this way before." His eyes fixed on the traveller, he stood rooted to the spot. Usually, he would rush down to the road and wait there for the passers-by, who went their way, some with a greeting, some without a glance.

The man walked very quickly. Halil waited, his face ashen. He would have made no move, if the wayfarer himself had not turned and come towards him.

"*Selam aleyküm*," the man said.

Halil swayed. He was tongue-tied.

"*Aleyküm selam*," Beardless Shahin returned the greeting.

"Have you got any water to drink?" the wayfarer asked. "I haven't had a drop of fresh water since this morning. My throat's parched."

Shahin ran to get their jug from under a bush. "Here you are," he said.

The man drank with long thirsty gulps.

By this time Halil had pulled himself together. "My granny . . ." he blurted out. "My granny, Anshaja . . . Tell me, how is she? And my mother? And what news of Ipekché?"

The wayfarer was quite young. He stared, then cried out, "Why Halil! I'd never have known you but for your voice . . . Whatever have you done to yourself? Your face, your hands . . ."

"Tell me, is my grandmother alive?"

"She is indeed."

"And my mother?"

"Yes, yes."

"Ipekché?"

"Why, she's waiting for you . . ."

"God bless you, Duran!" Halil cried, throwing himself at his neck. "Thank God for sending you to me. Thank God that I should live to see this day!"

Duran was looking at him with growing astonishment. "Why Halil," he said, "I can't believe this. I'd never have known you, not in a thousand years. Why, your own mother wouldn't know you. What on earth have you done to yourself?"

Halil was not listening. His face glowing with happiness, he looked at Shahin. "Come along," he said. "You too, Duran." It was as if he had put on wings. In no time they were in Memik Agha's yard. "Is the Agha upstairs?"

"Yes, he's there," a servant replied.

Halil made for the stairs, followed by Shahin and Duran.

"Well, well, Halil Agha," Memik Agha said with a supercilious smile. "You're early for the town this year. And how is it you've cleared so little land these last days? It's not like you at all. I hope you're not ill or something . . . And who's this young fellow?" He pointed to Duran. "Come to do some stumping too?"

"No!" Halil almost shouted. "No, no! This is Duran. He's from my village."

"Oh, is that so?"

"Yes Agha," Halil said defiantly. "And I'm going back home. So I want my money now, all of it. It comes to one thousand two hundred and seventy-three liras and seventy-seven kurush, not counting this year. And Shahin too has seven hundred and fifty-three liras in trust with you, besides this year's earnings."

Memik Agha gave him a long appraising look. "Certainly, certainly, Halil," he said gently. He produced his wallet, counted some banknotes, scrutinised Halil, counted them once again. "Here," he said, "this is what you've earned this year."

"We want all our money."

"Aren't you going to town now?"

"Yes . . ."

"Well then, you take this much with you and when you're back we'll see to the rest."

"We want it all. Now."

Memik Agha raised his voice. "You can't go gadding about town with all this money on you. Get along with you. Go," he added, his face suddenly dark and stern as Halil seemed about to insist.

This time Halil did not step backwards as he left. He turned his back on the Agha and went out without another word. The three of them made straight for the town.

First they went to the barber's where all three sat in a row to be shaved and have their hair cut. Then on to the kebab shop which was hazy with fumes and reeked of burnt fat, *sumac*, onions, tomatoes and dill. They ordered large portions of Adana-style kebab. Halil had begun to get over the initial shock of relief and he talked on and on as they ate. They drank coffee in the coffee-house, sipping noisily like the aghas did. Afterwards they walked through the town park to the ironsmith and cartwright marts, past the mosque, the Government House, the railway station and came to the grain bazaar which was crammed with pile upon pile of wheat, oats and cotton. And from there . . . On and on they went, Halil leading, through fruit orchards, vegetable gardens, rosaries, and stopped at last at the mill that smelled of freshly ground flour and where the water flowing down a high turbine came crashing down with a deafening roar.

"That was a good walk about town," Halil said as they squatted down, leaning against a wall. His eyes were shining with pleasure. "But Duran, we were so excited we never asked after you! What are you doing down here, brother, like this on the eve of the *Kurban Bairam?*"

Duran was all in a sweat and out of breath. "I'm in a bad way," he said. "The wolves got my oxen and devoured them . . ."

"Did they?" Halil laughed. "Yes, they do that, the wolves. A good thing they don't eat us too, the wretched creatures."

"Then the government levied the toll tax . . ."

"They would," Halil laughed.

"And soon there wasn't a morsel of food left at home."

"I know how it is," Halil said, still smiling, his white teeth gleaming.

"The children went naked. And my mother and my wife could not show themselves in the village for want of proper clothes to cover them."

Suddenly, Halil jumped up. "Come with me," he urged.

They set out at a running pace. In an instant the noise of the mill was left behind and they heard the sound of hammering from the smithies in the centre of the town. When they came to the clothiers market, Halil stopped a moment, then stepped into one of the shops.

"Measure me some of that blue cotton," he said. "Seven yards."

The shopkeeper slowly lifted down the bolt, picked up the iron yardstick and unfolded the cloth. Halil was sweating with impatience. "I want a length of that one too," he said pointing to a flowered print on the shelf.

This time, infected by Halil's eagerness, the shopkeeper was quicker.

"And some of this . . ." Halil kept pointing to the cloths and ordering three yards, four, five . . .

They went out. Halil, his excitement growing apace, handed the parcels to Duran. "Here, brother," he said. "I've earned a lot of money. These are for you." Then he fell to the road, the others following, and once out of the town he stopped under a plane tree and produced a wad of money from his pocket. He counted it, smiled and, setting aside some of the banknotes, he held the rest out to Duran. "Take this," he said. "I've got plenty of money. This is for you. It'll buy you a team of oxen and make up for the toll tax too."

Duran stood mesmerised, the money in his hand, his eyes wide open, glazed, staring unbelievingly as in the face of a miracle.

"Put that money where it will be safe on you. There's no end of thieves and evildoers on the high roads."

"I'll be careful," Duran said, his voice strangling.

"And now, don't stop. Go straight back home. And when you get there, go to my mother and my granny and to Ipekché too and tell them I'm coming. Coming on an Arab horse and with money enough to buy a team of oxen, a plough, five cows, fifteen sheep . . ." Halil listed all the things that came to his mind. "Go like the wind. You're young, you can do it. Don't waste a minute. Tell Ipekché . . . Tell her Halil's coming. In less than ten days Halil will be there . . ."

"I'll tell her," Duran said.

"Godspeed to you. Don't come with us. It's nearer to our village from here. Go without stopping, neither by day nor by night."

"I won't, I won't," Duran vowed as they left him there under the plane tree.

Halil pressed on as though he had wings to his feet. Shahin, stretching his neck, could barely keep up with him. They came to the river. The raft was moored on their side. Quickly, they got in.

"Don't wait for anyone else," Halil said. "I'll pay you what's necessary. I'm going back home, brother, I'm in a hurry."

The ferryman seized the cable and began to pull. Halil hurried to help him and Shahin lent a hand too, so that in no time they found themselves on the opposite shore.

"How much?" Halil asked, his hand in his pocket.

"For you, nothing," the man said. His eyes were smiling.

"How's that?" Halil wondered.

"Aren't you Halil?" the ferryman asked.

"Well, yes but . . ."

"Good-day then, brother." The man patted his back. "May Allah unite you speedily to your loved ones. You deserve it. You owe me nothing."

Halil was gratified. His eyes shone with emotion. "What good people there are in this world," he said.

They jumped from the raft and made for Memik Agha's house at a run.

Overcoming the initial shock of seeing them like this, panting and sweating before him, the Agha smiled. "Well, have you brought back your money? I hope you haven't spent it all like last time."

"I did. I spent it all!" Halil flung out with a touch of pride.

"All of it? Where could you have spent all that money? You didn't stay so long in town this time."

"I gave it to Duran. He needed it badly, the poor man. Anyway what I earn is enough for five men, and more even."

Memik Agha paled, his foxlike face grew longer, his lips tightened and beads of sweat appeared on his brow. "You gave away all that money, you fool? Don't you know how we earned it, you and I? D'you think I found that money lying around?" He rose and stepped forward angrily. "And you too, Shahin . . ."

"No, no," Shahin said calmly. "My money's with me here."

"Thank goodness!" Memik Agha drew a deep breath. Then he grabbed Halil's arm. "You fool, you enemy of honest labour, did you really give it to that man? All of it?"

Halil smiled. "I've still got a little, Agha. Don't worry so."

"Money you earned by the sweat of your brow! Quick, give it to me, now, right away, before you go distributing it to all and sundry."

Like a bird of prey he was now, Memik Agha, with his hooked nose and knit brows and his arms swelling out like spreading wings.

"We're quitting," Halil said. "Going back home. So will you please settle our accounts."

"What accounts?" the Agha shouted. "You've just gone and given away all my money, and now you ask for more? What money, man?"

"Why, the money I earned from the rice harvest and all that we earned these years stumping for you. The money you're holding in trust for us."

"First give me what's left on you. Then we'll talk."

"Very well," Halil said. He took his money from his pocket and handed it over to Memik Agha.

Shahin did the same.

"Good!" Memik Agha sat down with a sigh of relief. "Now speak, what is it you want?"

"The money you're keeping for us . . . We're going home . . ."

"What money, man?"

"The money we earned all these years working for you . . . And all that I'd earned in the rice paddies and orange groves . . ."

"How many years is it since you came here, Halil? You tell me this." Memik Agha frowned, his moustache bristled. "Come on, speak!"

"It's been six years, eight months and eleven days . . ."

"Right, and all this time didn't you eat, didn't you drink?"

"Yes, but . . ."

"So I've reckoned up all you ate these seven years and also what you spent each *Kurban Bairam*, and also what you went and gave away just now, and it comes out to this: you owe me fifty-nine liras and seventy-three kurush. That's how it is, Halil Effendi, my boy . . . You people are very good at adding up what you've earned, but you have no idea of what was spent on your food and upkeep. And how many sets of clothes did you use up in these seven years?"

"Three," Halil said, "but they were already used. Look here, Agha, you're joking, aren't you?" He stood there smiling unbelievingly, almost fawningly.

Memik Agha leaped to his feet. "Joking!" he shouted. "Joking, hah! You've eaten me out of *tarhana*, and what *tarhana*, *bulgur*, and what *bulgur*, *ayran*, onions, butter, and the best, and now you stand there and ask for a bonus to boot. After you've eaten me bare, after . . . And on top of that . . ." He was choking, beating at the wall, mad with rage. "Joking, hah? Joking!"

Halil's face was ashen, the smile frozen on his lips. "Agha, you're joking of course, aren't you . . . ?"

"So you think I'm joking, eh Halil, my lad?" Suddenly Memik Agha was quite calm, his face hard, expressionless. His eyes boring into Halil's, he spoke very softly. "So you're not doing any more stumping?"

"That's right, Agha."

"And you're thinking of going back to your village?"

"If God wills . . ."

"Is that certain?"

"I wouldn't stay another day, even if they gave me the whole of the Chukurova."

"But you'll have to stay, you'll be forced to."

"Not if they kill me, I won't."

"Then what about the fifty-nine liras seventy-three kurush that you owe me?"

Halil smiled again. "Agha, I swear you're joking."

"See here, Halil, you're not taking a step out of this village without bringing me that money." The Agha looked at Shahin. "And that goes for you too. You owe me thirty-three liras and sixty-two kurush."

Beardless Shahin, his neck stretching out like a bird's, stared at him blankly.

"Agha, you must be making fun of us . . ." Halil was no longer smiling. His mouth was dry.

"If you leave without paying your debts," Memik Agha said, "I'll have you arrested before you get beyond the Narrow Pass, and thrown into jail too. And as for that villager of yours you gave my money to, I'll have him stopped and brought back here and thrashed until he passes blood."

"But Agha . . . Memik Agha . . . For heaven's sake . . ."

Suddenly Memik Agha began to shout. "Ungrateful wretches, biting the hand that feeds you, lost to shame!" His voice rang through the air, enough to wake the dead. "Scoundrels . . . After seven years of feeding on my doorstep . . . Like mangy dogs they were when they came . . . And now they stand there and deny their debt! Ah, raw milk is what man has sucked, ah wretched humanity . . ."

"Stop, Agha. Please . . ."

"Get out! Out of my sight!" He advanced upon them screaming: "Out, and don't you dare go anywhere without bringing me what you owe me."

"Don't, Agha! Stop . . . For heaven's sake, Agha," Halil and Shahin repeated as they backed away. They stumbled down the stairs, broke through the crowd of labourers that had gathered and ended up sitting on the ancient inscribed marble slabstone in the yard.

They remained there till sundown without speaking to each other. Then they rose and went up to the castle ruins. There they crouched down side by side against a rock. The air smelled of scorched thyme and an unaccustomed wind was blowing from the east. Darkness fell abruptly, the plain below was wiped out. Beyond the shadowy ranges of foothills, rising out of the darkness, swaying slightly, bathed in light, Mount Düldül seemed to reach for the sky, its brightness increasing, shimmering like blue-spangled crystal. All night through hundreds of thoughts revolved in Halil's mind. So many years of blood and toil . . . Wasted . . . So many dreams gone with the wind. Years spent imagining his grandmother smiling with her toothless mouth, greeting him with boundless relief, his mother's embrace, Ipekché standing before him, arms hanging limply, eyes cast down . . . All these seven years every day, morning and evening, stumping, eating and drinking he had visualised how he would return to his village in a cloud of joy.

All night through, the peak of Düldül Mountain had been bathed in light and as dawn broke the mountain was veiled in a snow-white cloud glittering with millions of tiny pinpoints of light.

"Did you ever see the like of this mountain, brother?" Halil said, turning to Shahin for the first time since the night before. "Whirling through the darkness like a shooting star . . ."

"Never," Shahin murmured.

"Isn't it a sign, a divine mystery? A huge mountain bathed in light all night long . . ."

"It must be."

Halil smiled suddenly. "All right then," he said as he rose. "Come, let's get going."

They hurried down to the village and made straight for Memik Agha's room.

Startled at first, the Agha quickly composed himself. "How

now, young men?" he exclaimed. "Have you come to pay me your debts? Or do you want to start working again?"

Halil's eyes were fixed on him and in that gaze was concentrated all his anger, his frustration, his blighted hopes.

Suddenly, the Agha felt a twinge of fear. He was on the point of giving way, of saying, I was joking with you of course, just testing you, Halil, to see if you were as good at standing up for your rights as you are at stumping. Then he took a hold on himself. For heaven's sake, Memik, careful! Show them one weak point and you're lost. They'll eat you alive. They're wild beasts, these people, you must be five times as wild or they'll never let you live . . .

Halil had felt a weakening in the Agha. Quickly he took a stand. "Give us our money, Agha," he said, his voice loud, razor-sharp.

"What money?" the Agha said opening out his hands innocently. "God knows, this is the first time a debtor makes himself out to be a creditor."

"For the last time, Agha, will you or won't you give us our due?"

"What due, man, are you crazy?"

"Very well then, Agha. On your own head be it."

Memik Agha, old jackal that he was, felt his blood run cold. He jumped to his feet, he swayed, his eyes went dark for a moment, then he began to shout. "Ungrateful wretches! After all I've done for you . . . Bloodthirsty scoundrels!" Shouting more loudly than ever in order to stifle his mounting fear, his voice echoed from the crags beneath the castle ruin, but in his ears ever more insistently rang Halil's words, on your own head be it . . .

After a while he realised that he was alone. He ran to the window and looked at the inscribed marble slab. It was bare. Halil and Beardless Shahin were nowhere to be seen.

"So that's how it is . . ." he said, trying to feel confident. "Well then, I'll show them." He pondered a while, then smiled and called to the Arab who came rushing up the stairs.

"Here I am, Agha."

"You've heard all that's happened?"

"I have, Agha."

"You're to take Sadi and Ömer with you . . ."

"I understand, Agha."

"They'll be on their way back to their village now."

"I know, Agha."

"Their bodies must never be found."

"We'll burn them, Agha."

"Up on the mountain . . ."

"Nobody'll smell anything. And the bones we'll throw into a well . . ."

"That's right. A well," Memik Agha approved with a smile.

8

NOW THE VILLAGE abounded with chickens and chicks, and Salman swelled with pride. If a single eagle happened to show itself above the rocky crest of the mountain, he was ready with his rifle. This morning, just as the sun was rising, three eagles began to fly into the village, side by side. Under the pomegranate, his finger on the trigger, Salman waited eagerly for them to draw nearer. They were right above Ismail Agha's house, wheeling lower and lower, heads bent towards the yellow fluffy chicks that swarmed about the yard. Suddenly, gathering in their wings, they dived and in the same instant Salman took aim and fired and the three eagles flopped down helter-skelter to be caught by the children, two of them still half-alive, and dragged on towards the river. The villagers who had rushed out of their houses at the sound of shots, saw Salman strutting up and down, his head held high, with the air of a victorious general.

Today was the day when Ismail Agha's new phaeton was expected from Adana. People had been talking about nothing else for days. The sun was quarter high and already getting hot when a carriage hitched to a pair of spotless white horses appeared at the ferry pier on the opposite bank of the river. At once the villagers hurried to the landing stage and the children left off playing with the eagles. The carriage was embarked, several hands grabbed the wire cable and in no time the raft was ferried across. There was no sound from the onlookers. They stared in awe-struck silence. The carriage seemed to have been oiled all over. Its folding hood glistened. The horses were well-fed beasts, each one held back with difficulty by two men. Part of their harness, in particular the rings and buckles of the reins, was of nielloed silver. Gold spangles sparkled among the blue beads that adorned their foreheads. The brass of the steps and of the lanterns was polished till it shone like gold and flashed blindingly under the sun. The slim wheels had been painted a very bright red, with blue, black and white stripes. The interior of the carriage was lined with yellow leather. Süllü, the coachman and the grooms, too, were gaily apparelled.

The carriage disembarked easily, the horses champing the bit, pawing the ground, eager to break into a full gallop. Süllü gave them full rein and off they went in a cloud of dust, among cries of admiration and followed by running children. They entered the village at full speed and reined up in the yard. Ismail Agha and Mustafa came smiling down the stairs. At first Mustafa stood at a distance, entranced, devouring the carriage with his eyes. Slowly, very slowly, savouring every moment, he approached and breathed in the odour of new leather and grease. He had never smelled anything like it before and it made his head whirl. He touched the wheels, the harnessing, the folding hood, the lanterns, then, without knowing how, he found himself inside, sniffing around like a cat, then out again, exploring underneath and about the wheels while Ismail gazed on proudly and smiled at his son's excitement. The elderly villagers who had met the carriage at the ferry now returned to join the crowd assembled outside the walls of the yard.

Salman was sitting at the foot of the rocks under the pomegranate tree. He made no move to get up. Not once did he turn to look at the new phaeton.

"Süllü," Ismail Agha said, "take Mustafa for a ride around the village or wherever he wishes to go."

"Right," Süllü said. He jumped into his seat and steered the phaeton expertly out of the yard. The silent crowd divided to let them pass and the children fell in after them again with shrill cries.

Mustafa sat in the middle of the carriage, very straight, overflowing with joy, feeling he must be the happiest boy in all these villages, the proudest creature on earth. Closing his eyes, he savoured his happiness to the full as the carriage swayed slowly through the village. After a while he opened his eyes. "Drive more quickly," he said to Süllü. "Whip up the horses, make them fly. Quickly, quickly."

Süllü plied the whip, the horses reared. In an instant they were off, scattering chickens out of their path. They left the village in a cloud of dust, rounded the old castle and went tearing along the riverside. At the Gökburun crags, Süllü turned back without reining in at all. On his feet now, clinging to the brass handrail, intoxicated by the furious wind of the speed, Mustafa was shouting enough to split his throat. "Faster, Süllü, faster! Whip them up . . ."

Süllü had given the horses a long rein, he cracked his whip again and again and at a crazy pace the carriage flew through the village and out onto the road above the blackthorn scrub. They stopped beside the stream under a spreading mastic tree. The horses were foaming at the bit, breathing loudly, their flanks rising and falling, their snow-white coats dark grey with sweat, yet still straining at the reins, still eager to be off.

"Go on, Süllü, go on!" Mustafa screeched. "Don't stop . . ." And Süllü, stirred by the boy's enthusiasm, was off again.

Ismail Agha had rushed in alarm to the roadside. He tried to stop them, but they neither saw nor heard him as they hurtled past, the horses' hooves striking sparks on the stones, in and out of the village, until winded at last they began to slow down.

"Stop Süllü!" Ismail Agha shouted.

Süllü reined in, startled. "Yes, Agha . . ."

"You're driving much too fast, Süllü."

"No, no! Don't stop, Süllü. Go on, go on . . ." Mustafa was jumping up and down and screaming like one demented.

"Home, Süllü!"

"No, no, nooo . . ."

"Son, the horses are tired . . ."

"No, no, nooo . . ." Mustafa clutched the brass handrail as though he was going to tear it out.

Ismail Agha gave in. "Go ahead, Süllü," he laughed. "Do whatever Mustafa wants."

"Haydaaa!" Süllü whooped, and off they shot with Mustafa hanging on to the rail and laughing his head off.

Mustafa's infatuation with the phaeton lasted a week or ten days. Even when it stood unhitched in the yard, he never left it, climbing in and out, opening and shutting the folding hood, dusting and polishing the brass fixtures, the lanterns, the gaily coloured wheels, and when he was tired, curling up on the seat and falling asleep there. He had quite forgotten his friends, the hunting for kingfishers, the game of hidie-hole, even the fear of Salman.

One morning as Süllü was taking the horses from the stable and harnessing them to the phaeton, Mustafa came face to face with Salman. He drew up short, frozen by the look in Salman's eyes.

"Get in, Mustafa," Süllü called when the carriage was ready. "We're going to town with your father."

Mustafa did not move. His face was pale, his teeth clenched.

Süllü was alarmed. "Mustafa, what's wrong?" he cried.

"He's going to kill me," the boy moaned.

"Who?"

"Salman . . ."

Süllü laughed. "He'd kill everyone if he could, that one, even Allah. Never you mind. All that reptile can do is kill poor eagles in the sky. What's there to be afraid of in a skunk like that? Is it because he goes around with a gun? Just look at him, a dwarf, no less! Look at that face, is there anything human about it? What's there to be afraid of in a creature who does not even look like an animal?"

"I'm afraid," Mustafa said.

Ismail Agha appeared on the balcony. "Are you ready, Süllü?" he called as he came down the stairs, thrusting his ivory-handled gold-encrusted gun into his waist. He held himself very straight, with proud confidence.

Mustafa grasped Süllü's hands. "Please Süllü, please! Don't tell father I'm afraid. Besides, why should I fear Salman? I was just pretending . . ."

"I won't tell him," Süllü said. "But you mustn't be afraid of him at all. Why, your father could squeeze his throat with only one hand and his eyes would pop out like this and he would die." He mimicked Salman's face and bulging eyes. Diverted by Süllü's mummery, Mustafa burst out laughing.

Salman was standing behind the cactus hedge. He heard every word and saw Süllü mimicking him.

Ismail Agha got into the phaeton. He put his arm round Mustafa and held him close. "Dear child, father's little falcon, father's handsome, brave son . . ."

Süllü whipped up the horses and they were off and out of the yard. And Salman stood there, very still, looking after them.

* * *

After returning from the town that time, Mustafa never again went near the phaeton, not even when his father called him for a ride. Of this fear that had taken root in him, he never spoke to anyone, hardly daring to admit the reason even to himself. Now and again his father would go away, sometimes taking Salman along, and he would be absent for a week, ten days, even a month. They've gone to Adana, Zéro would tell him, or to Mersin. But all the time they were gone Mustafa knew no peace. He would wake up terrified in the night, seeing Salman killing his father, stabbing him with a dagger and slashing him to pieces. Or locking him up in a wooden shack and setting fire to it and as the shack went up in flames, he would hear his father's screams from inside. Salman would also cast Ismail Agha's dead body into a dry well. Thousands of green flies would be buzzing over the mouth of the well and all around earth and sky would be green with flies.

And so Mustafa would waste away until his father returned home at last, safe and sound. As for Salman, he would come back quite changed from these outings, his usually sullen face open and pleasant, even quite talkative. He would always bring a present for their very old neighbour, Lame Hatché, and sit by her for hours. What they talked about no one ever found out.

Every month or so, from down south tall white-robed Arabs with chequered *agels* binding their *keffiyehs* would visit the mansion. Ismail Agha treated them with the greatest deference. They brought with them thoroughbred horses for sale and they also had gifts for Mustafa in little caskets beautifully carved with roses, gazelles and cranes. There were dates, toys, shoes, clothes, and once, in a larger casket, a sumptuous, silver-embroidered *mashlak* and *agel*, a dagger with a gold-encrusted handle, pointed Arab shoes and even a tiny revolver. Mustafa had quickly donned the *mashlak* and *agel*, put on the pointed shoes and, thrusting the dagger and revolver at his waist just like the Arabs did, he had gone out into the village, carried away with joy, and for a while he wore nothing else until one day he came eye to eye with Salman, went pale, undressed at once and never wore the Arab clothes again.

When the Arabs arrived word was sent to the Old Groom who lived in a neighbouring village. He never failed to come and together with Ismail Agha and Süllü they inspected the horses thoroughly, taking their time, riding them, feeding and watering them, before making their choice. The newly bought horse was put in a stable apart and Ismail Agha placed a Turcoman saddle on it, delicately filigreed and emblazoned, a paradise of colours, he fastened the silver-nielloed and gilded reins, and then lifted Mustafa onto the saddle. And Mustafa would live again the exhilaration of riding the new phaeton. Holding fast to the pommel, he would let himself be led by Süllü up and down the village, proud as a young god. But one day, he suddenly refused to be mounted on a new thoroughbred and no amount of urging could make him change his mind.

Mustafa's greatest pleasure was when his father took him up to the thyme-scented crags beneath the castle ruin. From there they could watch Mount Düldül, visible even in the night, glittering like a star in the first light of day, and the river meandering in the plain below, brimming, rising and floating between earth and sky, while eagles hovered among the crags, bees hummed all around them and his father struck up a song. Even the sight of Salman always planted nearby, rigid as a statue, could not mar his happiness. Aaah, it would have been better if Salman was not with them. But he had to be because he guarded his father from those men who wanted to kill him. Who those men were, Mustafa had no idea. Before his eyes there always rose the image of Salman, they were each one of them the spitting image of Salman, hands, legs, ears, clothes, guns and songs, the swaying from side to side, the eyes that looked at you as if to kill . . . Halil Zalimoglu too was just like Salman, a twin brother. Mustafa had never seen him, but that was how he visualised him. It was because Salman safeguarded his father from those other Salmans that Mustafa did not tell what Salman did to him, not because he was afraid of him . . . Sometimes with a band of children they went up to the castle ruin yelling at the top of their voices, we're not afraid, we're not afraid, stopping to listen to the returning echoes, then after a while, gazing at the grim sharp crags, feeling the immense solitude all around, they quickly scampered back to the village, still shouting, we're not afraid, we're not afraid.

And Salman was aware of the fear he inspired. It gave him a pleasant feeling of power.

On the very night the phaeton arrived, the village youths again went foraging in the Forsaken Graveyard. They turned the knoll upside down with pick and shovel and uncovered a lot of inscribed marble slabs and some marble heads with broken noses. The slabs they carried into the village square and the frizzy-haired broken-nosed marble heads they sold to Cheté Ali for a lira and a half each. But no one found a jar full of gold like the one Ismail Agha was rumoured to have unearthed. They were sorely disappointed for they knew now that the Forsaken Graveyard was really the remains of an ancient city. So the gendarme sergeant had told them. Such a city could only have one treasure and obviously this one had already gone to Ismail Agha.

"To think he was dying of hunger when he first came here!"

"If it hadn't been for the villagers, for Memet Effendi, he would indeed have died of hunger, that Kurd who came from God knows where . . ."

"Why did he refuse the Armenian mansion and a farm large as a whole county? Tell me that!"

"Why did he call the Armenian a bird?"

"As if he could fly, that Armenian!"

"But after refusing that huge farm, he came and seized the gold treasure that was in that other Armenian's land right here."

"Because he had heard of this Forsaken Graveyard back there in the old country."

Ismail Agha had a friend there, named Onnik. This Onnik was a geomancer. He could see all that existed up to the seventh heaven and down to seven leagues under earth and sea. From far-off Van, Onnik had seen this treasure lying hidden here in the Chukurova. He told his friend, Ismail the Kurd, about it. And so, on pretext of the war, Ismail lost no time in coming to the Chukurova. He pretended to go stumping for Memik Agha during the day, but in the night he set to digging the Forsaken Graveyard, together with his brother Hassan and Halil Zalimoglu.

"Didn't you ever wonder why Halil killed Memik Agha, just like that, for no reason at all?"

"After working for him and eating his bread for seven years?"

"To kill a man who had been so kind to him . . ."

"To wipe out his family too, root and stem!"

"Even the babes in their cradles!"

"Why did he set fire to his house, burning everyone in it alive, horses and dogs too?"

Onnik had given Ismail Agha some old maps with strange

signs and inscriptions and he had taught Ismail to decipher them. And so without wasting another minute in Van, Ismail Agha made straight for the Chukurova. There for a whole year he spent his nights searching. He searched and searched looking at his maps in the moonlight and finally he located the Forsaken Graveyard. And then under the cover of stumping on Memik Agha's land together with that dim-witted Zalimoglu, they found the treasure. But Memik Agha got wind of it and that is why Ismail the Kurd had Zalimoglu kill him.

"And now, beyond Mount Düldül . . ."

"In his village . . ."

"With the gold from the treasure, Zalimoglu has built himself a mansion . . ."

"Just like Kurdish Ismail's one here . . ."

"Much bigger, much more splendid . . ."

"Zalimoglu took the greater portion of the treasure in exchange for killing Memik Agha."

"They say Ismail Agha fell at Memik Agha's feet. Agha, he begged, we found the treasure, half of it is ours by right."

"Never! The land is my land."

"But Agha, if I hadn't got that map of Onnik's, this treasure would have remained buried for aeons. Come, let's settle for one third to us."

"Never! This treasure belongs to me."

"One fourth then . . ."

"No!"

"So that's your final word, Agha?"

"Memik Agha, you're riding for a fall . . ."

"Yes indeed! If it wasn't for this treasure business, why would Zalimoglu want to kill Memik Agha?"

"Why indeed, poor Memik Agha."

"And now this Zalimoglu has horses brought to him from Arabia, no less!"

"They say he's got three sons . . ."

"All of them nursed in golden cradles!"

"The Vali of Marash himself comes to visit him."

"They say he's bought one of those Armenian farms, Zalimoglu, and made the Vali of Marash his partner."

"What's more, he's going to buy another one with Mustafa Kemal Pasha as his partner this time!"

"He's bought a phaeton too, Zalimoglu, with wheels of pure gold."

"Harnessed with horses, white as Düldül . . ."

Now that half the treasure was his, Ismail Agha went straight to Arif Saim Bey and told him the whole story. Here, Bey, he said, is the treasure . . . Wait, the other said, let's buy a farm with this money and hide the rest . . . And now Arif Saim's admiration for our Kurd knew no bounds.

He sent a telegram to Mustafa Kemal Pasha, saying we've got a man here, and what a man, he knows the secret of all the buried treasures on earth. Mustafa Kemal Pasha was delighted. He sent word to Arif Saim Bey ordering him to buy all the farmland available in the Chukurova with that money and to give him a share too . . .

This is how it is told:

Onnik was tracing his divining patterns on the sand when he heard booming sounds from under Lake Van. He put his ear to the ground and the booming came loud and clear, all from under the lake. Suddenly Onnik was overcome by sleep. And sparkling bright before his eyes, there appeared a vast plain of yellow-spiked corn. And from under the corn, one by one, there rose ancient cities. And clear as day, he saw their many hidden treasures.

On waking, Onnik called to Ismail, saying, here Ismail, you saved my life once, so now I give you the key to the Chukurova. All its treasures will be yours. Ismail would not believe him. Put your ear to the ground, Onnik said, listen to the sounds coming from under the earth and you will hear a rolling booming sound . . . Ismail Agha did as he was told and Onnik then unfolded before his eyes all the treasures of the Chukurova. Forty-one Anavarza rattlesnakes keep guard over these treasures, he said, and there lies the difficulty . . . Not to worry, Onnik brother, Ismail Agha said. I'll freeze those forty-one guardian rattlesnakes one by one, you'll see . . . They say they turn green, those snakes, crystal green if any man draws near the treasures, they start rattling away in a chorus and guardian rattlesnakes from other buried treasures of the Chukurova join in and make the plain tremble as if with an earthquake.

"Ismail the Kurd killed Salman's mother, the monster . . ."

"He filled a bottle with her blood."

"And this bottle he gave to Salman."

"And that night . . ."

"The night he went digging in the Forsaken Graveyard . . ."

"Together with Zalimoglu, Hassan and Salman . . ."

"At the first stroke of the pickaxe, the earth shook, the whole of the Chukurova shook as the rattlesnakes broke into a deafening chorus."

"A dark pall spread over earth and sky hiding the moon."

"Salman, Ismail the Kurd shouted, open this bottle and sprinkle the blood all over the barrow."

"Salman did as he was told."

"His dead mother's blood."

"A deathly stillness fell over the land . . ."

"And so they started to dig . . ."

What Onnik told Ismail was this: Listen brother, he said, only a woman's blood will silence these snakes. And the best blood is your own wife's. A beautiful woman . . . Kill her while you're on the road, pour her blood into a bottle and give it to her son to hold. And then the treasure is safely yours. One woman, this Zéro here, is more than enough for you . . .

"That's how it was. Or how could a Kurd from way-off Van find this treasure that had been lying buried here for a thousand years?"

"Salman should take his mother's revenge. Blood for blood . . ."

"How could he know, the poor innocent, that Ismail killed his mother, that he gave him her blood to hold in a bottle!"

"Salman doesn't even know that he's Ismail's own son."

"They want us to believe they found him on the road . . ."

"Dying . . ."

"Who would swallow that?"

"Ah, what the poor child has to bear . . ."

"And him ready to give his life for that Kurdish Ismail . . ."

"Standing guard for him night and day."

"His mother's murderer!"

"A father who has disowned him . . ."

"God forbid that anyone should be brought to this!"

"In freezing winter . . ."

"Come wind, come weather . . ."

"Without batting an eye . . ."

"There under the pomegranate tree . . ."

"Still as a statue . . ."

"Not so much as a fly can get past him."

"It's not Allah Salman worships, it's that Kurdish Ismail!"

"The way he says father, it's like a hundred thousand fathers . . ."
"Such adoration in his eyes . . ."
"If Salman only knew Ismail had killed his mother . . ."
"He knows, he knows it!"
"If Salman only knew that he wasn't found under a bush in the forest . . ."
"That he is Kurdish Ismail's very own flesh and blood . . ."
"He knows it, he knows . . ."
"Ah, if only he knew!"

Every year Ismail Agha offered sacrifices for Mustafa. He had made a vow to do this until the day he died. And the number of sacrifices increased with each passing year. They were chosen out of the thousands of sheep and other herds tended by Hassan for his brother. All through the year, Hassan took special care of the sheep, goats and young bulls he had marked.

The days of the *Kurban Bairam* were days of joy and festivity. Minstrels, bards and rhapsodes flocked into the village with their *sazes*, their drums and fifes. They came from the Taurus Mountains and from neighbouring villages to celebrate the festival in Ismail Agha's mansion. Arif Saim Bey came all the way from Ankara with his companions, and many Turcoman beys too, friends of Ismail Agha arrived from Adana, Kozan, Kadirli and Osmaniyé. The sacrificial meats would be spread on the festive board and distributed all over the village. No home was left without.

While all this was going on Salman was nowhere to be seen. Mustafa was the only one to notice and he could not rest until he had found out what Salman was about. This time he came upon him crouching in a secluded corner of the barn. Salman started at the sight of Mustafa. His eyes were bloodshot from crying. Mustafa stood rooted to the spot, his eyes locked with Salman's. Neither of them moved for a while. Then Salman rose and lurched forward, his face contorted, mad with rage. Somehow Mustafa felt no fear any longer. Drawing himself up, he faced Salman defiantly, ready for anything. Salman stopped one pace in front of Mustafa his hands lifted, clawlike, ready to strangle him. His lips quivered and twitched, and suddenly from the depths of his being came a cry: "Go Mustafa, go!"

Mustafa did not stir.

The voice came louder: "Go away Mustafa, go!" Entreating

almost: "Go Mustafa, go, or how will I face my father, what shall I say to him . . . Go, Mustafa, get away from here . . ."

Suddenly Salman shot out through the open door of the barn. Slowly Mustafa followed him out into the yard. Salman was running between the pomegranate tree and the cactuses near the entrance gate, back and forth, back and forth, then as if it had only just occurred to him, he opened the gates and rushed down the slope towards the mosque and on along the river away from the village.

Afterwards machinery began arriving for the farm. Tractors, harvesters, threshers flowed into the village, red, yellow, shining bright, as though in a big parade and stopped for a whole day in the square before the mosque. The villagers, old and young, came to look at these strange creatures that seemed to them like the giants in the old folk tales, examining them on all sides and touching them timidly.

The mechanics were men with pleasant faces and hands and clothes stained with grease.

Every time a new machine arrived, the village youths were off again at the Forsaken Graveyard, digging for all they were worth. As usual they unearthed inscribed marble slabs, broken-nosed statues, earthenware and bronze objects that they sold for a few kurush to Cheté Ali who had got wind of the fresh digging and was already waiting in the village.

With the arrival of machinery that year, all the available farmland was cultivated and sown. The earth which had for years been tilled with wooden ploughs that reached only a span deep, was broken a yard down by the new disk-ploughs attached to the tractors. That year it rained abundantly too. Never had such a crop been seen before with five to six long spikes on every corn-stalk. And soon the whole plain undulated like a sea of gold, rustling deeply and flashing in a luminous haze. People came from neighbouring villages and towns to see this unheard-of sea of corn.

"There never has been the likes of it in the Chukurova!"

The fame of the crop travelled all the way to Ankara and Arif Saim Bey came over in his automobile, accompanied by some deputies, close friends of his, to see for himself. Nobody had expected such a crop, for the land was stony or swampy in parts and a great deal of it covered with blackthorns. But Ismail Agha had tried uprooting a patch of blackthorns with the large disk-plough drawn by a tractor and this had worked wonders, so he had been able to add quite a large portion of land to his farm. Ismail Agha had also learnt to drive the tractors himself and had helped the labourers to gather the uprooted blackthorns and heap them up at the foot of the hill where they formed a new hill and this could now serve as firewood which he gave away freely to those villagers who needed it.

The yield that year was beyond belief. The threshing floors overflowed and it took all the trucks, horse- and buffalo-drawn carts and even camels to transport the harvest to the Toprakkalé railway station.

After this the gossipmongers knew no limit and people believed all that was told about Ismail Agha. Even Zéro, Hassan and Hazal were shaken at times by what they heard. As for Mustafa, he believed anything implicitly. About Onnik the Armenian he had often heard talk at home, so he believed the story of the buried treasure, and also that Salman was his very own brother, that his father had killed Salman's mother, that he would make Salman kill Arif Saim Bey one day so that the estate would be wholly his own.

These rumours had somehow reached Arif Saim Bey's ears in Ankara.

"Bey, he's a deep one, that Ismail Agha! Didn't he discover by means of alchemy a four-handled cauldron full of gold, there in the old castle?"

"Alchemy?"

"There is such a science, you know. And there are geomancers who place the holy books under their bottoms and sleep on them and so everything becomes manifest to them. How else could he have found so much money, this Kurdish fellow?"

"It's because he worked so hard."

"Could he have built that stupendous mansion in only a few years?"

"Why not?"

"And what about all those horses? And the flocks and flocks of sheep he owns . . ."

"He says, Arif Saim Bey entrusted me with land that was nothing but swamp and stones and blackthorn brush and I turned it into this rich farm."

"Well, that's the plain truth."

"Onnik traced his divining patterns in the sand, back there in Van. And he saw golden insects flitting under the ground, thousands of golden insects flitting here and there, filling an underground palace . . ."

"Only a man with blood on his hands could find this treasure. So Ismail Agha killed his wife. He drowned his cousin in the lake of Van, he saved an Armenian's life, he tied his own brother to a tree up in the mountains on a snowy winter's day and left him there to freeze . . . Only such a man could find the treasure in the seven-handled cauldron. Yes indeed. Ismail found it and sent half of it to the geomancer Onnik in Syria. And as for that Salman who mounts guard over him all night, a Mauser rifle in his hand, ask him if you don't believe me, let him tell you all about how Ismail the Kurd killed his mother."

"And d'you know who made Zalimoglu kill Memik Agha?"

"Who?"

"Why, Ismail the Kurd of course!"

"But why?"

"Because of the seven-handled cauldron full of gold that was found on his land."

"Listen, Arif Saim Bey. Ismail the Kurd is going to have Salman kill you."

"Oh come on!"

"Just ask Salman, let him tell you."

"And all those horses coming from Syria . . ."

"All stolen booty!"

"Sold all over the world by way of Kurdish Ismail . . ."

"Indeed?"

The season of the forty afternoon rains began, when the days dawn clear and bright, but grow swelteringly hot towards noon, and afterwards, in the west over the crest of Aladag Mountain a cloud appears, it spreads along the crescent of hills that surround the plain, swelling so rapidly that by early afternoon the whole sky is black and lowering, and a chilly wind blows in, whipping up whorls of dust, and from far off beyond the mountains thunder rolls, lightning flashes drowning the blue level plain in brightness, thunderbolts crash over the land one after the other, forming balls of light like so many suns, and large, luminous, lightning-filled drops of rain fall to the ground.

It was like this always in the afternoon. Some days the

lightning was so intense that the whole plain, the clouds, the river, the rain itself were bathed in a dazzling radiance.

As soon as the rain started Salman, darting wary glances about him, made straight for the stable and flung himself with longing at the bay filly. And the villagers, oblivious of the driving rain, stuck their eyes to chinks in the brush wall and watched until he had finished and had fallen back, his penis still stiff, and was drawing up his *shalvar*-trousers and tying the cord and creeping furtively away. And even before he was out, the snoopers had dispersed and were strolling innocently between the houses.

And so it went on all the while the rains lasted, twenty-five to thirty days, and Salman never caught on. He must have suspected something, but somehow he did not seem to mind.

One day Salman did not appear at the stable as usual. The villagers watched out for him in vain. It had stopped raining too, the earth was fast drying up and a smoky haze spread over the village. Tired of waiting the villagers had retired to their homes, leaving a boy to watch the stable.

The days went by and there was no sign of Salman any more.

And slowly the talk began.

"Uncommon amount of rain we've had this year."

"A real deluge . . ."

"And the lightning . . ."

From right and left, from the Mediterranean Sea, from above the distant rain-sodden mauve mountains ringing the plain, streaks of lightning followed by the rumble of thunder tore through the sky and gathered right over the plain, flashing all at once, drowning the world in a wonderful radiance, razor-sharp, multiplying like so many large flowers opening and closing among the clouds.

Every autumn the *agel*-coiffed men coming from Urfa, Aleppo, Kamishli and Irak would appear on the opposite bank of the river with their herds of purebred colts aged from six months to one year or a year and a half. Ismail Agha aided by Süllü would make his choice. This year he bought fourteen colts. These were then scrupulously tended by Süllü and his helpers who in a final choice kept only the very finest and sold the rest. Each year some of the very best of these horses would be offered to Arif Saim Bey.

"A real flood that was!"

"Never seen such lightning . . ."

"And those thunderbolts scorching the earth!"

"Salman suspected something."

"With all those eyes fixed on him."

"The things these villagers do!"

"It all came out of that chit of a Mustafa."

"One should wring his spindly neck."

"Lording it on that phaeton . . ."

"Riding richly-saddled Arab horses . . ."

"Like the son of God . . ."

"Without a look to right and left . . ."

"And then he does this to Salman."

"Poor Salman!"

"Shaming him in everyone's eyes!"

"How could Salman know, the poor lad . . . ?"

"How could he know that a huge village had their eyes stuck to the brush wall . . . ?"

"All watching him!"

'Old and young!"

"How could he know that while it was raining . . ."

"As the lightning flashed . . ."

"As balls of lightning gathered in the highest heavens . . ."

"Flaring like a huge sun . . ."

"Earth and sky in a turmoil."

"How could he know . . . ?"

"How could he know that even the bedridden had themselves transported and found chinks in the brush wall!"

"Poor chap, all the while he was at it with the filly . . ."

"How could he know that the villagers, mad with curiosity . . ."

"Even the snake will not attack a man who's drinking water!"

"Salman will kill Mustafa."

"And Bird Memet too . . ."

"What did they want with poor Salman? Why shame him like this?"

"Ah, Salman will kill them for this!"

"And Ismail the Kurd too."

"Let him!"

A cloud of dust canopied the village. Creamy dust coated the surface of the river. Thistles tossed in the air and chaff and straw swept across the roads, covered the roofs and walls of the earthen huts, the hedges, the cactuses, the crags, got into people's mouths and noses, stuck to their clothes.

"A youth his age! Not yet married! He's bound to take to a bay filly."

"What else can he do, poor thing?"

"When a young man can't find a woman . . ."

"He finds a bay filly instead."

"Makes of the bay filly his woman . . ."

"Did you see how he kissed its eyes?"

"Just like a lover!"

"How he caressed its rump?"

"Just like a lover."

"What else could Salman do?"

"Every youth's done the same since time out of mind."

"Where's the youth who hasn't had a young filly as his first woman . . ."

"So why not Salman?"

"What vast farmlands he has, Kurdish Ismail!"

"And the crop he got this year!"

"It took him more than six months to transport it to Adana."

"And Arif Saim Bey . . ."

"Mustafa Kemal Pasha's bosom friend."

"The apple of his eye . . ."

"Isn't that farm Arif Saim Bey's really?"

"That Kurd's getting too big for his boots!"

"He's refused to give Arif Saim his due!"

"The farm's all mine, he said!"

"And he said, who does he take himself for, that measly Arif Saim Bey . . ."

"A pasha he may be, Mustafa Kemal, but he's not God, is he . . . !"

"If he's Arif Saim Bey, I am Kurdish Ismail of name and fame in the Chukurova."

"Let him try and take the farm away from Kurdish Ismail!"

"Why, Kurdish Ismail will have him killed in no time!"

"Never mind if he's a deputy in Mustafa Kemal Pasha's Grand National Assembly!"

"There's no stopping Kurdish Ismail."

"Take that Salman now . . ."

"All the world, earth and stones, tremble at the sight of him."

"But when Kurdish Ismail says to him . . . Son . . . My son Salman . . ."

"Light of my eyes . . ."

"He springs to attention, stiff as a poker. If you please father . . ."

"You're to set fire to the Chukurova . . ."

"Burn it to ashes . . ."

"As you wish, father."

"Kill everyone on the plain . . ."

"As you wish, father . . ."

"Go to that stream and stop its flow . . ."

"Very well, father."

"Go, kill Mustafa Kemal Pasha."

"At once, father . . ."

"And Arif Saim Bey . . ."

If you please father, as you wish father, very well father . . . Salman is the ground on which you stand, father. Trample him and pass on. May Salman lay down his life before he lets a stone touch the nail of your little finger, father. So it is with Hassan too, and Süllü, and Blind Habip the tractor driver, and all his men, his grooms and servants and Zalimoglu, everyone . . . Everyone loves this Kurdish Ismail. He's got the devil's own charm. But Salman's love is a thing apart. That look of adoration . . . Go Salman, lift that mountain and put it atop the next one . . . At once father . . . Never for a moment doubting it can be done. What is there about this Kurdish Ismail? After all, he's only a Kurdish shepherd . . . Starving when he first came to the Chukurova . . . And now he owns a huge farmland, he rides in royal phaetons, all the villagers of the Taurus Mountains work as labourers in his fields . . . Threshers, tractors, motorcars, disk-ploughs, harvesters, all operating full speed, round the clock. And Fair Eminé dying for the love of him . . . The daughter of a noble Turcoman Bey . . .

"Worshipping him . . ."

"Even more than Salman . . ."

"That Salman whose mother he killed."

Doesn't Salman know? Doesn't he know that Kurdish Ismail killed his mother and threw her into a dry well in Urfa? What was it Kurdish Ömer said, the spindly fellow with the scraggy neck who ran away from the village? Wasn't it he who said Salman was Ismail's son begotten from his very own sperm, whose mother Ismail had killed and cast into a dry well in the desert of Urfa?

And when Ismail had no money left . . . When they all went hungry . . .

Ismail's mother was ailing. He had to carry her on his back for years. Well, why not, he's a huge strong man. Look at him, look at those wide shoulders! Why he's three yards tall! Anyone as huge would carry his mother not on his back but on his head . . . He sold his wife, Salman's mother, to a man in Urfa for three gold pieces. But after a week she was back. So this time Ismail sold her to another man for five gold pieces. Three days later there she was again. Such a dazzling beauty she was, Salman's mother, men went crazy for the love of her. But Ismail kept selling her to all and sundry. Then one day, down Antep way, a Kurdish bey by the name of Hashmet fell for her and bought her for a thousand gold pieces.

"One thousand yellow Osmanli gold pieces!"

The Kurdish Bey lost his head when he saw her. I must have that woman, Ismail, he moaned. How can that be, Bey, Ismail protested. How can you ask for my own wedded wife . . . I'm sorry Ismail, but I've fallen in love with her. At this, Ismail flew into a rage. You dare to do this to me, to trample my name underfoot . . . And he drew his gun . . .

"No, no, it wasn't like that."

"He didn't draw his gun or anything . . ."

"He simply pocketed the thousand gold pieces."

"She's yours Bey, you can use her as your own wife."

"And he went his way, the money in his pocket . . ."

"Because she was bound to come after him."

"In a couple of days or more . . ."

So when Ismail came to the Chukurova he stopped at Toprakkalé and waited. But she never came. Just then, his mother whom he'd been toting on his back all the way, his mother died and her last words to him were, you must kill that woman who for one thousand gold pieces went to lie under another man. That woman's no good for you, she said. But still Kurd Ismail went back to Antep, straight to Hashmet Bey's house. Look here Bey, take your money and give me my rightful spouse. I can't, Hashmet Bey said. At that Kurd Ismail whipped up his gun. I'll kill you, he cried, and the woman too, rather than go without her. She broke her promise to return to me, so kill her I will. Hashmet Bey wept and pleaded. Listen Ismail, he said, you can keep the thousand gold pieces and on top of it I'm giving you my sister Zéro. But this woman here is mine.

"And you can have her son Salman too . . ."

"And so Ismail accepted."

"He took away Zéro."

"And Salman too."

"How the woman grieved for her son Salman . . ."

When they came to Toprakkalé, Ismail was consumed with longing and that very night he was dashing back to Antep. Entering Hashmet Bey's house what should he see? – there was a moon you know – but the two of them locked in an embrace, the woman's naked thigh gleaming in the moonlight, Hashmet Bey's hands clasping her breasts. Kurd Ismail aimed his gun . . . Bang, bang, bang . . .

"That's how he killed Salman's mother."

"This Salman who worships him."

"He adores him as the one who saved him when he was dying."

"Well so would I, even if he wasn't my real father."

"Yes, but a man who killed his own mother!"

"If it were me I wouldn't wait another minute . . ."

"I'd grab my Mauser rifle . . ."

"And when he's asleep, Kurd Ismail . . ."

"Deep asleep . . ."

"I'd aim the rifle right at his eye . . ."

"I'd pull the trigger."

"The bullet would smash his brain to smithereens."

"Remember how he came here, that Kurd, dressed in rawhide?"

"Sheepskins . . ."

"And here he is now, rich as Harun el-Rashid."

"Poor woman! It was all right that she came back again and again. But the one time she loved another man . . ."

"How could a man kill a pair of star-crossed lovers!"

"A low-down man like this one could."

"Well, Salman will kill him in turn."

Black-cloaked swarthy men with gold watch-chains and patent-leather shoes had arrived from Adana. They talked without a break, gesturing constantly as they inspected the horses that were being led out of the stables. They looked into their mouths, at their teeth, under their tails, at the hooves and eyes, and those that they liked they led to the groom who was waiting beside the cactuses. Ismail Agha was nowhere to be seen. He must have been away from home or he would surely have made an appearance to greet the visitors. Perhaps he had gone to Adana or to the farm or to Arif Saim Bey's estate down south. These last days

Arif Saim Bey's car had not been seen in the village. Instead, he summoned Ismail Agha to his side when he needed him. Rumour was rife that Arif Saim Bey had got wind of what Kurd Ismail had said about him and about Mustafa Kemal Pasha and that he had flown into a rage. The powerful Arif Saim Bey whose voice was like thunder in the heavens would surely settle that Kurd's accounts now. Why, he'd have him torn to pieces and thrown to the dogs and wolves . . .

The villagers crowded around and watched in admiring silence as the horse sale proceeded. But when Salman's bay filly was brought out of the stable a murmur and a wave of movement passed through the crowd and all eyes turned to Salman who was standing on the balcony, motionless, his chin resting on the mouth of his rifle that glinted in the sun. As the bay filly appeared a violent spasm ran through his body. He blanched and turned away into the house.

The horse trading lasted till sundown. Süllü drove a hard bargain and always obtained the price he wanted. If not he simply had the horse put back into the stable. But when it came to the bay filly there was no bargaining at all. The filly changed hands in silence. And by twilight the men from Adana left with the horses strung behind them. It was then that the villagers saw Salman, his rifle on his shoulder, rushing up the mountain to the craggy summit. And suddenly a rattling noise rent the air. From behind a large flinty rock Salman was firing away, shot after shot, without a break, whizz whizz whizz . . . All night through bullets rained over the village raising the echoes.

The startled villagers cowered in their homes.

"What can he do, poor lad . . ."

"What can he do but go crazy . . ."

"The ant that sprouts wings is bound for destruction!"

"It'll come tumbling down from the high heavens."

"Just like Kurd Ismail will."

"Buying up the whole of the Chukurova!"

"Just wait and see . . ."

"Whatever he touches turns to gold."

"Just wait and see . . ."

"That poor Panosyan . . . All those years he spent cultivating this land!"

"And what did he get? Hardly the seed he planted."

"But when Kurd Ismail sowed, earth and sky overflowed with his crops."

"A tiger couldn't pass through . . ."

"They say Mustafa Kemal Pasha summons him to Ankara every so often."

"To ask his advice."

"The advice of a barbarous Kurd!"

"Who can hardly speak properly!"

"Just wait and see."

"It was a lucky day for him when he came to this village."

"And when he uncovered the treasure that had lain buried a thousand years in the Forsaken Graveyard."

"All those mighty Turcoman beys, Ramazanoglu, Kozanoglu, Karamüftüoglu, Kurdoglu, and even the powerful bey of the Jerids, Kurdish Ali Agha . . ."

"All those proud Turcoman beys come to visit him . . ."

"To visit this Kurd who only yesterday had to go stumping on other people's lands!"

"They flock to his house as though to a holy shrine . . ."

"And how he swells with pride, that Kurd!"

Like he created these mountains! Every day he sends men on horseback to Osmaniyé or Adana, every day! To get a new pair of shoes for his son, every day! And every day a new suit too! Cases and cases of lokums and coloured candy. Once, a green sugar horse came from Antakya, the gift of an Arab sheikh, just like a live horse it was . . . And from Izmir came a pink sugar camel, with eyes like a real camel, its neck stretched down to pluck mauve flowers from the roadside. And a sugar mosque, the size of a child, with six minarets, all glittering blue, and mollahs sitting inside, their Corans open before them, swaying as they recited the verses, and the Corans of sugar too . . . A red greyhound chasing a yellow rabbit among the bushes, all of sugar . . . An elephant sitting on its haunches, its trunk in the air, white as milk, with tiny twinkling eyes. Someone sent a pigeon from Holy Mecca with a red beak, yellow legs and feathers of gold. A lofty plane tree, a model of the one at Eyup Mosque in Istanbul with a stork walking underneath . . . And what did that snotty Mustafa do? He started eating the minaret! Does one ever eat a minaret, even if it is a sugar one! He'll see what's what . . . The head of a mollah he bit off, didn't eat it even, just threw it into the mud. The head of a mollah reading the Coran, all mud-stained! Ah, the godless wretch . . . He'll soon see what's what . . . Then he invited all the children to lick the mosque. Were they horrified! What! Lick Allah's mosque! Why not? he said, that reprobate, this house of God is made of sugar, so are the mollahs, the Corans, just things of sugar. That's what he said, the graceless one. So all the children, himself at their head, fell to licking, their tongues sticking out like so many spades. First they finished the minarets, then they ate the golden dome, then the *shadirvan*, may it stick in their throat. And even the Corans on the mollahs' knees, may it choke them . . . And all the while Salman stood watching, still as a rock, his rifle in his hand. And Mustafa never once asked him to have a lick too. Poor Salman, he remained there his mouth watering. Poor lad, how can he help hating that snotty Mustafa? They've killed his mother and now they make him wait at their door, come wind come weather, like a mongrel . . . All day long, right before his eyes, they licked the mosque . . .

"All the village children . . ."

"They licked it clean."

"And Mustafa said, tomorrow, he said, we'll lick the plane tree of this holy Eyup Mosque and the stork under it too."

"Let them! They'll see what's what!"

"And the next day we won't lick, we'll eat Holy Mecca itself . . ."

"Let them! They'll see what's what!"

"Munching and crunching the holy city!"

"And Ismail looked on, splitting his sides at his son's antics."

"Let him laugh away!"

"The ant that tries to fly . . . Why did he sell the lad's bay filly?"

"Why indeed!"

"What has Salman done but keep guard on his house year in year out?"

"Keeping the brigands away . . ."

"Guarding him from his enemies . . ."

"It's on purpose he sold the bay filly."

"Just to torment Salman."

And what had the poor lad done? Just falling in love with the bay filly! What youth hasn't done so in this village when he comes of age? Why, a man is not called a man here in the Chukurova if he hasn't done a spell of dallying with a bay filly! And now here comes this wild Kurd from the mountains, who can't even speak properly, and he wants to impose new rules on us!

"He sells poor Salman's bay filly."

"Well, see if you can escape Salman's vengeance now!"

"With that German carbine . . ."

"In his anger . . ."

"In his anger he's right to fire at the whole village."

"A thousand times right!"

"He'll kill Ismail . . ."

"First Mustafa, then Ismail."

"He'll see, Ismail, what comes of selling the bay filly."

"A poor lad's truelove!"

"As though he needed the money!"

"Why, if he wants to, Ismail can have all his doors made of gold!"

"And the stairs . . ."

"And the pillars . . ."

"So why did he sell Salman's filly?"

"Out of plain cruelty!"

"The poor lad . . ."

"Lovelorn . . ."

"His mother dead, killed by Ismail . . ."

"All alone in the world . . ."

"No fiancée . . ."

"No wife."

"Not even a bay filly."

"What is he to do now?"

"He'll run amok."

"Today he fired on the village."

"Tomorrow he'll attack Ismail's mansion."

"He'll set fire to it."

"With Ismail inside . . ."

Salman would never do that! Salman wouldn't touch a hair of Ismail's head. He worships him. Even though he killed his mother. Even though he cast him into a dry well on Harran plain in the desert of Urfa. A week, ten days, a month maybe Salman remained in that well. Some shepherds found him there, agonising. They took him out and brought him to Ismail. Take this child and mind you don't throw him into a well again. Ismail's mother was alive then, a good woman, she took care of the boy. He was covered with sores and vermin. It's to Eminé Salman told this, only to her . . . That when he would be old enough to hold a gun . . .

"Still, he didn't kill Ismail or Mustafa."

"Why now?"

"Just because of a bay filly?"

"He'll kill them, never fear."

Way down south, above the Mediterranean white clouds were slowly rising, swirling in a flood of light, growing whiter and whiter, then turning blue as they gathered in the middle of the sky.

Beyond the first shadowy foothills a second range trembled in a mauve haze, a third was veiled in blue, while the fourth and fifth ranges were only dimly visible, blending into the sky. In the west snow-capped Aladag Mountain stretched high above the vaporous ranges, the rainclouds swept past it, spreading over the Chukurova plain. Suddenly the sky darkened. A cool rain-wind stirred up the dust, lightning forked down over the mountains that circled the plain. The thunder rolled and the lightning-torn clouds flashed and faded again and again like so many huge flowers of light. Such a fulguration erupted in the sky, it was as if light had penetrated the earth and filled the very essence of the trees, grasses, crops, rocks and streams. And the pebbles on the bed of the stream, the fish, the tortoises, the weeds stood out as clear as though the water had been drained away. Then raindrops began to fall, denting the dust. A keen earthy odour rose from the ground and the rain poured down with gathering strength.

Mustafa was crouching under the cactus hedge. It was not long before Memet came creeping up to him. They did not speak, their teeth were clamped tight. It was almost time for the midnight cocks to crow, and still the sound of shots echoed and re-echoed over the village. Eagles startled out of their rocky eyries were circling above, round about the old castle ruins.

Memet was the first to be able to speak.

"He's going to kill us. He was looking for us, then he went up into the rocks. You see there? Those flames shooting out of his gun?" He held Mustafa's hand. Both the boys' hands were ice-cold. "The villagers are saying, I heard them talking, my mother, the women, they're saying Salman's going to kill all those children who licked the mosque, ate the gazelle, the eagle, broke the horse . . . All of them . . ." He snuggled up to Mustafa. "Why don't you speak?"

Mustafa tried, but could not utter a word. A tiny spark fell and died out under the pomegranate tree right opposite them.

"The villagers say your father ran away for fear of Salman. They say, my mother says, the other women . . . That now your father's gone Salman will kill you instead. So that your father may make moan like a deer whose young has been taken away from him, that he may go mad with grief and kill himself . . ."

"My father didn't run away," Mustafa forced his mouth open. "He's gone to Adana. If he were here Salman would never dare to kill me."

"But he isn't here now," Memet said. "We must hide until he comes back."

"Wherever we hide he'll find us. He'll kill us."

"He'll kill us . . ."

They crept out of the cactus hedge. The thorns tore through their shirts, but the pain shook them out of their numbed state. Just then five bullets blasted out one after the other from the crags.

"He'll kill us," Mustafa said. They broke into a run. Under cover of the sheep-pens they reached the river bank and waited for a while in a crevice, listening to the firing, then, unable to keep still they rushed on to the Pass, but the sound of shots followed them. On and on they ran and the harder they ran the more they panicked. The whole village was roused. There was a deafening uproar, but the boys rushed through all this, hearing nothing, seeing nothing, drenched in sweat, their legs weaving, their breath coming in short pants, and suddenly they found themselves on the edge of Osman's pit. They clambered down without thinking. Then they realised where they had come to, but they had no strength left to climb out.

"Osman . . ." Memet whispered.

"His bones!" Mustafa moaned.

"Salman . . ." Memet began.

"He'll be afraid."

"He'll be too afraid to come here . . ."

Locked together in a frenzy of fear, drawing closer and closer as though their bones would stick to each other, a strange shapeless heap in the pit, beside the skeletons of horses, cats, dogs and oxen, deaf now even to the noise of shots, they waited, their ears straining for the dawn sounds.

The first cocks crowed, the first rays of light struck the mountain tops, but still Mustafa dared not open his eyes, dared not move, as though if he did Salman would appear there, right before him.

Suddenly the jangle of cartwheels and the tinkling of horse-bells roused them. Without opening their eyes, they flung themselves out of the pit, on to the open land behind the castle ruins and stopped, cowering against each other in a hollow under the Sheldrake Rock. As day dawned they drew apart and sat on the rocks facing the river.

"We're saved," Mustafa said as he grew warmer. "We'll run away, we'll escape."

"We'll escape," Memet said.

They both knew how they were going to escape. Oh yes, to the other end of the earth . . . Neither Salman, nor Ismail Agha, not the villagers, not anyone in the Chukurova would find them, not if they searched for a thousand years . . . Nobody would be able to kill them. They had given Salman the slip last night, hadn't they? The rest was easy. Wouldn't one of the timber rafts that passed this way, at least half a dozen of them every day, come by today? And if not today, they could wait, couldn't they? Nobody could find them here. The tip of the rock jutted out far over the water and its shadow rose from the bottom of the river like a minaret. On their left a whirlpool swirled and eddied with great speed and noise as it splashed and foamed against the rock. Nobody coming from either left or right could see them. Besides, they could always get back into their cover. They were well hidden from the opposite bank too, for the river here widened considerably with a vast expanse of white pebbles spreading all along the shore. And right in front of their own craggy promontory a mauve rock rose out of the water like a small pointed hillock. The timbermen always moored their rafts here on their way down from the mountains into the plain. Some of the rafts were large, some small. The large ones drifted along rather slowly, but the smaller ones, aided by their long white oars, were carried away on the current in the twinkling of an eye. Up in the dense primaeval forests of the Taurus Mountains, where the trees were felled, half a dozen trunks were laid on the ground at intervals of one or two metres, these were secured to each other by long flat planks over which more logs were trussed with thick ropes and chains. There could not be more than two or three layers of logs, otherwise the raft would be too heavy, it would sink or run aground in the shoals. Log rafts that were set to float up in the mountains would reach the Chukurova and the Mediterranean in a week or ten days and were then easily transported to the timber yards.

Mustafa had once travelled on such a raft with his father from up the Zamanti River down mountains and waterfalls to the Chukurova plain. He had been very young then, but he remembered the pleasant timbermen with their laughing faces and handlebar moustaches each one armed with a rifle like Salman. He remembered the white foaming waters, the vast star-studded sky, the white pebbles strewn far and wide along the shores, the pink, red, white flowering oleanders on the banks between which they were sailing. How it happened that the raft ran into some rocks and the timbermen struggled a whole day to free it. How he nestled under his father's silver-embroidered greatcoat, drunk with the intoxicating smell of wood-resin. How tenderly blew the wind, carrying the scent of marjoram and other scents too from the fields along the river . . . How the timbermen had baked *böreks* in the ashes, the savour of which one could taste only once in a lifetime. How those huge, mustachioed men had sung as they floated on, their deep-toned voices resounding from the countryside, how hard he had tried not to fall asleep, how mortified he had been when sleep had overcome him. He remembered the huge-antlered deer with their glowing red coats, erect on a rock, how Ismail Agha had stopped the timberman just as he was aiming his rifle, saying see how beautiful it looks there in the dawnlight . . . And the deer had stood unmoving, its wet antlers tilted over its back, looking steadily at them until the raft had glided by. And then a haze had fallen over the river and for perhaps three days they had flown on without a glimpse of the shores, the sun like a dying ember behind the haze. Yes, all this Mustafa remembered ever so clearly, and many other things too. How the river had overflowed its banks, turning quite red and carrying uprooted trees from up in the mountains down to the sea . . . He remembered how the mouth of the river had seemed like a forest of roots, how the sea had been red almost half way, the tall waves beating the shore. And beyond, a boundless expanse of blue, bathed in brightness, stretching to infinity.

In front of the timber mill, three large ships were anchored, rusty, their paint peeling. The mill smelled of resin and rust. The shining saws, the bucksaws, the milling machines, the oily rotating straps, the hundreds of greasy men . . .

Such good kind men they were, those lumbermen. Never since had Mustafa seen the like. How they looked up to his father, ready to do his every wish, even before he said anything. And how good they were to Mustafa. Every noon they baked his favourite ash *börek*, sometimes stopping the raft to do it. Once he had heard partridges chirring on the shore. Even before the word partridge had come out of his mouth, the head lumberman had called out: Stop mates, stop the raft! And this, in spite of the fact that they were sailing through swift turbulent rapids, between tall narrow crags. In an instant they were alongshore, but with such an impact as might have severed the chains and ropes and shattered the raft. Off you get mates, the head lumberman ordered, and shoot me some partridges, and mind you bring back mushrooms from the woods too . . . Soon the men were back with a dozen partridges, their heads hanging limply, and a sackful of mushrooms. A huge fire had been lit and the head lumberman had also cooked ash *böreks* with his own hands for Mustafa, and they tasted so good that Mustafa had eaten too much and his stomach had rumbled all night through, preventing him from sleeping. Many other things Mustafa remembered from this journey on the raft. A huge black snake he saw again in his mind's eye, coiling up a plane tree towards the nest on the tree-top and the nestlings, their mouths open wide, twittering madly, while a wide-winged bird was whirling above. Wait men, Ismail Agha had cried, let's save those chicks. The men had stayed the raft on the spot with their long oars. Swiftly Ismail Agha had drawn his gun and fired and the snake had shot up into the air, all coiled up, and had fallen back stretched out in all its length on the shingle. We've rescued the chicks, Ismail Agha had laughed. And in the same instant the chicks who had been raising hell all the time fell suddenly silent.

The head lumberman treated Mustafa with the same respect as he did Ismail Agha, addressing him as my sultan, my agha, just as though Mustafa was a big grown-up man like his father. How could Mustafa ever forget the warm gaze of his black eyes, so full of love . . . They were all like him, the timbermen who passed by the village, tall, broad-shouldered men with genial sunburnt faces, handlebar moustaches, crinkled narrowed eyes, large hands, and whenever they stopped to moor their rafts here, near the whirlpool, that was a festival day for Mustafa. Often they would go up to the old castle with Bird Memet and watch out for the rafts to appear on the shining river round Gökburun's craggy point. And as soon as they spied a raft, they would rush down to the Sheldrake Rock where the birds always returned to nest at one time of the year. Strange birds they were, these shelducks, their eggs much coveted by the village children. Only Mustafa and Bird Memet never touched them. The Sheldrake Rock always crawled with snakes also covetous of the eggs.

Way off at the point of Gökburun, three rafts came into view.

Eagerly the boys waited for the rafts to come up. Here they were, about to be saved while it must be hell to pay, back in the village with Salman rounding up the children, shooting them . . . Wiggler Yusuf, though, must have taken refuge in the craggy hill where the eagles nested. He was surely safe. And so were Bald Mistik and Minstrel Ali. Hidir's son certainly had a bullet in him, however much his mother must have begged Salman, throwing herself at his feet, crying, kill me Salman, instead of my son. But of course Salman wouldn't, he only killed children . . .

"Look!" Mustafa cried. "Look who's coming!"

"It's Uncle Haji Hassan," Bird Memet exclaimed. Bird Memet's father was a hunter. All the year round he was up hill and down dale with his two dogs, one a greyhound. He laid snares and caught rabbits, partridges and francolin which he sold to the rich aghas of the region.

"Uncle Hassan!" Mustafa shrieked from way off to the timberman who was standing on the raft looking at the shore.

Hassan recognised Mustafa and waved to him. For the past couple of years Mustafa had been in the habit of meeting the rafts here and bringing the timbermen whatever he could lay his hands on at home, butter, honey, sugar, molasses, meat, chicken, onions . . . And all the timbermen hereabouts knew him and Bird Memet. They loved them like their own children and brought them presents from the forest, carts, bears, horses that they had carved from pine barks. Once his Uncle Hassan had given Mustafa a small pinewood cannikin carved with birds and flowers and engraved with Mustafa's name. Mustafa had been wild with delight, not even drinking from it for a while, taking it wherever he went, even to bed. And now, at home, he never drank out of anything else.

The first raft drew alongshore and Haji Hassan called out: "Well well! If it isn't Mustafa and Memet! We stopped just for you. We're behind time on this trip. Why don't you hop in and we can talk a little. But we have to get on."

"We're coming with you," Mustafa announced.

Haji Hassan stroked his handlebar moustache. "Where to?"

"Down there. My father's waiting for us at the Bey's farm. They wanted to take me in the car, but I said, you go father, I'll join you in Uncle Haji Hassan's raft. It's sure to come by these days."

"Well, get in then, mates," Haji Hassan said. He had always wanted to take the boys down on his raft and show them around the timber mill and the town. Ask your parents for permission, he would say, and I'll bring you back in three days. And now the boys were coming at last. "Have you asked for permission?" he said.

"Oh-ho, Uncle Haji Hassan," Mustafa said, "as if we wouldn't! It's mother brought us out here. She wanted to hand us over to you herself, but she had pressing work to do, so as soon as she saw you coming round Gökburun, she went back. I have great confidence in Haji Hassan, she said, he'll get you to the Bey's farm. Look, there she is, near the castle."

And indeed there was a woman trudging up the hillside under the castle.

They boarded the raft. "How are things at the village?" Haji Hassan asked. He was a very tall, dark man, a long scar on his forehead and a dark mole on the edge of his right eye. Haji Hassan was in the habit of laughing all the time, even when he told of the saddest things. His clothes were stained red from the bark of pines and the raft smelled strongly of resin. Whenever the rafts passed along the river, the whole village would smell of wood and resin, of pine and cedar, instead of the usual odour of manure that was stacked all over the place.

"We came in a hurry and I haven't brought you anything," Mustafa said. "Father was away and he had the key to the cellar."

"Why, that's all right, Mustafa," Haji Hassan said. "You've always brought us so many good things in the past."

"Yes indeed," the other men laughed. "Mustafa and Memet are our good faithful friends."

"Right," Haji Hassan approved. "And today we're going to treat our honoured guests to a real feast. What would you like to eat, children?"

"Ash *böreks*," Mustafa said promptly.

"Oh yes," Memet said, his mouth watering. "I've never had some, but Mustafa once ate so many his belly was all swollen, like a balloon."

"Ash *börek* it'll be then," Haji Hassan said. "That's one thing we timbermen know how to cook. And also mushroom pilaff."

"I want mushroom pilaff too," Mustafa cried.

"Me too," Memet said.

"We've got three days to go before we get to Gökbujak farm. You'll have mushroom pilaff every day and ash *böreks* with fillings of onions and partridge meat." He looked at his men. "Hey mates, do we have enough onions and mushrooms and partridges for our very dear guests?"

"Eleven partridges, three sacks of mushrooms, a basket of onions, a can of cheese, two cans of butter," a long fellow with a sparse beard and slanting eyes replied. "Will that be enough?"

"More than enough," Haji Hassan said. "We can treat our dear guests like sultans . . . Well, start pulling the oars, let's get going." Then he hesitated. "Tell me truly boy, do they know at home that you're coming with us. If not there'll be hell to pay."

Mustafa flared up. "Come Memet, let's get out, we're not going."

"But Mustafa," Memet pleaded, "if we go back . . . Salman . . ."

Haji Hassan did not hear him. "Don't be cross Mustafa, dear friend. I just asked. There's nothing to get angry about."

A red-headed beardless timberman intervened. "Don't mind him, Mustafa. He's just an old dotard who doesn't know what's what. As though you'd come without your parents' permission. Why you old fogy, didn't Mustafa tell you his mother brought them here?"

"Why, I forgot! It's old age has come upon me. Forgive me, my dear guest, my dear Mustafa."

"It's all right then," Memet cried eagerly. "We're coming with you. Mustafa's forgiven Uncle Haji."

The lumbermen were trying hard not to laugh. This did not escape Mustafa's notice and he grew more and more sullen, although Haji Hassan was talking twenty to the dozen in order to mollify him. It was only as they left the whirlpool and moved past the village that Mustafa's face cleared.

The three rafts glided one after the other along the flatness of the plain, their oars glinting as they rose and fell. The river widened gradually now, the water became shallower and the raft sometimes scraped the pebbles on the bed. Haji Hassan's eyes were fixed on Mustafa. Would the boy be hurt if he insisted on questioning him . . . They had heard an unusual noise coming from the village as they went by and, even now, though the village was left well behind they could still hear loud clamorous cries. His curiosity got the better of him. "Dear guest, please don't take it to heart, but I just have to ask you. Is there something untoward in your village? Such a din there was as we went by! Why, we can still hear it from this far. Has something happened?"

Taken unawares, Mustafa felt as though a boiling cauldron had been poured over him. "No," he shouted, "nothing's happened . . ." Then he hung his head and thought. He must say something to the timberman, something to convince him. Suddenly he raised his head and smiled, as if to say, I'm telling a lot of lies, you just pretend to believe me. "Last night Zalimoglu, the bandit, came to our village . . ."

"Why should they make such a noise because of Zalimoglu?"

Mustafa was launched now. He could go on for ever inventing stories. "Zalimoglu came last night. He was looking for Memik Agha's son, Muslu. Muslu hides in a different house each night because Zalimoglu will kill him if he finds him. Didn't you know?"

"I didn't know that," Haji Hassan said.

Mustafa, beginning from the very first, related the story of Memik Agha and Zalimoglu and then went on to tell about the sad fate of Muslu.

"When the bandits raided their house, Muslu let himself out through a back window and ran to Memet Effendi's house, save me, he said, Zalimoglu Halil is killing my father, my mother, everyone in our house . . . Even before anything happened, even before Zalimoglu had fired a single shot, before he'd set fire to the house, Muslu had known that he would kill his father. Even before the raid began . . ."

"Even before . . ." Bird Memet said.

"He came to us, Muslu, to us children. He was dying of fear. He's going to kill my father, that stumper . . ."

"Which stumper, we asked him," Bird Memet chimed in.

"Zalimoglu, he said," Mustafa went on. "And Wiggler Yusuf asked, how d'you know. And Muslu said, I saw his eyes. Muslu had understood everything from the look in Zalimoglu's eyes."

"Just like Mustafa from Salman's eyes . . ." Memet bit his tongue at the angry look Mustafa gave him.

"And so," Mustafa went on, glaring at Memet, "he escaped through the window, and the others set fire to the house."

"Who?"

"Zalimoglu. And the other stumpers . . ."

"They killed everyone, burnt everything in that house."

"They shot at the tree too, it started bleeding, they set fire to it, it screamed, it struggled to escape, but it couldn't tear itself from its roots."

"Its branches reached out and clawed at the sky, the tree was burning, bleeding, its blood streamed through the flames right down to the river. The river flowed red with blood, bubbling crimson blood. Mother Hava said so, would she ever lie! The branches beat against the sky like the wings of birds, madly, straining and struggling for dear life. In vain. The tree remained there, rooted to the ground, half bleeding, half burning . . ."

"The whole village saw this with their own eyes. My father saw it too."

"Everyone's father and mother saw it," Mustafa said. "And then one night, Zalimoglu came to our house. Never in my life, he said, did I see such a pitiful sight as this tree, wrenching at its roots desperately to escape death. All my life I've spent uprooting trees, stumping, but never have I heard such loud crackling sounds at the roots, as this tree strained to tear itself out of the ground, aflame, its thousand arms writhing, its thousand mouths open, moaning, shrieking. And glory be, the blood pouring down the trunk like human blood . . ."

"Mother Hava always tells it this way when the jinx takes her . . ."

"Always," Mustafa said. "So when Memik Agha's son, Muslu, escaped, he went to hide in Osman's pit. And Salman saw this . . ."

"That same Salman," Memet said, "that Mustafa read in his eyes . . ."

"Don't interrupt me," Mustafa scowled. "Salman with his brand-new rifle, his cartridge-belts strapped all over him . . ."

"And his two huge revolvers, and his two long daggers," Memet put in quickly.

Mustafa glared at him. "And the binoculars too," he hurried on. "Now this Salman stood there all night long on the edge of the pit where Muslu was hiding and no one dared approach."

"Because Zalimoglu like everyone else feared the pit, Osman's pit, and he feared Salman too."

Haji Hassan and the other timbermen were fascinated. They

had heard of this event before, but the way the children told it, feverish, carried away, was like listening to some old-time story-teller.

"And so that night, after killing everyone in Memik Agha's house, Zalimoglu, the stumper discovered where Muslu was hiding, but he could do nothing for fear of Salman."

"I'll kill that one later, he said, and he went away."

"But now, every fortnight . . ."

"He comes to the village, this Zalimoglu."

"He comes and looks for Muslu."

"He searches all over the place."

"But he can't find him."

"He can't because Muslu sleeps in a different house each night."

"How can Zalimoglu know which house!"

"Once he searched every single house in one night."

"But the villagers spirited him away from house to house."

"I'll get him one day, come what may I'll kill that Muslu."

"They call me Zalimoglu, I'm an outlaw, my shroud is round my neck, I have taken a vow before God almighty, to wipe out from the face of the earth all the offspring of that tyrant Memik Agha, so that never again shall poor people be treated so wickedly."

And now, last night Zalimoglu descended upon the village with fifteen men, bent on finding Muslu. He rounded up the villagers in front of the mosque . . . Why didn't Mustafa and Memet think of taking Muslu along with them to the timber raft . . . ?

"If only we'd brought him with us . . . We could have saved his life."

"Ah, if only . . ." Memet said.

"Would you have taken him up on your raft?" Mustafa asked Haji Hassan, looking earnestly into his eyes.

"Of course," Haji Hassan said, "since you wished it, dear guest, why ever not?"

"But," Mustafa said, "but aren't you afraid of Zalimoglu?"

"Afraid? No," Haji Hassan said. "This one soul I have I owe to God and he'll take it back in his own good time."

"But Salman . . . Aren't you afraid of him?"

"Who's that?" Haji Hassan smiled.

"Salman," Memet announced, "is Mustafa's father's very own son. Only Mustafa's mother isn't his mother. He's the one who killed all the eagles in the sky over the village. And then, when the bay filly . . ."

Mustafa nudged him.

"Salman kills not only eagles in the sky, but people too. Really truly, you're not afraid of him?"

"No, I'm not." Haji Hassan laughed.

"Then you're not afraid of Osman's pit?"

"No, I'm not."

"And of the bleeding burning tree?"

"Not at all." Haji Hassan and the other timbermen were splitting their sides.

"And of God . . ." Bird Memet was about to say when Haji Hassan's huge resin-smelling hand was on his mouth.

"Everyone fears God."

"Everyone," Mustafa concurred, angry with Memet's stupid talk.

The rafts were now sailing through a deep green stretch of water, like a lake, with willows and tamarisks all along the banks, their branches drooping over the water. Here the river did not flow so quickly and the men had to use their oars.

The villagers had gathered in the square before the mosque and the place was all in an uproar, people shouting, swearing, weeping, beating their breasts, for since last night not a single child was to be seen in the village. They had all vanished into thin air the minute Salman had started shooting from up in the crags. Mothers and fathers who had missed their children, some in the evening, others in the middle of the night or in the early morning, had searched everywhere, up in the hills and around the old castle, but with no result. And so they were all there in the square trying to decide what to do.

In the midst of all this hullabaloo, Ismail Agha appeared followed by his two bodyguards, riding hell for leather, his bay horse black with sweat, foaming at the bit. Cleaving through the crowd, without stopping, he came to his house, jumped off his horse and rushed up the stairs.

"Zéro!" He shouted in a terrible voice.

Zéro stepped into the hall at once. A black kerchief was bound round her forehead and her eyes were red and swollen.

"Zéro, is it true what I have heard?"

Zéro hung her head.

"What! That he rained bullets over the village all night through?"

"Yes . . . Everyone was up . . ." She could not bring herself to tell her husband that Mustafa was missing.

"Has he gone mad that boy? Where is he now?" Ismail hissed through clenched teeth.

Süllü was standing there at attention. "He's downstairs in his room," he said grimly. "Sleeping as though nothing has happened."

"Go and tell him to come to me," Ismail Agha said. He looked about him as though searching for something, someone he had missed. His face softened, his eyes brightened. "Where's Mustafa?" he asked, smiling.

Zéro hung her head.

Ismail Agha's smile froze. "Where's Mustafa?" he repeated hoarsely.

Zéro was in tears. "He's disappeared. Süllü, me, everyone, we've been looking for him everywhere. He's nowhere to be found. Mustafa . . ." Her voice came in a moan, as though keening. "Memet can't be found either. None of the children . . ."

Ismail Agha was thunderstruck. "God, oh God," he cried as though his heart was being wrung out of him. He whirled and staggered to the sofa at the foot of the wall. His face was ashen.

Suddenly Salman stood before him, dark, defiant. This came as a shock to Ismail Agha and for the first time he was seized with a strange misgiving. The face before him was the face of someone whose mind was made up, who would never forgive, razor-sharp, pitiless.

Ismail Agha bridled his anger. "Salman, my child," he began in a quiet voice, "whatever took hold of you, raining bullets all over the village last night? Has anyone done something to you? Tell me."

Salman's eyes were on the ground. He said nothing. His yellow moustache had been coiled to needle point and curled upwards. It was the first time Ismail Agha had seen him like this. He wore a pair of yellow accordion-pleated boots. His cartridge-belts were crossed over his breast, as usual, his daggers hanging from his sash almost to his feet. His *shalvar*-trousers were of blue English cloth, of the kind that came from Antakya. He had a new pair of binoculars too, longer, more powerful.

"Well my child, why don't you answer me? Why don't you say something to your father?"

Salman was trembling imperceptibly.

"Aren't you going to speak?" Ismail Agha's anger was mounting. "While you were shooting all over the village, your brother Mustafa suddenly disappeared. D'you know this?"

Still Salman never said a word. His teeth were clenched to breaking point, his cheeks twitched.

Slowly Ismail Agha rose to his feet. "You must know, Salman," he said softly, "you must know that if anything has happened to Mustafa I could not live. This you know better than anyone, Salman, my child, don't you? And you know too that I would never let anyone live who would touch a hair of his head. Now then, tell me, what possessed you last night. Give me a reason. How could a son, an elder son, who should be the head of the house when his father is away, to whom the household, the whole village has been entrusted, how could a son when his father is away start shooting all over the village the whole night through? And if the father doesn't know the reason for this what can he say to the villagers, to the gendarmes? Come my child, won't you tell your father why you did this?"

Salman's countenance was still black, but he was sweating now. Beads of sweat ran down his face.

"Very well, I won't ask you any more. Sooner or later I'll find out. What I want to know now is this, is there any connection between your firing on the village and Mustafa's disappearance? Because if anything's happened to Mustafa . . ." His voice strangled. He waited in silence, his eyes fixed on Salman, who just stood there, rigid, frozen, as though all the blood had been drained from his veins, the only sign of life in him was the sweat pouring down his face. Ismail Agha waited and the waiting seemed to last a year. He felt like trampling Salman under his feet, like breaking his bones. At last he slapped a hand over Salman's shoulder.

"So you won't speak then," he said in mocking tones. "Lord of the eagles . . . Anyone wielding that rifle of yours and using up all the ammunition you have in the past three years would have been able to shoot not just an eagle but a tiny fly in the sky. With a rifle like that and a father like me to back him anyone would have raided not just a small village, but Adana town itself. Playing heroics with a gun is no big feat. Any child can do it and kill the whole village too. The truly brave man shows his valour by fighting hand to hand. Who do you take yourself for, raiding villages and all . . ." His voice was like a vibrating wire, tensed to snapping point. He fell silent and for a while scrutinised Salman from top to bottom with contempt, as though looking at some insect. Then he turned to his men. "Take away this fellow's weapons, all except for one dagger. Let's see him attacking a whole village again, shooting at his own house . . ."

Süllü, Hassan and Hüseyin hurried up, removed Salman's bandoliers, his rifle, his revolvers and laid them aside. Salman made no resistance, he was like a man turned to stone.

"And never again will he be my bodyguard, never till I die," Ismail Agha said as he left the room.

Salman stood there for a while, staring at his weapons piled on the floor, then he took off the binoculars that hung from his neck, put them over the weapons and slowly walked away down the stairs.

Ismail Agha heard him closing the door to the courtyard. I haven't done right, he thought, I shouldn't have treated Salman so hardly, I shouldn't have punished him without first getting to the bottom of this affair. Who knows what induced him to do this, who knows where that little rogue of a Mustafa's gone to. He regretted what he had done, but he could not turn back now.

As for Salman, he did not stop when he came to the crowd in front of the mosque. People held their breath as he pressed forward without looking to right or left and they fell apart as though at the stroke of a sword to let him pass. When he came to the river beyond the graveyard, he stopped a moment, looking back at the village, then he began to climb up into the crags and was lost to sight.

As soon as he had gone the crowd came alive. Everyone started talking at once.

"Just look at him."

"That weaselly face . . ."

"Those cold snaky eyes . . ."

"Damn him!"

"They've taken his rifle from him."

"Ismail Agha . . ."

"Of course he would."

"Shooting all night all over the village."

"Well, look at him now . . ."

"Without all those weapons . . ."

"He's like a wet mongrel."

"All his swagger gone."

"So he's taken himself away, up into the mountains."

"Let him go to the pit of hell!"

"Why are all the children so frightened of him?"

"A mere dwarfling . . ."

"Wall-eyed too."

"Pot-bellied."

"Pumpkin-nosed."

"Scraggy-necked."

"Like he's been flayed now he's without his weapons."

Without his rifle, without his bandoliers he's just a midget. A man wouldn't want to waste his spittle to spit on him. What makes a man is his horse, his weapons, his woman. Salman had a horse, he had weapons, but he had no woman. Well, he had the bay filly, but Ismail Agha sold her, and a good thing too. Making use of that poor dumb filly like a whore!

"Who knows, maybe the bay filly enjoyed it . . ."

"No filly would ever enjoy it."

"With that dirty fellow . . ."

"It's a sin for men to have intercourse with mares."

"The hodja said so."

"It's written in the Coran."

"Ah, the bay filly was afraid of him."

Everyone feared him when he wielded a gun, the eagles in the sky, the children, even Ismail Agha. Even the bandit Zalimoglu Halil. That's why Zalimoglu didn't come to this village. If it wasn't for Salman, Zalimoglu said, I'd raid that Kurdish Ismail's house, he's a nobody, I'd carry off his woman Zéro, I'd burn down that mansion of his. I'd gouge his eyes out. Aah, if it wasn't for that accursed Salman . . .

"But now that Ismail Agha's stripped him of his arms . . ."

"Zalimoglu might come any time."

"And lay waste our homes."

"Carry off our wives, our daughters . . ."

"Run our children through . . ."

Still, God forbid anyone should be like that accursed Salman . . . Taking himself for the lord of the Chukurova, raining bullets over the village all night long. Glowering at the children with those snaky, poison-green eyes. Wouldn't the children be afraid, wouldn't they run away?

"And now they've disappeared, all of them . . ."

"Where can they have fled to?"

"Could they have jumped down the cliffs?"

"Terrified . . ."

Not a single child was to be found since last night. Shepherd Veli searched the old castle ruins. The young men went up into the cave on the other side of the hill, it was empty save for its usual company of bats hanging upside down. Riders combed the countryside up to Gökburun and Endel, down the Valley of Hawthorns, around the Dédé shrine, the Alaja crags and even way across the river. But there was no trace of the children.

Ismail Agha had dispatched his own men on horseback and he was waiting in his room, his heart in his mouth.

As the afternoon advanced the crowd in front of the mosque was growing ever more worried. Evening came and one search party after another returned empty-handed.

"A monster . . ."

"To think we took him for a human being, this Salman!"

"Making us believe his mother was Ismail Agha's first wife!"

"They simply found him on the roadside, this skunk. Eaten up by lice . . . Crawling with lice and worms, he was, a fair sight! Festering . . ."

"And here he went strutting around, passing himself off as Ismail Agha's very own son!"

"Hah, he couldn't even be Ismail Agha's dog!"

"He said, my father killed my mother back in Urfa, in Harran town as she was trying to flee to some Arab sheikh."

"Pretending his mother was the daughter of an Arab pasha!"

"Inventing all these lies, the gypsy . . ."

"And not only him, but Fair Eminé too . . ."

"Wouldn't she do that too, with that incurable wound in her heart?"

"Never, not until she dies will Fair Eminé forget Kurdish Ismail."

"On her grave . . ."

"Revenge will grow instead of flowers."

"Revenge against Kurd Ismail."

"Who but Fair Eminé would want to invent such stories?"

"Does Salman look like any son of Ismail Agha's should?"

"That skunk . . ."

"That worm . . ."

"That viper . . ."

"Just wait and see if he doesn't do it with Fair Eminé!"

"Like he did with the bay filly . . ."

"All his bluster is against little children . . ."

"Poor innocent mites!"

"Where can they be now?"

"What if . . . ?"

They could not bear to say it aloud. What if the children had thrown themselves down those cliffs into the water? And the river had carried them on to the Mediterranean and they had become food for the huge fishes of the sea? All kinds of horrible things passed through their minds that they dared not voice. They began to light fires in the square, while search parties and riders came and went.

As dawn broke the half frozen crowd roused itself, waking the echoes, and as one man they made for Ismail Agha's house.

Ismail Agha's face was chalk-white. "It's unbelievable," he said. "How is it possible that every single child in this big village should vanish into thin air?"

"Why don't you ask your precious son?" a white-bearded old man countered. "That evil-gotten Salman?"

"But my own son is missing too," Ismail Agha said.

"Serve you right," the old man said. "If you go picking up all kinds of brats left lying on the roadsides, gypsies or what, and bring them up as the apple of your eye, this is what it comes to. He'll carry off all the children into the mountains and shoot them one after the other, and your own son too, Ismail."

Ismail Agha could not utter a word. He just stood there, his hands in the air as though lifted in prayer.

"You should hear what they're inventing about you, Ismail, Fair Eminé and your precious son Salman, spreading gossip all over the Chukurova."

"What can I do, Mahmut Agha, against such evil, ungrateful wretches?" Ismail Agha's hands fell limply to his sides.

"Let's go, folks," Mahmut Agha said. "There's nothing to be expected from this Kurd, he's at his wit's end. There's nothing for it but to keep searching." His green eyes were red with weeping. He had five grandchildren among the missing. "Look, look if you can see where that Salman's gone to after doing away with all those children. On your way." He brandished his stick at the crowd.

And so the villagers resumed the hunt. Ismail Agha leapt onto his horse and rode out into the plain without quite knowing where he was going or what he was doing.

The plain, the mountain, the river banks rang with cries and calls.

"Ahmet, Ali, Yusuf, Nuri, Talip . . ."

Sounding and resounding.

"Salman's gone. He's gone!"

"Ismail Agha's taken away all Salman's weapons."

"Come back children. You can come back now.

"Mustafa, Memet, Halil, Veli!"

"The gendarmes have taken Salman away . . ."

At close of day the search parties returned, tired, silent, and the waiting began anew.

The sun set and darkness fell and suddenly the cry rang out: "The children! The children are back!" In an instant the village was alive with joy and relief. Fathers and mothers, even the sternest, did not utter a word of reproach, did not lift a finger against the fugitives. The children who had feared what might await them on their return, had never expected to be greeted with such rejoicing. That evening the tastiest dishes were prepared, the liveliest songs were sung, the warmest words of love exchanged. In all the houses except two, Mustafa's and Memet's . . . Ismail Agha remained stuck to the balcony railing all night long, waiting, waiting in vain.

The children were playing dumb. Not one of them let out where they had gone to. Ismail Agha went from house to house questioning, trying to make them reveal their hiding place in the hope of finding Mustafa and Memet there too, but it was impossible to get even a clue from them. Many simply lied, saying they had hidden in a water well, in a granary, in caves, in the cliffs and the mountains, among the reeds on the river bank, in the Valley of Hawthorns, in the old castle, in the shrine way off on Anavarza hill. But these were all places that had been turned inside out by the search parties. As a last resort Ismail Agha tried putting the fear of Salman into them. "If you don't tell me where you've been hiding," he said, "then I'll give Salman back his rifle and have him shoot the lot of you." At the name of Salman the children paled and trembled and Ismail Agha's hopes rose, yet still not one of them confessed. He tried everything, pleading, threatening, offering them money, and with him the mothers and fathers pressed and questioned. It was no use.

"The children don't know where they went."

"Wouldn't they tell if they knew?"

"One night, the jinn . . ."

"The jinn who dwell in the cave beyond the hill . . ."

"The jinn carried them off to Anavarza."

"The Peri King has his palace there on the Anavarza crags."

"They took the children to a peri feast."

"They say that Shahmaran, the king of the snakes has a palace up on Yilankalé."

"They say the jinn gather at Dumlu Castle too."

"The peri folk have always loved children."

"They say that every three years the peris carry off the children of a village to feast with them and take part in their merry-making."

"It's Mother Hava tells of it."

"The peris live in sparkling crystal palaces."

"In the land of the peris it is always bright and fair."

"Neither cold, nor hot."

"All the year round the trees, flowers and grasses are abloom."

"All the twelve months of the year it's never winter, not autumn, not summer . . ."

"Only springtime all over the land."

"And the wind blows with the scents of spring."

"Softly like the dawn breeze . . ."

"Fresh and mild."

"The children were wonder-struck."

"A land of milk and honey . . ."

"A feast was spread before them . . ."

"In the Peri King's royal gardens."

"The children fell to and ate their fill."

"The peris took Mother Hava along too . . ."

"And beautiful birds came in from Zanzibar . . ."

"From the land of Serendip."

"Each bird carried a titbit on its wings."

"The green bird, bright green figs picked in Paradise."

"And bunches of grapes."

"All bright green."

"Shedding a green glow as they flew round and round the feast."

"And then red birds, glittering, crystal red . . ."

"And bright blue-winged ones too."

"A blue that covered the sky."

"The blue you see of an evening . . ."

"That fills a man with love."

"A blue rapture . . ."

"A velvety glistening blue."

"Would the children ever tell where they went!"

"The Peri King said . . ."

"When you go back, children . . ."

"If you ever tell about the peris, then you'll never see us again."

"Would they ever tell then!"

"I wouldn't if it was me!"

"Ismail Agha had a cousin back there, near Lake Van."

"A cousin who loved a peri maid."

"Every day at dawn he would go to an island on Lake Van . . ."

"And make love to the peri maid till nightfall."

"He was so handsome this cousin, this Hüseyin, that not only the peris but ordinary people would be spellbound at the very sight of him."

"And the peri maid said to him, be careful, Hüseyin, never to tell anyone about me."

"I'm going to bear you children."

"Half peri, half human."

"But if you tell our secret to anyone . . ."

". . . the spell will be broken and my father will kill you."

"That wretched Ismail! He never rested until he had wormed poor Hüseyin's secret out of him."

"And one day the Peri King killed Hüseyin."

"His body was found floating in the lake."

"Bluebirds hovering above . . ."

"Shedding a blue light over him."

"Would the children ever reveal where they've been!"

"And suffer the same fate as Hüseyin."

"Of course they wouldn't!"

"Good for them."

"At least they can get away from this hell of a place once every few years . . ."

"And live in the land of the peris."

As the days passed and there was still no news of Mustafa and Memet people began to talk. Could it be that Salman had killed them? And thrown their bodies into the water with stones tied to their necks?

"Why shouldn't Salman kill?"

"The way Ismail's always treated him."

"Like a mangy dog."

"A man wouldn't treat even a dog like that."

"How many years is it, God knows, that he's stood guard at his door?"

"Come wind, come weather."

"Never stirring."

"Not blinking an eye."

"And on warm summer nights, while himself sleeps peacefully under a mosquito-net . . ."

"With his son . . ."

"Salman is out on guard, devoured by mosquitoes."

"Shivering with malaria."

"His bones racked with pain."

"His belly swollen like a drum."

"Never complaining."

"Not only do you kill the poor lad's mother . . ."

"But you hand him over to a stepmother."

"That cruel Zéro."

"Who kills him with blows."

"Neglects him."

"Lets his wounds fester . . ."

"Of course he'd kill Mustafa!"

"You kill his mother and throw the poor woman's body to the dogs . . ."

"Before the eyes of the boy who's old enough to understand . . ."

"And on top of all that you don't marry him off, a man of his age!"

"So he falls in love with a bay filly."

"And your son Mustafa spreads this all over the village."

"And people rush to watch him . . ."

"Their eyes glued to the brush wall of the stable."

"And then what do you do but sell the poor lad's filly!"

"Of course he'd kill."

"Who knows what else that Kurdish woman, that Zéro, did to the boy that we don't know of . . ."

"Who knows what pushed poor Salman to kill his own brother, the apple of his father's eye!"

"Who knows?"

Ever since that day Salman had not been seen anywhere. He

had simply disappeared, like Mustafa and Bird Memet, and this gave rise to more rumours that spread like wildfire and finally reached the ear of Arif Saim Bey in Ankara. He jumped into a train and was in the village in no time having roused all the gendarmes in the province with this order: "I want you to find the son of my brother Ismail, dead or alive, at once, or I'll set fire to all these villages with everyone in them lock, stock and barrel."

Lightning forked over Aladag Mountain, flash after flash. The snowy peak was bright with light one instant and plunged into darkness the next. Clouds spread along the surrounding mountains, a roiling tenebrous mass shot with lightning, and advanced over the plain to merge with another bank of clouds rising from the Mediterranean. Sky and earth trembled and thundered as streaks of lightning zigzagged through the clouds ever more quickly in swirling bolts like so many suns, drowning the world in a blinding radiance. And then the rain began, black torrents streaming from the sky and down the mountainside, tearing the rocks from the soil.

It was in this downpour that two horsemen came galloping hell for leather into the village. One was Haji Hassan and the other Dursun. Haji Hassan had Mustafa riding pillion behind him and Dursun Memet. Without reining in, they turned the horses towards Ismail Agha's house, stopped at the gate, only for a moment, set the children down and galloped off out of the village like the wind.

Ismail Agha went wild with joy. He offered sacrifices for his son's return. A great feast was held, with celebrations such as the village had never seen before.

Some weeks passed before Ismail Agha attempted to ask the children where they had been hiding, but both Mustafa and Memet remained mute as stones. They were determined to keep their secret and never give away their timbermen friends for fear of getting them into trouble.

After Mustafa had turned up, Salman came home too and was seen wandering about the village, pale and listless, like a bird with a broken wing. One day Ismail Agha summoned him to his side.

"You can have your rifle again, Salman, my son," he said in his warmest, most affectionate voice, "and all your other weapons as well. You can be my bodyguard too as you always were. I'm sorry, my boy, if I hurt you, you must forgive your father. Go now and take your rifle."

9

THE MOON HAD risen and the shadow of the castle fell across the river right up to the opposite bank. Halil and Shahin, keeping low under the cover of brush walls and cactus hedges, came to Ismail Agha's. It was the hour of the evening prayer.

"No one's seen us, have they?"

"No one," Shahin said. "And anyway no one would recognise us."

"They would," Halil said. He knocked on the door a few times.

"Who are you, what do you want?" someone called from inside.

"We're old hands of Ismail Agha's."

"Come on in."

A big man carrying a Mauser rifle led them up the stairs and stopped outside the hall. "You've got guests, Agha," he said.

"Show them in," Ismail Agha called.

At the sight of the two men his face changed. Rising, he embraced Halil and, with his hands on Beardless Shahin's shoulders, he said, "Welcome, my friends," and led them to a sofa near the fireplace. It was piled with snow-white embroidered feather cushions that smelled pleasantly of soap. Seeing that Halil hesitated, Ismail Agha made him sit down where he himself had been sitting. Shahin perched himself diffidently on the farthest end of the sofa.

"Have you had any dinner?" Ismail Agha asked.

"Many thanks, we've eaten," Halil lied. He was in a strange state, exalted, radiating gladness all about him.

"Many thanks, we're not hungry," Shahin said.

Ismail Agha was surprised. Instead of the melancholy, introverted Halil that he knew, he now had before him a man buoyant and carefree as a child. He knew what Memik Agha had done to Halil, he knew it, down to every word that had passed between them and it struck him with force that Halil would never be the same again.

Coffee was brought in and a fragrant aroma filled the room. The young servant deposited the tray in front of the fireplace and left. Halil took his cup from the tray and began to talk and every other sentence was punctuated by a loud burst of laughter. He told about the rice paddies, about his grandmother back home in the village, of his mother, of how he used to extract honeycombs from hollows in old trees, of how he had gone hunting for deer, lynx and leopard, of the orange groves where he had worked and even of Ipekché about whom he had never told anyone before, of how she had been waiting for him for years now, how she would hardly recognise him, Halil, in the raggle-taggle stumper that he was now. On and on he talked without a break, in a fever of excitement, and the more he talked the more astonished Ismail Agha became at the extraordinary change in the taciturn man he had known not so very long ago. He listened open-mouthed to this torrent of words that seemed to come from the lips of an old-time storyteller.

It was long past midnight when Ismail Agha finally put in a word. Halil started, he came to himself, but did not lose a whit of his good humour. "Ismail, brother," he said. "There's something I want to ask of you."

"Anything you wish," Ismail Agha said.

"Nobody's seen me come here tonight. No one must know I entered this house, that I talked to you, no one."

"Nobody will know," Ismail Agha assured him. "But . . ." He lifted his hand before the other had time to go on. "Listen to me Halil. I know what that man did to you, the worst a human being can do to another. But still I say, don't do what you're going to do."

Halil was taken aback. His face froze. He tried to speak but Ismail Agha stopped him again.

"Don't do it, Halil. I'll help you. We're buying a new farm. You can take charge of it. Go to your village and bring back your family, Ipekché . . . If you don't want it this way, aren't you the world's best stumper? I'll buy some land for you and you can clear it, together with Shahin, and then set up your own farm on it, the title deeds I can procure in no time. If you like . . . You know that you're dearer to me than a brother . . . If you like, I could give you money, as much as you need, and you could take yourself away, far away beyond Mount Düldül and build yourself a house with farmyard and orchard. If you like . . . Don't do it, Halil. One doesn't get into a cage with a serpent, a wild beast, a madman . . . Don't do this, it'll lead you nowhere . . ."

Ismail Agha argued and pleaded in this way until the first cocks began to crow, but never by a single word did he indicate that he had guessed what Halil was about to do. And Halil listened quite calmly as though Ismail Agha was talking about something that had nothing to do with him. Dawn was about to break when he suddenly rose to his feet. "I've come to you because I know you won't turn me away empty-handed. Could you give me one thousand four hundred and twenty-three liras?"

"Of course," Ismail Agha laughed. "Right away." He took a purse from his waist and counted out some banknotes under the light of the night lamp. "Here you are, Halil," he said.

Halil's face brightened, he recovered his good humour of the previous evening. Tucking the money into the pouch tied under his armpit, he embraced Ismail Agha and held him awhile in his steely stumper's arms. "Thank you, Ismail," he said, "thank you my good Kurdish brother. I'll repay you in less than a couple of months."

Ismail Agha realised that nothing more he could say would be of any use. This was a very different Halil he had before him now. He accompanied the two men to the door. "Farewell then, my friends," he said and turned back hurriedly to the stairs. He did not hear Halil calling after him: "Forgive me everything, Ismail, my good Kurdish brother."

The two men passed under the pomegranate tree and, scaling the crags, stopped under the old castle ruin. There they sat for a while and watched Mount Düldül trembling in a coppery haze, gradually turning to mauve and then, as the sun struck its snowy crest, glittering like a many-hued crystal cone.

"Shahin," Halil said suddenly, "d'you know what I think?"

"What?"

"That Arab . . . He must be on the look-out for us at Aslantash or at Dikenli, on the road to my village."

"I know."

"With half a dozen armed men, waiting to kill us."

"I know."

"And until he hears from them Memik Agha won't get a wink of sleep."

"Yes, he was scared of us . . ."

"He was almost saying I'll give you what you want, only spare my life . . ."

"Why didn't he say it?"

"He depends on that Arab. He's sure he'll find us and make short work of us."

"He knows too that it's too late, that we'll never forgive him."

"Maybe he thinks so little of us, a fly is worth more in his eyes . . . And then he's such a niggard. Parting with money is a thousand times worse for him than parting with his life."

"Maybe . . ." Shahin said.

They fell silent. Then Halil spoke again. "What shall we do now?"

"Have you forgotten? We were going to the town," Shahin said. "To buy a few things for your people back home."

"Right then, let's go."

A pale light reflected from the mountain top was falling over the dusky plain.

"We'd better cross the river at the Gökburun ford."

"Yes, they might have someone on the look-out for us at the ferry."

They walked down into the fields at a running pace. At Gökburun they took off their clothes to cross the ford. The water reached up to their chest. Then, keeping away from the villages, they reached the railway track, passed through the orchards and entered the town market. In and out of the shops they went, Halil, still in a joyful mood, carefully inspecting the goods in every shop, then quickly making his choice, handing over the money and casting about the market for another likely shop.

And so it went on until the time of the evening prayer. They each carried a bulging bundle tied in a length of red silk. Stopping in front of the coffee-shop under the plane tree, they watched the little stream in which shoals of tiny fish darted hither and thither.

"I'm hungry," Halil said.

Shahin licked his chops. "My stomach's churning . . ."

"To the kebab shop!"

They made their way to an adobe building a little further off whose walls were covered with vines, ivy and gourds, and from which swirled fumes of greasy kebab and *sumac*. A strong smell of raki met them at the door.

A sullen-faced handlebar-moustached waiter in a blue apron, a dirty towel thrown over his shoulder, showed them to an empty table in a corner. As they sat down a cloud of flies rose from the table and the waiter swore long and loud. "What d'you want?" he asked sourly.

Halil gave him a hard look.

The man quickly changed his stance and smiled ingratiatingly. "What shall it be, aghas?" he said again.

"Two Adana kebabs, double portions each."

"Certainly, beys . . ." As he went to the cooking range, the waiter turned again and again to stare at Halil's hands, his eyes widening.

Two platters piled high with parsley, water-cress, black radish and green peppers were brought in together with two large bowls of freshly beaten frothy *ayran*. Halil drank his *ayran* at one go with long gulps, his Adam's apple bobbing.

"Another *ayran* for me, brother," he called as he set the empty bowl down.

The waiter left the client he was serving and quickly brought a fresh bowl which he placed carefully before Halil. "Here you are, bey."

Shahin could not but notice how differently people were treating Halil now. Even Shahin himself was a little diffident towards his friend, more respectful, careful not to anger him. There was something about him that made people almost rise to their feet before him as he walked through the market place. The shopkeepers too, after one look at him, brought out their best quality goods and even allowed him a sizeable reduction on the price. And the aged cook at the charcoal range who was pressing the ground meat in longish balls onto the skewers, kept looking at Halil, taking extra pains, and sent over two large copper plates of kebab nicely browned and done to a turn. And before Halil had time to order it, the waiter hurried over with another bowl of frothy *ayran*.

Slowly, savouring every morsel, while listening to the talk around them and watching with pleasure the other clients eating and drinking raki, they finished their meal. Halil paid the waiter, adding a handsome tip. They rose and left, the waiter looking after them his eyes still fixed wonderingly on Halil's hands.

There was a bakery next to the coffee-shop under the plane tree and the odour of warm freshly-baked bread spread through the market. They crammed some warm loaves into their bundles and bought a kilo of black olives, and without more ado they took to the road in the direction of Mount Düldül. They walked on till darkness fell without talking, without looking at each other. As they ascended a slope they came to a vantage point from which they could see camp fires down below. They heard the barking of dogs and the tinkling of bells, but it was nearly midnight before they came to the camp. They were greeted by some Yörük shepherds.

"We're God's visitants . . ."

"And very welcome to us are God's visitants," the shepherds said.

The nomad encampment consisted of a number of tents set up side by side. In front of each tent a fire was burning and a bird of prey was perched dozing on a forked post.

The shepherds hurried to put a meal before their guests, warm milk, butter, molasses, yogurt and *yufka* bread. Then they were shown to an empty tent and were asleep the minute they lay down on the felt floor of the tent. In the morning they were off before daybreak, the road unrolling like a ribbon under their feet. And, always before them, way in the distance, stretching into the sky was Mount Düldül in a coppery mauve haze, its snowy summit glittering in the sun.

At last, on a midday they came to a small town that was only a day's distance to Halil's village. Here they found their way to the market again and went on a spending spree, buying anything from coloured candy to silk kerchiefs which they stuffed into a new sack. After this they speeded on, eager to reach the Kiraz spring where they intended to stop for a bit and drink of the ice-cold, marjoram-scented water before entering the village. Halil's impatience knew no bounds. His neck stretched forward and with Shahin straining to keep up, he seemed to be flying. At the spring he flung himself down and drank long and thirstily.

"How many years, how many," he said heaving a deep sigh, "since I've drunk of such a spring." He held his head for a while under the water which spouted from the foot of a rock. "Thank you God, thank you for letting me see this day," he murmured as he rose to his feet, his eyes still on the purling spring, the white pebbles glittering on its bed and the violet, orange and white reflections of the flowers surrounding it. "God be praised for this day, God be praised . . ." he repeated. Three gold-speckled green butterflies floated gently on the water, their shadows fell over the white pebbles below. Further off a bee careered round and round a tree in a crazy joyous whirl, drowning the world with its buzzing. A tall plane tree with a trunk so thick three men could not have joined hands around it, spread its branches over a red-veined rock opposite the spring. And above, at a height of three poplars, a rufous raptor, wings outstretched as though nailed to the sky, breasted the wind that could not be felt down below. Shoals of tiny fish clustered over the pebbles, then shattered suddenly as though a bomb had been dropped in their midst, leaving shimmery trails in their wake. Reflections from the shining water rippled over the red-veined rock, the fresh green moss and the tree trunk.

Halil could have remained there for days.

The sun was sinking fast. Dark shadows spread down the flinty crags of the valley in front of them and from its far depths came the loud echoing boom of a waterfall. The insistent cry of a strange bird sounded from where it perched, now on a crag nearby, now from down where the valley opened into the plain.

Suddenly Shahin saw stars falling into the spring, tossing, flashing like a thousand suns. And the trees, the craggy valley, the sky above were all alight, twinkling with millions of tiny sparks. And afterwards a vast deep blueness settled on the closing day, a golden velvety blue.

"Halil! Something's happening . . ." Shahin cried. The sky was aswarm with screeching swallows darting here and there with unbelievable speed.

"It's evening time," Halil said, still smiling. "God be praised . . . Thanks be to the Creator . . ." He leaned against a rock. "Shahin, I'm not hungry. You eat something if you like." His head fell over his breast and he was asleep in an instant. Shahin sat down beside him. Opening his food bundle he ate his fill, then curled up on the ground.

They woke up to the loud clamour of birds, perched in hundreds on every branch, greeting the day. A dense haze fell over the spring, hiding the water that had been dancing with light the evening before. Quickly they swallowed some breakfast and set out at once, Halil leading as though he had wings to his feet. The sun was quarter high when they came to the village.

Halil's grandmother was sitting on the threshold of their house, spinning wool. She was a tiny figure shrunk to the size of a fist.

"Mother," Beardless Shahin said as they approached, "is this the home of Halil? Is he here?"

The old woman looked up screwing her eyes. Her face was a maze of wrinkles. "Halil isn't here," she said with a sigh. "And who are you, where are you from? Halil hasn't come yet," she added as though Halil had only just gone out and was expected any time.

Just then the mother appeared at the door. "It's Halil you're asking after?" she said.

"Yes," Shahin said. "We're comrades from the military service."

"Why don't you come in and sit down?" she said. "Halil's gone out."

Inside, she quickly spread a felt mat and threw a pallet over it. Then she set the coffee-pot over the embers on the hearth.

They took off their shoes and sat down cross-legged on the pallet.

Halil began to speak. "He hurried on before us, Halil . . . We thought he'd be here already. He said he couldn't wait, he would run . . . So he gave us these to carry for him, all the things he bought for you."

The mother put the bundles down against the wall and for a long time she sat silently looking at them. "What news from my Halil?" she said at last. "How is he? We haven't heard from him since he went away. Only once a fellow, Duran or something, who'd returned from the Chukurova, told people that Halil had showered him with money. That's what the villagers said, we never saw him."

"Mother," Halil said, "would you know Halil if you saw him?"

She laughed. "What are you saying lad! What mother wouldn't

know her own son!" But she had begun to sense something unusual in the visitors. She looked at them more closely as though sniffing a familiar smell.

"So you'd recognise Halil, would you mother?" Halil drew a deep sigh. "No one would recognise Halil any more, mother, not even his mother, not even his grandmother. Halil's changed, mother. He's a different man altogether. Not even human any more, a strange creature that no one would know."

Suddenly she threw herself at him. "Halil, my boy, my son! May I sink to the bottom of the earth! As if your mother wouldn't know you! Everyone would know you . . . Just let me tell Ipekché." She rushed off, her white headscarf flying.

Ipekché was outside under a tree weaving a *kilim* on her loom. She started up anxiously. "Mother! Has something happened?"

"Halil . . ." the woman panted.

"He's come!"

"He's here, at home, waiting for you."

Ipekché began to run, but when she came to Halil's house she stopped, she simply could not go on. The mother came up and shouted, "Halil, damn you, come out, just look who's here . . ."

At first Ipekché could not recognise Halil. Then her knees gave way and she sank down at the foot of the wall. Halil crouched down beside her and for a long time they remained side by side leaning against the wall without speaking.

At last Halil began to laugh. "You didn't recognise me, did you, Ipekché?" he said a little reproachfully. "I'm changed so much even mother, even granny didn't recognise me at first . . . Look, I've got many things to tell you. Let's go somewhere and talk quietly before the villagers hear I've come."

"All right," Ipekché said, rising. Halil had not taken his eyes off her since the first moment, as though etching her every feature, her whole figure on his mind's eye, as though he would never see her again, never, never until the day he died.

They walked down the valley and found a sheltered place and Halil began to talk. He told Ipekché all the turns his life had taken since they had last been together. And then he went on to outline his future plans.

"What do you say, Ipekché?" he asked when he had finished, relieved, glad to have told all.

Ipekché's blood was boiling. "Don't stay, go! Go back to that village at once, this minute. I've waited for you all these years, I'd wait a thousand years if I have to. Don't stop, go. You're right."

"I know I am."

"Then go, don't stop."

"I was thinking that we could get married before I go."

"No," Ipekché said. "Tomorrow morning you'll set out. Before daybreak. You'll do what you have to do and then we'll get married."

"But what if I should die?"

"You won't die," Ipekché shouted. "You've got right on your side. You won't die."

"But still . . ."

"All right then," Ipekché said. She took off her headscarf and laid it over a bush. Her thick red-gold hair fell about her shoulders. Her blue eyes were wide, glowing with passion, her face flushed. Quickly she undressed and lay down in the shelter of a rock, her legs slightly parted. "You want to get married," she murmured. "Here then, we're getting married now. Come . . ."

Halil had also thrown off his clothes. He bent over her, his head whirling, burning with desire. And they came together.

The next morning it began to rain and the roar of torrents crashing down the ravines filled the whole world. Mount Düldül was hidden in a dense haze. Only its summit emerged, glittering in the sunlight, and all around it lightning flashed, fork after fork.

That night Ipekché and Halil had slept together in the same bed just as if they were married. "I'm staying here, mother," Ipekché had told Halil's mother. "You must go home and tell my people that Halil and I are married now. Halil's got some business to finish off down in the Chukurova. He'll soon be back."

And so Halil and Beardless Shahin took to the road that very morning under the driving rain and made straight for the town where they found Kurdish Hamza, who sold weapons in contraband.

"These rifles you want are very expensive," Hamza said. "The newest. You'd be the first to use them. I've got some that are cheaper."

"I want these, the new ones," Halil said. "Because I'm in the right."

"Of course you are," Kurdish Hamza said. "I never knew anyone in your case to be wrong. Do you know how to use these rifles?"

"During military service," Halil said diffidently, "I never missed a shot. It runs in our family. My grandfather was a soldier at Sarikamish, my father fought against the Greeks. On my mother's side, my uncles were drowned in the Nile fighting the English and then there are some who were at Çanakkalé too."

"And you?" Hamza asked Shahin.

It was Halil who answered. "This Beardless Shahin you see here, Uncle Hamza, can shoot the flying crane in the eye, the running hare in the hind leg. I've seen with my own eyes what a splendid marksman he is. Without a comrade like him I wouldn't set out on this business. I do have all my wits about me!"

"Well my lads," Hamza said, entering into Halil's buoyant mood, "I've taken a liking to you. Have these rifles then if you want them. You can pay me when you've done that business of yours."

"With this business there's no knowing how it may end," Halil said. "Thank you Uncle Hamza, we've got enough money."

"Well then, I'm giving you these rifles at cost price."

"Thank you, Uncle Hamza."

"You want ammunition too."

"As much as you have."

"I've got plenty."

"And we want knapsacks. Have you got that?"

"I have."

"Just like in the army."

"And you'll need fezzes too."

"One each," Halil said. "Like Gizik Duran, the famous bandit."

"Yes," Hamza approved. "Things don't go right without a fez. Red, with tassels like everyone used to wear before Mustafa Kemal Pasha came. And what about binoculars? I'll lend you a couple and you can pay for them after your first hunt."

"All right," Halil said. "And while we're about it, let's have two Circassian daggers too."

They left the arms smuggler's house changed men, fully equipped from top to toe. Joy lent them wings as they walked on to the steep woody crags of Asarkaya. There they spent the night and tried out their rifles in the first light of dawn, making the red rocks of Asarkaya tremble and echo with their shots.

Halil's good spirits knew no bounds, the smile never left his face. Beardless Shahin shared his joy. And so one night they raided the house of Salih Agha, one of the richest men in the Chukurova and said to be as miserly as he was rich.

The Agha was an old man with a stern face, hook-nosed, and eyes like a bird of prey under bushy eyebrows. They found him sitting on a sofa in a room entirely panelled with carved oak. He lifted his head and his deep-set eyes scrutinised them from head to foot.

"Greetings, Aghas," he said. "Sit down here and welcome."

"Thank you," Halil laughed. "But we're in a hurry. We've no time to sit. We've just got one little thing to ask of you. Three thousand liras, if you please."

The Agha seemed to partake of Halil's good humour. "Since when did I borrow this sum from you? Or have I forgotten . . ."

"True. Your memory's failing you, Salih Agha, or how could a man as lordly as you, all-powerful, forget a debt?"

"Pity," the Agha said. "Seems I forgot." Then as if it just came to his mind: "Look here, my boys," he said, "you won't mind if I ask you something . . ."

"Ask away, we don't mind, but be quick about it, we're in a hurry."

"I'm going to give you the money you want. I've no choice, I see that."

"I'm glad you do, Agha," Halil laughed.

"I know that if I refuse you'll shoot me without a second thought."

"Right you are," Halil said. "And now ask what you want to and be quick about it."

"You see these . . ." He waved his hand towards the east. "Under every bush is a bloodthirsty, ferocious bandit, the mountains teem with them, but not one has ever tried to rob me, not in all these forty years, no one's crossed my threshold with bad intentions. Did you know this?"

"Don't we know it!" Halil grinned.

"You think you'll get away with this?

"Now, that's enough talk." Halil's voice rang loud and harsh. "We know who we're robbing and we know very well why. And you, Agha, you'll have understood us by now."

"I have," the Agha said. "And I've got this to say to you, take my money but don't do what you're going to do. You're angry, you're raging mad, but still don't do it."

For an instant Halil's face was devastated with grief, but he recovered immediately and burst out laughing. "The arrow's long left the bow, Agha," he said. "But thanks all the same. I shan't forget your kindness."

"Is this your first time?"

"The first," Halil said. Behind him Shahin was standing, his back to the wall, his finger on the trigger.

Salih Agha rose, a tall gaunt figure of a man in a silver-embroidered *shalvar*, a naked gold-inlaid Nagant revolver thrust into his sash. He unbuttoned his waistcoat, from a secret pocket he produced a large wallet, counted out six banknotes, these were five hundred notes newly put into circulation, and handed them to Halil. "I can give you more if you want."

"You shame me, Agha. This is quite enough, thank you."

As they were about to leave the room Salih Agha said: "Could I mediate and patch up your quarrel?"

"Even God Almighty would find it difficult to do that," Halil said. "God forgive me but this business is already finished and done with."

"A pity," the Agha said, as he watched them pass through his armed men, the clustering women and children and out of the yard. "What a pity . . . Soon we shall hear of whose hearth has been destroyed."

"Shall we trail them?" his men asked. "We could lay an ambush."

"Don't bother," Salih Agha said. "You'd better keep out of this."

"But why?" asked his nephew who also acted as his principal bodyguard.

"Look," Salih Agha pointed at the two men who were disappearing down the slope. "You couldn't kill those men, or ambush them. Those men are already dead . . . They're dead, risen from their graves for a short turn on earth. If you try and shoot them and if you miss, if they escape from your ambush, then you may be sure this village here is finished, not a living creature will be left in it."

"But they're only two," his nephew objected.

Salih Agha laughed. "That one in front with hands as large as my body, that man is capable of mustering a thousand men in a day and leading them against an army, of telling them die and they will die at his command."

"Why uncle!"

"Why uncle indeed! Would any other man have been able to rob me in my own house with all my armed guards about me?"

"But uncle, we could easily have . . . They're only two . . ."

"How do we know they're only two?" Could that be possible . . . Quickly he dismissed the idea. That man with the huge hands had a crazy look about him, but he certainly was not mad. And his countenance overflowing with a strange joy also exuded a certain magnetism. Never in his whole life had Salih Agha been so unnerved, even afraid. Heaving a deep sigh, he sank down on the sofa. From his tobacco case he rolled himself a cigarette and sparked the flint of his lighter. A pleasant odour of flint spread through the room. "Oooh," he said as he breathed in the smoke, "thank God that's over." The more he thought of Halil, the more the idea that he had had a narrow escape struck him with increased force.

There was a moon that night. Eagles circled above the craggy peak of the mountain. The two men crossed the Narrow Pass and came to the village which was plunged in silence. Before Ismail Agha's mansion they stopped and Halil said to Shahin, "You go inside and give Ismail back the money we owe him."

"Let's finish our business first," Shahin said.

"But what if we're killed?"

"But what if that one learns we're in the village and escapes?"

"You're right," Halil said. "Ismail will absolve me if I die. Even Salih Agha did so." He laughed.

They jumped over the wall into Memik Agha's yard. Shahin went to the barn. He was soon out with a can of paraffin and some rags.

"Let's sit a little on that slabstone," Halil said.

It was the same old slabstone inscribed with a script nobody had ever been able to read, neither the Imam, nor Ismail Agha, not even Arif Saim Bey. These stones dated from pagan times and the treasure hunters kept digging them up in the Forsaken Graveyard. This one had somehow turned up in Memik Agha's yard.

They sat down for a while, back to back as they used to. Then, "Come on," Halil said. They drew up to the house. "Memik Agha, Memik Agha," Halil called.

The faint gleam of a night lamp came from inside. Memik Agha's head appeared at the window. "Who is it? What do you want?"

"I'm Halil. Halil the stumper, and this is Shahin the stumper."

"What do you want at this time of the night? Go away and come back tomorrow."

"We're not going," Halil's voice sounded out joyfully. "As to what we want, it's your life we want, tonight, right away. If you come down and give yourself up, we'll spare your family and the Arab. We've got you surrounded with fifteen men . . ."

Memik Agha drew back and in the same instant a volley of shots rang out.

"All right Agha," Halil shouted. "On your own head be it. Go ahead Shahin."

Shahin quickly stuffed the rags into the threshold, emptied half the can of paraffin and struck a match. Then he rushed round the house and emptied the can here and there, immediately setting fire to the paraffin.

"What about the barn?"

"Set fire to everything. And shoot whoever tries to escape."

Memik Agha and his men were raining bullets on Halil who had positioned himself behind the trunk of a large mulberry tree. Halil did not respond, he just kept to his place without moving. A strong north wind was blowing, tossing the whirling thistles before it and kindling the fire. The door was ablaze and the flames had reached the upper floor. The barn caught fire. Long flames swirled into the sky. Suddenly, the Arab's long figure appeared at the flaming door. He rushed out into the yard, his hand over his eyes, blinking, stupefied. From the burning stable came the neighing of horses and the bellowing of cattle.

"Don't kill me Halil, don't kill me! I'm a stranger, a fugitive," the Arab pleaded as he darted this way and that. "I haven't done anything to hurt you. I was just doing my job, don't kill me. I've got a mother back in Tripoli waiting for me, just like you have. Don't kill me."

Halil's first bullet pierced him in the shoulder. The next shots hit him in the arm, the belly and the neck. He whirled crazily round and round, then threw himself at the mulberry tree and clasped the trunk. Halil retreated to the shelter of the slabstone. Strangled sounds came from the Arab. "You shouldn't, Halil," he was saying, "you shouldn't kill me . . . Why me . . . Me . . . Halil, Halil!" Round and round the tree he went, gnashing at the bark, nails clawing, his raucous screams echoing from the crags. Halil stopped firing. The village was all in an uproar. No one dared approach the burning house. The terrified villagers watched from afar as the flames rose high into the sky, illuminating the castle and the sheer mauve crags that reddened in the glare and swayed with the shadows.

Some villagers had climbed up into the crags behind Memik Agha's house and from there they had a good view of the front and back yards. They could see Halil darting here and there with his rifle and Beardless Shahin sitting on a rock ready to shoot anyone coming out of the back door. Screams came from the burning house. All the dogs in the village were howling, the cattle lowed, horses neighed, and the cocks too crowed by fits and starts in a chorus.

The north wind fanned the flames, tore them from the fire, spewed them above the village. A long flame touched the tree the Arab was clinging to and set it ablaze, but still the Arab held on to the trunk. Then the brambles around the root of the tree caught fire and the flames covered the whole tree. The Arab was seen no more, his screams were silenced.

"You didn't do well, Halil, why kill me . . ."

He had been on the run all the way from far off Tripoli, this Arab. Halil knew his story very well, so did the whole village and the surrounding villages as well. One night his tribe was attacked by an enemy tribe. Everyone was put to the sword. The Arab escaped into the night and came to a town on the sea with whitewashed houses, but the enemy's vengeance would not be complete without killing this Arab too, and only a few days later the Arab saw three of his enemies, all riding white Arab steeds, each with sword and dagger and revolver, tall, lean men, hook-nosed, eagle-eyed, white *agels* flowing in the wind. The Arab took to his heels and came to another town. There too, those men were after him. One night the Arab cornered the three and killed them all. But he was soon hunted down again. So he fled on a ship that landed him in a town he had never heard of. He joined a caravan that was leaving the town and deep in the desert he took refuge with a Bedouin tribe. He lived with them for a few years, married a girl from the tribe and even had a child, when one night he woke up and there they were, three more men on white horses, swords drawn, ready to pounce on him. He escaped. And so from place to place he came to the village and stopped in Memik Agha's yard. Because Memik Agha's house was exactly like the one a soothsayer had once described to him. Go, she had said, until you come to a rocky village, death by the sword cannot reach you there . . .

"You didn't do well, Halil, to kill me . . ."

Memik Agha leaped out of the burning door. He was wrapped in a wet *kilim*. "I surrender," he cried, holding out his hands.

"Too late," Halil said. "The time of surrender is over. I even killed that wretched Arab because of you." And he lunged at him. Memik Agha's hand went to his revolver. He fired once, but Halil was already behind the burning tree, shooting away. At every shot, Memik Agha leaped into the air, screaming. He threw himself back into the flaming house from which came the cries of women and children, then out again. In and out, until he stumbled back one last time and was seen no more.

At the back of the house Shahin had been shooting anyone who tried to escape. All except one, and that Muslu, the Agha's son. Shahin loved the lad and would have died rather than harm him.

Halil and Shahin sat down again on the inscribed slabstone, back to back as before, and remained there until the house was burned to ashes. Dawn was breaking and the first light fell on Halil's face. There was no trace now of yesterday's childish joy, the exaltation. "Not one of them's left alive," he said harshly. "Root and branch we've destroyed that godless miscreant's progeny."

"Yes. Only . . ." Shahin hesitated.

"Only what?"

"Muslu. I let him go."

"But why?"

"I just couldn't kill Muslu, Halil. Would you when he stood there speechless, looking into your eyes?"

"I would!" Halil roared. "Yes, Shahin, I would. There's no village beyond death . . ."

"Yes, there is," Shahin was incensed. "There's the beyond. If not I'd have shot Muslu too."

Halil sprang to his feet. "Let's go. The gendarmes will be here any minute."

"What about Ismail Agha's money?"

"No time now. We'll come back for that one night."

With the light of day the villagers had drawn nearer. They stood about silently, hands folded, frozen. The neighing of horses, the lowing of cattle, the barking of dogs had stopped. There was not a sound as the two men walked through the crowd and up into the crags, their rifles swinging on their shoulders. After they had gone the noise broke out again, louder than before.

And the keening began for Memik Agha, his wives and children and all those who had perished in the fire. In time strange stories began to circulate about the mulberry tree that had burned with the Arab clinging to it, how every night, all night long, it ran with blood, how the blood flowed gurgling down into the river, how it emitted a scintillation of light as it flowed, how ever so many people had seen this sight, how the women especially vouched for it. Somehow Ismail Agha's name was brought into the affair. Much was known about the friendship between him and Halil. Why had Halil visited Ismail Agha before leaving the village, and in the dead of night too?

The talk did not stop at that. Soon it was rumoured that Memik Agha had found out about Kurd Ismail's gold mine. See here, Ismail, he'd said, let's go partners in this, there's a world of gold here. But Ismail's eyes were blinded by greed, not an iota would he yield. Here, he said to that mountaineer Halil, take this rifle and rid me of that fiend, root and stem and all. I'll give you three thousand liras for it. And Kurd Ismail had his eye on the land Memik Agha had cleared by stumping, this land of which each span is worth blood. Sell me this land, he said, I'll give you as much gold for it as you ask. And Memik Agha shouted at him, you could set ten gold pieces on each span of this land and still I would rather die than sell it to you. So Kurd Ismail Agha laughed. He laughed and laughed. So be it Memik Agha, so be it. You will give me your life and the lives of all your progeny and your land as well. You will be wiped off the face of the earth, leaving not a sign, not a trace that you have ever lived.

Do you know Zalimoglu Halil?

I know him well.

Together we went stumping on your land, a whole year and a half . . .

10

SALMAN WAS BACK in the village now. He went from house to house, from one person to another, eager for someone to talk to him, anyone, even visiting strangers, even the children. And always the villagers spoke of Ismail Agha, of the killing of Salman's mother and one and all they asked him the same thing, where had Ismail Agha found all that gold, where, in the Forsaken Graveyard, in the ancient tombs on the Anavarza crags, in Yilankalé, the Snake Castle . . . ?

"Who was that man whose house your father looted on the journey down Antep way?"

"He was a Kurdish Bey, wasn't he?"

"They say he had a chest full of gold."

"A big room crammed with jade."

"A treasure of rubies . . ."

At Antep they had nothing left to eat and on Ismail's back the mother was moaning with hunger.

"Is it true, Salman, that Ismail Agha didn't kill your mother? That she starved to death on the road?"

What could Ismail do? He had five brothers. One of them, crazed with hunger, cast himself into the turbulent waters of the Euphrates, the others all perished with hunger, groaning aloud, sobbing. Of his two wives, the one, Salman's mother, weak with hunger begged to be allowed to see her son, her own Salman, until she breathed her last, she begged to be buried when she died and her body not left a prey to wild birds and beasts. But what did Ismail Agha do, he took Salman by the hand, Salman who was very sick too, and led him away, leaving the poor woman to agonise there in the forest under some snake infested crags.

Salman, this very same Salman here, when night fell, sleep would not come to him, furtively he rose and ran back. A mother! How could any son bear it! He ran and ran barefoot through the vast forest looking for his mother, calling to her, mother, mother, raising the echoes from the crags, hungry, thirsty, for three days and three nights he searched. And then one day, one morning he heard a faint cry coming from the foot of the crags. Fear overcame him, only a child he was then Salman. All around, wolves howled, snakes hissed, poor mite, of course he was afraid, riveted to the spot. If he had been the Salman he was now . . . Not even of Azrael is Salman afraid now. He fell asleep, the sound of wailing, the howling of wolves, the hissing of snakes in his ears. And when he opened his eyes, what should he see? Earth and sky swarming with eagles, wing to wing, pressing down. Not a wolf howled, not a snake hissed. The wailing had stopped. His heart tightening, he ran to the crags. Only his mother's head remained there. The eagles had her bloody bones in their beaks. Salman fled, the eagles after him. In the nick of time, before they could tear him to pieces, he found refuge in a cave, but the eagles crowded at the entrance, flapping their huge wings, screeching . . . Salman crawled in to the depths of the cave, cowering in a crevice. Night fell, the eagles gave up and went away. Salman slept, exhausted. Even as he woke up he was running, running in a desert and there a horseman took him up behind him.

"That Ismail Agha . . . Performing his five *namaz* prayers a day . . . Holier than thou . . ."

"He never once went to look for Salman."

"The horseman was a tobacco smuggler. He set Salman down on a bridge . . ."

"So that passers-by should provide for him."

"So that someone might adopt him, the poor orphan."

"But days went by and no one passed by that bridge."

"The child crept under a bush."

"His flesh rotting."

"Moaning."

Such is fate that Ismail happened to be passing just that way carrying his mother on his back. He put her down beside a spring at the head of the bridge under a spreading cedar tree. His wife Zéro, his brother Hassan and wife Péro were all drinking at the spring, for of food there was nothing left, when they heard a sound of moaning coming from the bushes. Ismail Agha recognised the voice at once. He hoisted his mother onto his back and ran. Stop Ismail, his mother said, can't you hear your own son crying, I won't go anywhere without him. Ismail ran on even faster on his long legs. But his mother kicked and struggled so, he could not get the better of her. I must kill that Salman first, he thought. So he put her down, hungry as she was, her stomach churning, and went back. Such a fetid smell struck him as he bent over Salman to strangle him that he had to hold his nose. Don't kill me father, the child pleaded, maybe somebody will come by and save me. Ismail, beside himself, was at his throat when suddenly a horseman stood looking down at him. What are you doing, friend, he asked. I'm tending my son, he's sick, Ismail answered, so the horseman went his way. Father, Salman said, what will you get out of killing me, just let me be, Allah doesn't want you to kill me, that's why he sent the horseman . . . So Ismail left him there and to his mother he said, I was just bringing him when he died on the way. Did you bury him, she asked. No I didn't, he had to admit, and the result was she refused to stir without first burying her grandson. Willy-nilly Ismail took her up again and went back, praying that Salman should have died in the meantime. But he was there, very much alive and sleeping peacefully under the bushes. The mother knew all about the healing plants that grew in the forest. She brewed ointments for Salman and in the space of one month she had nursed him back to health. How did they live for a whole month? Well, there was this tobacco smuggler, he who supplied the Yörük Bey, Hashmet Bey, with black-market tobacco. They had been smugglers in the old country together with Kurd Ismail and Onnik the Armenian. It was the tobacco smuggler who supplied them with food there in the forest all that month. And when Salman was cured the tobacco smuggler said to Ismail, "Look here Ismail, there on the hillside you'll see Hashmet Bey's seven-poled tent, each pole chased with gold and ivory and rubies, and diamonds too. These poles were given to Hashmet Bey's ancestors by Sultan Murat during the Baghdad campaign. He's got chests full of money too. You can be his guest and then one night . . ."

"But such a rich bey, this Hashmet Bey, wouldn't he have people living with him?"

"Such a great bey all alone in a huge tent!"

"With those chests full of gold!"

"Ismail was his guest that night."

"Hashmet Bey took to him . . ."

"They'd known each other before that."

"Salman said so."

"Salman saw the bey with his own eyes. He says he was a tall man with a handlebar moustache, eyes that looked at you like a wolf's . . . That he wore yellow boots . . ."

"Salman says, even my father was afraid of him."

"Salman says he saw that gold belt."

"It glowed and glittered so, you could see it from a three days' journey away."

"It was the sight of that belt led Ismail into temptation."

"Did anyone see us enter this tent, friend, he asked the tobacco smuggler . . ."

"No one, friend, the other said. So you'd better be quick."

"There was never a shortage of guests in that majestic tent . . ."

"That night, Ismail put them all to the sword."

"And as for the tobacco smuggler . . ."

"That infidel . . ."

"Ismail strangled him on the spot."

"And he put the bloody sword into his hand . . ."

"Then Ismail took all these chestfuls of gold and went down to the Chukurova plain."

"With all that gold, of course he wouldn't deign to take that Armenian's old tumbledown house and his neglected land!"

"Then why did he go stumping for Memik Agha?"

"For the treasure trove in the Forsaken Graveyard, of course!"

"What would he want with the treasure trove when he already had so much gold?"

"Abundance of goods never did anyone any harm . . ."

Every day Salman ate in a different house and listened to all kinds of gossip about his father and Zéro, Arif Saim Bey and the farm. He himself had suddenly become loquacious, relating events he had heard of or imagined, thus feeding the gossip that travelled from village to town with much embellishment, and came to the ears of Arif Saim Bey. How Ismail Agha was determined to find a way of doing away with him, and if not, how he was planning to discredit him in the eyes of Mustafa Kemal Pasha. How he intended to appropriate the whole farm for himself, to supplant Arif Saim Bey as member of Parliament for Adana. Certainly Arif Saim Bey did not believe all this, but he was a worldly-wise man who had been through the mill and who had succeeded in finding a place in the Pasha's close entourage. He did not trust his own eye, and life had taught him to take everything, everyone with a pinch of salt. There was another rumour too that went round in the Chukurova, that he, Arif Saim Bey, was plotting to kill Mustafa Kemal Pasha and take his place. Could it be Ismail Agha who was spreading this rumour? He had been hobnobbing with all those powerful beys recently, Kozanoglu in Adana, Kurdoglu in Kozan, Canbolatoglu in Antep . . . Thick as thieves they'd been. What was behind all this? How could such talk, that he intended to kill the Pasha he loved more than his life in order to supplant him, how could such talk be spreading around the country? Something was brewing against him. Someone audacious enough to plot this must be at the bottom of it all. Could it be Ismail Agha, this Ismail Agha who seemed so devoted to him? . . . Ah, but it's raw milk that man has suckled at birth . . . There's no telling . . . Hadn't the idea of getting rid of the Pasha and supplanting him crossed his own mind now and again? Why shouldn't Ismail think of doing the same to him? Was Ismail the kind of man to kill, such an honest, upright, kind man, a staunch friend . . . Yes, but then why had he had his stumper friend kill Memik Agha? And in such a horrible manner too . . . It was said that Memik Agha had treated him badly, that Ismail had set his heart on the land he had cleared of blackthorns for the Agha. But the Chukurova is full of empty land. Ismail Agha could have taken his choice. Why then have Memik Agha killed by this stumper? No one could put any meaning to it. Don't forget, he had already killed once, his first wife, the mother of that youth who stood guard at his door every night, stiff as a poker, that youth he denied was his son . . . And then what about the army of men he kept? At least fifteen of them at his door every night, all armed to the teeth.

All these rumours came to the ears of Ismail Agha too. There was this rumour too about a bay filly that he could not understand and that nobody could really explain to him. It seemed it was talked about with awe in the villages.

Salman never had enough of listening to all this. It was an endless pleasure for him. In the space of a few days, he had learned all there was to know about the ins and outs of the village and the fifty years of its history. Halil's story he knew as though he had heard it from Halil's own lips, why he had killed Memik Agha, his home village on the other side of Düldül Mountain, Ipekché, the old grandmother Anshajé, the mother Döndülü, how Ipekché had been waiting for Halil these last seven years, how Memik Agha had appropriated the money Halil had earned in Adana, how he had let Halil wait for days at his door, begging for the money that was only his due . . . Yes, he knew all this. How many were the men from the mountains who had worked for Memik Agha, stumping and clearing his land for sometimes as long as fifteen years, without being able to obtain their money in the end. He remembered seeing those huge gaunt men wandering about the village, imploring help from anyone they came across, and finally taking themselves off, wasted, broken, in rags, their faces, hands, bodies scarred, lacerated. Empty deserted hives with nothing human left about them. Yes, Salman knew all this. So why, how was it that people said Ismail Agha had made Halil kill Memik Agha? People were witness to Halil laughing, exulting as he burned down the house, shot the Arab, killed Memik Agha. Salman himself had watched Halil as he went out of the village and up into the hills. His face was calm, happy, as though he had just woken from a pleasant dream. But then, Salman had seen something else too. Before this event, Halil had come to the mansion and had remained shut up with Ismail Agha till dawn. No one but Salman had seen them. If Salman told the villagers then there'd be hell to pay among the gossipmongers.

"I saw your mother in a dream, Salman. Your mother! A thing of beauty, she was. My son, she said, don't let my blood go unavenged. In a dream I saw her, Salman, your mother! A dagger was planted deep between her breasts, right to its gold-studded hilt. Your mother, draped in white silk, came rippling out of a blue cloud, a vision as bright as day."

Old Jennet's hennaed hair fell in two heavy red braids down her back. She wore silver bracelets on her withered arms and blue beads interspersed with gold round her neck. Her thick lips were dry and cracked. And she never stopped telling Salman about his mother.

"She was like Fair Eminé, your mother. Do you remember your mother, Salman? Well, I've seen her, I've held her hand. She stood there large as life, in all her beauty, her eyes opened wide, shining. Have you seen my son Salman, she asks, as she floats on the deep blue cloud in her white robes. Your son Salman's grown, he's a brave sturdy youth now, I tell her, and she smiles, she's happy, oh so happy, her face blooms like a flower."

And Salman listens spellbound to the telling of his dream mother. Every morning he goes to Old Jennet's house. In my dream I saw her . . . I saw your mother, the living image of Fair Eminé. She was in a sea of blood, swimming, swimming and could not get out. They've killed me, sister Jennet, they've made an orphan of my son. Tell him not to let my blood go unavenged . . . The sea of blood frothed, tall waves rose up high and swallowed up your mother . . . In my dream I saw her, in my dream . . . It rained for days, for months, the bloody dagger was plunged to the hilt into your mother's left breast and she stood there bleeding under the rain, stark naked, all by herself in the middle of the plain. I drew up to her, Zeynep, I said, Zeynep, don't you worry about your son, Salman's a grown man now, a German rifle on his shoulder he keeps guard at his father's door. Suddenly she was angry, the blood spurted from the dagger and frothed over the green grass. She flung out her arms and shouted, he's not his father, he's not! Salman must not call him father, never, never, never! He killed me, it was he who killed me and he would have killed Salman too. And then Fair Eminé came to stand beside her, stark naked too. Dear God, how alike they were! There they stood, both stark naked in the middle of the vast plain, each with a dagger plunged into her breast. Planted by the same man . . . Both of them so like each other . . . Two of the loveliest creatures . . . All of a sudden I saw the sun blazing. All of a sudden I saw flames flaring from the four corners of the plain. And I saw the two naked women enveloped by the flames and rising to the sky, holding hands, the daggers still planted in their breast, waving to me from out of the flames, the world's two greatest beauties. Both killed by the same man. All a dream it was . . . In a dream I saw her, Salman, your mother.

The thistles were like a forest on the edge of the desert, dense, thick-growing, with large mauve flowers that turned red, pink and pale mauve towards the centre. Long black snakes swarmed through the thistles and slithered out into the desert in the coolness of the night. The corn had dried and was trampled underfoot. Timid gazelles raced from one end of the desert to another, leaping and bounding, in a reckless quest. Hordes of people fell upon the abandoned broken-eared crops. They came with knives, swords, daggers, some with sickles, and in an instant, as though devastated by a swarm of locusts, the vast field that had been glittering gold under the sun was left bare, empty of stalks and ears and all. Fires were lit along the desert and the plundered stalks were beaten over rugs, coats, dresses, mats or whatever could be spread on the ground, and even as the grain was separated from the chaff and boiled, and even before the pans were taken off the fires, it was devoured by the famished hordes that had been stalking Harran plain for days in search of some small patch of sown land, wheat, oats, barley, rye, and which, when they found, they laid waste in the twinkling of an eye. Not a single blade of grass, not the root of a vegetable, not even the stalks of melons and water-melons did these starving armies of locusts leave behind them. And worst of all were the children, ruthless, pitiless children who had lost their parents in the upheavals, been driven from their homes and villages by forays and incursions, had fled before the advance of enemy armies, gone through fire and water, and were band-ing together on the plain of Harran and Urfa, along the banks of the Tigris and Euphrates, all over Mesopotamia, half naked, ravaging fields and gardens and orchards, decimating the flocks of sheep and goats, killing and being killed, thieving, resorting to the most unimaginable means to fill their hungry stomachs. And as they rushed through the plain, from village to village, from town to town, they died like flies, and many were the dead children that were found lying in dry river beds and in hollows about the desert, half-naked bodies of children between six and fifteen years old, over which vultures and other birds of prey whirled wing to wing, young bodies already reduced to skin and bones, attacked by jackals, hyenas and wolves, all day, all night.

And though they died like flies, their number increased daily. They came from different nations, different tribes, from the Chechens, the Terekemé, the Karapapak in the Caucasus, the Afshars, the Kurds, the Armenians, the Yezidis, the Arabs, Assyrians, Nestorians and countless others.

At first, when they came together, they all spoke different tongues, but in the space of a week or ten days they had already made a choice and had all begun speaking that same one chosen language. Some of these child bands had armed themselves and had become quite dangerous in their forays on villages and towns. By the first week of July all the gardens and orchards in the vicinity of the Tigris had been laid waste and their watchmen killed in their sleep with knives plunged into their belly. It was soon clear that the perpetrators were children, so the landowners started to scour the countryside on horseback, hunting for children and killing every stray child they came across. Soon all the region around the Tigris River was strewn with the bodies of children, mercilessly exterminated like insects. And this only served to make the children wilder, more bloodthirsty and more ferocious in their forays. And far more cunning too. After a while there were no children to be seen anywhere in the daytime. They had learned to protect themselves and devised a thousand and one hiding places from where they pounced upon their prey unawares like savage wolves or venomous cobras. And it came to this, that a most implacable war raged in the desert between children and grown-ups.

And it was in one of these rampaging bands of children, one of the wildest that Salman found himself and though he was the youngest among them, he was also the most hardened, the most resolute, the most daring of them all. Much later, one day, he had boasted about this to Ismail Agha in order to curry favour with him. Father, he had said, you don't know who I am, if you did, if you knew the things I've seen and gone through in my life, your blood would run cold, you'd be struck dumb. But Ismail Agha had given him such a look that Salman had stopped short. And so the memory of those terrible days would remain forever locked in him until the day he died. With his gang of hundreds Salman had swept like a hurricane through the valleys along the Tigris and the Euphrates. One night they raided a large Bedouin tribe, killing all but a few children whom they took along into the Tektek Mountains together with all the tents and belongings of the Bedouins, including the camels and the flocks of sheep. For a while they lived in these tents and ate the food of the Bedouins until they had consumed everything, even the animals, and then they left the tents just as they were and made off for fresh nightly raids. Ah, if only his father could have heard all this, if he only knew what his life had been . . . It would not matter then that he was short and bow-legged, that his eyes were greenish like a snake's, no, he would be proud then of his son. Ah, Salman must tell him everything one day, he must . . . But what if he was displeased, what if he understood him wrong? Who else did he have in this world? His father was everything to him, his whole existence . . . If he were to die one day . . . The very thought made Salman tremble from top to toe. He longed for his father to know him well, to love him a little, just the thousandth part of the way he had loved him before Mustafa was born. He wanted his father to know that no one in this world loved him as much as he did, not even Fair Eminé, even though she was a woman, even though she was not his daughter . . . And always, when he thought of his father, from the first moment he had seen him as he lay with his wounds festering, stinking, when everyone turned away from him holding their nose, when he was ready to sink with shame, he remembered how his father had caressed him with love, held him to his breast, and the very thought was like a dream of paradise and lifted him out of this world in a wave of pride and bliss. Even though Eminé was a woman, even though she resembled his own mother, Salman had for days nursed the idea of killing her one night in her bed just because she bore this love for his father. Yet who knows, maybe his father desired her secretly, without even confessing it to himself . . . Salman knew this for certain, even if his father didn't. He knew that if he killed Fair Eminé his father would grieve. All right then, just let anyone look askance at Fair Eminé . . .

And so the children lived on in the desert, inexorably caught up in a deadly whirlwind, some of them exultant, some sobbing their hearts out, but mostly frightened to death. One night Salman fell asleep in the forest of thistles where black snakes pullulated. When he opened his eyes in the morning he saw snakes all about him, some coiled up, some hissing loudly, their red tongues flickering, as they slithered slowly by him, some hurtling through the air, flying. With a bloodcurdling scream, he rushed out of the thistles and began to run in the desolate immensity of the desert, shouting madly until his voice gave out, night fell and he dropped down in a faint. It was the same with all the children. They were frightened even when banding together, crazy with fear and this made them wilder, more reckless, courting death in order to conquer their fear. It was this kind of fear of his father that Salman felt at times, a lancinating fear that sapped his strength, that he could not overcome. What if one day his father had enough of him? What if he did not want to see him any more? The very thought was enough to cast him into the tenebrous depths of a bottomless pit.

Was Salman's mother really like Fair Eminé? He tried to imagine how she looked, but he could never summon her up as a whole. Sometimes it was only her eyes he saw, wide-open eyes, very black, that somehow veered to a deep blue and then to an iridescent moss-green. And sometimes it was a tall slim figure . . . An orange silk headscarf, a gold nose-ring, a red coral necklace with gold coins . . . Lovely hands . . . Long slim fingers . . . And also strangely enough those perfect white teeth that in every woman's smile brought back her smile to his mind. And most of all it was Fair Eminé's smile and her large laughing black eyes that stirred up the memory of his mother. He devised a thousand ways of coming near her, and when she smiled he was in seventh heaven. But recently he had begun to be afraid she would realise how he longed to look at her, to see her smile, to watch the dimples that lit up her face . . .

His father had been very tall. He wore a military cape, a long one, he carried an old Mauser rifle, a kerchief was tied round his forehead, his feet were bare, mud and blood had dried between the toes. Suddenly he was there, dragging his mother by the hair. He was beating her . . . Salman called to mind a many-walled place, thick walls, a bell tower, a long minaret . . . The east was lighting up. At one end of the desert a crowd is gathered, men and women and children, kneeling, waiting for the sun to rise. As the tip of the sun appears, they all bend down and kiss the ground. Their lips are moving in prayer. Gradually the murmuring grows louder, swelling into singing and the sound fills the empty desert as the sun rises. Horsemen come galloping in, their bare swords glinting in the first light. They set upon the kneeling people . . . Again and again they wield their swords. Blood spurts. There is no sound, no move from the kneeling crowd, the singing goes on. The horsemen gallop away, rein in, return and charge at the kneeling crowd once more. Blood drips, steel-blue under the sun, sparkling red. The horsemen do not come back. Slowly, the worshippers rise after singing one last song, they kiss the earth one last time and with heavy steps they make their way on along the desert, leaving behind the dead, the severed heads and bodies. They do not look back. As the day draws to a close they stop and face the west. They stand with their hands clasped, watching until the sun has quite set

and the murmuring begins anew and the chanting. It spreads
through the desert night. And again they come, the horsemen, at
full gallop, they slash at the worshippers with their swords. Not a
cry, not a sound from those attacked. Blood flows, heads fly . . .
The horsemen depart and the crowd moves on, still chanting, and
walks towards the west without looking back at their dead
companions. A terrifying clangour of chains, a clamorous outcry
in the night. "The Yezidis are going! The Yezidis are escaping!"
The clanging of chains fills the night, draws nearer, louder.
Day dawns, the kneeling crowd is now ten, twenty times larger,
joined by those who came clanging their chains in the night, the
chanting is louder, amplified. They do not move when the men
with swords charge at them. They wait until they have gone
and then walk on, still chanting, towards the sun. And as the
sun reaches its zenith they stop. They are on a hill, and more and
more people flock in from all over the desert. They come chanting and kneel about the hillock. Then Salman's mother flings
herself over him. His father is among the horsemen. Salman
sees him. His mother's hand is holding another hand, the hand
of a man with red hair, a small man with a pleasant laughing
face. She draws him closer. The horsemen are now attacking
more fiercely. This time the Yezidis put up a fight. Shots ring
out. There is screaming and bloodshed, dust and confusion.
Salman sees his father, his terrible glowering eyes . . . His sword
plunges into the red-headed man's back and pierces right
through. His mother, a blood-stained sword in her hand, lunges
at his father. He laughs, seizes her long raven braids and slashes
off her head. His eyes bulging, crazy, he looks around for Salman.
But Salman has crawled under a heap of dead bodies. His father
gives up. Grabbing his mother's blood-soaked head by the hair,
he rides away. And night falls. The whole sandy hillock moans,
one long continuous plaint. When day dawns Salman is lying on
a pebbly patch like the dry bed of a river, dazed, half asleep. He
hears the sound of voices. A group of children is passing by,
running. Instinctively, he joins them. And when night falls the
children huddle against each other and sleep. Then another
night all together . . . And one day, as the east begins to pale, he
kneels down and kisses the earth before the rising sun. The
children wait for him. They are patient. He murmurs a prayer,
rises singing and joins the children. They fall upon the first
village they come to and are out again in the twinkling of an eye,

leaving behind some casualties, but each of them carrying a few loaves of bread, onions, cheese, curds, and they make their way to a distant well.

And so Salman embarks on the great adventure of his life.

Numb, rigid, coiled into a ball, his body ached as though the bones were being wrenched from the flesh. Sounds reached his ears, very faint, they came and went. His ear was stuck to the ground. Could he but hear those sounds again, he would be brought to life, the silence about him would be dispelled, the echoing emptiness . . . A bird-call, the buzzing of a fly, the creeping of an insect, even the hissing of those snakes he had fled from a while ago would be welcome now. An ant, a tiny lizard, a hawk on the wing, its shadow falling darkly over the desert sand . . . Something that breathed, that moved . . . Anything . . . Maybe there was such a thing out there. He only had to open his eyes and . . . But they were sealed tight. Suddenly he heard a noise, quite loud, very near him. He jumped to his feet, his eyes wide open now. A pack of dogs was coming his way, tails erect, muzzles dripping with blood, large well-fed sheepdogs, orange, black, yellow, many-coloured . . . Without a second thought Salman ran up to them. The huge animals, each one a behemoth, glanced at him for a moment, then went on their way without paying any more attention to him. And Salman, relieved of his fears now, fell along with them, adapting his pace to theirs. Ling-a-ling-a-ling they went, and in the evening they came to a watercourse. There the dogs stopped. Silently, they sat on their haunches, heads lifted towards the setting sun, and listened. A booming sound, very faint, was drawing nearer. The dogs' eyes shone, they jumped up, milled around, and as though they had only just seen him, they came to Salman one by one and sniffed him all over, some of them licking his face and hands. Then they were off again, ling-a-ling-a-ling . . . And Salman went along too. Sometimes they stopped for no apparent reason, sitting, their tails curled beneath them, ears cocked, quite still. And each time before going on, they first came to sniff at Salman and lick his face and hands and feet.

Salman remembers how night would fall all of a sudden. He remembers the ferment in the night sky, those huge shooting stars tossing and plunging through the star-studded sky, then breaking up to rain down on the far horizon of the desert. He remembers how terrified he had been, how he had snuggled close to the dogs and how he had then slept peacefully, as he had not done for many nights. A fearful tumult roused him. Barking and snarling, the dogs had rounded up a herd of gazelles and were pursuing them as they bounded this way and that and ran for dear life all over the desert sand. When a dog got one, it quickly tore the animal to pieces with the help of three or four other dogs, then left it where it was and went on to catch another one and another . . . There were hundreds of gazelles in this herd and many kids too, little ones, skipping daintily round and round in the midst of all this melee. Soon not a living gazelle was to be seen. Their mangled bodies lay all over the sands. Some, still agonising, lifted their heads and with large sorrowful black eyes looked sadly at their own lacerated bodies, their severed legs, then slowly, gently lowered their heads again. Others lay on their backs, legs stiff in the air, quivering. The dogs fell upon the dismembered gazelles, snarling, gnashing their teeth, breaking into fights, and feasted long and sumptuously, but they never touched the gazelle kids who even as the dogs devoured their mothers, snuffled about eagerly for their mothers' teats. Nothing was clear in Salman's memory after that. Only the snarling and crunching of bloody teeth grinding away like millstones . . . And also the blood-steeped dogs. For a long while Salman saw everything dyed crimson, the dogs, the desert sands, the sky, the sun and stars . . . He remembers the gazelle kids wandering between the scattered white bones, still searching for their mothers, while the dogs, satiated, licked themselves languidly without a look at them. Salman had caught one of the kids, it was soaked with blood, he let it go at once.

They were now in a green well-watered place. All about him the dogs lay fast asleep, heads on their front paws. Some way off, eagles were approaching, circling in the sky, nearer and nearer, and soon they were swooping upon the gazelle kids, clutching at them with crooked claws, gouging their eyes out before devouring them.

The little gazelles sensed that something terrible was stalking them from out of the sky. They attempted to hide, to escape, they bounded this way and that, but the eagles soon had them nailed to the ground, beaks jabbing savagely. They kept coming in, the eagles, from the distant blue mountains that hovered palely in the north, they drew themselves into a tight black ball and swooshed down, devouring their prey in an instant. The desert was all in a turmoil, a confusion of wings as the eagles fell to fighting, snatching the kids from each other's beaks, clawing, tearing, ten, fifteen eagles all in a flurry, screeching, rending the air, while still more eagles kept winging their way out of the sky and joining the fray. Feathers flew, sand was whipped up and tossed through the air. It was like a day of doom in the desert. And suddenly Salman saw a young gazelle that somehow had escaped the eagles. It was coming towards him, skipping and after it, wing to wing, were some fifteen or twenty eagles in hot chase. Without thinking, Salman rushed forward, but before he could reach the gazelle, one of the eagles shot out and was already upon it. In a moment the other eagles were down in a huge writhing screeching mass. Salman remained there, dazed, utterly drained, until he crept back to the haven of the sleeping dogs.

The first meal he ate was in a water-melon patch on the banks of the Tigris. Salman signalled to the dogs to stop before they entered the field. They obeyed him. He walked to the *chardak* where the watchman was standing, a Mauser rifle on the ready. The man wore an old tattered military uniform and his long jet-black beard glistened greenly under the sun.

"I haven't eaten for days," Salman said. "Have you got some food, uncle?"

The man rattled the barrel of his rifle and introduced some more cartridges. "I've got nothing for you. No bread, not a melon, not a water-melon . . . Get the hell out of here!" he said as he pointed the rifle at Salman. "I'm sick of all you beggars."

Salman pointed to the dogs. "You see these?" he said quietly to the watchman. "There are more of them than you can count. I only have to whistle and they'll tear you to pieces."

The man slowly lowered his rifle. He laughed. "All right, lord of the dogs, come along!" He climbed down the ladder. Under the *chardak* an earthenware pot was simmering over a fire, smelling temptingly. "I killed a gazelle yesterday," he said proudly. "A large one . . . Look . . ." he had spread a few ropes right down to the riverside and hung up the meat of the gazelle in strips to dry. "See? This'll keep me for a whole month, this meat. Provided your pack of wolves don't get at it first."

"They won't," Salman said. His cheeks were sunken, touching each other. He was nothing but skin and bones, a mere wisp ready to blow away. His feet were bare, his hair bristled stiffly on his head and the shirt he wore was torn to shreds. "They ate a whole herd of gazelles only yesterday."

"And you just stood by as they feasted, your gang, is that so?"

"What could I do?" Salman said.

"Come," the man said as he took the pot from the fire. "Such a stew I've cooked, you'll eat your fingers with it too . . ."

He emptied the hot steaming stew into a large platter and handed Salman a wooden spoon. From a bulging sack leaning against one of the *chardak*'s poles, he drew out some *tandir*-baked loaves of bread, each with a hole in the middle and set them beside the platter.

"Don't start at once," he said. "Wait a bit."

Suddenly, the man's face changed, his brow furrowed, his greening beard quivered.

"My name is Abdülvahit," he said hoarsely. "It's done me good to have you here to talk to . . ." And he began to tell his tale. "Fifteen years ago, I loved a Bedouin girl. I abducted her from her tent and brought her here. For the fifteen years that she was my wife, her brothers, six of them, all mounted on Arab steeds, never stopped hunting for us and in the end they tracked us down. I was wounded fighting them right there, in that dry river bed. I could not move. They killed our six children before their mother's eyes and carried her off screaming and weeping and left me there for dead. I opened my eyes. I was bleeding. From the village they heard the sound of shots and they came and saw. Side by side lay the bodies of my six children, all dead, their throats cut . . ."

He could not go on. Silently he motioned to Salman to start eating. But Salman had no appetite left. For a while they remained face to face, holding their spoons, until suddenly the man fell upon the no longer steaming stew. It was clear that he too had not had a proper meal in a long time.

They did not speak as they ate. When they had finished, Abdülvahit leapt to his feet. His face was full of menace. "Get up, child, go!" he growled. "Quick, go. If you stay here another minute I'll kill you."

Salman understood. He whistled and was among the dogs in that instant, and they were all trotting away, running along the banks of the Tigris towards the upper reaches of the river.

Some days later they encountered a large group of children. They were all naked, save for a few who had tied a narrow cotton string to their waist. They stopped and took each other's measure for a while, the dogs and the naked children, then seeing Salman standing among the dogs the children joined him without any qualms. And these ferocious dogs never once barked at the stark-naked children. They banded together, children and dogs, and from that moment turned into so many wild fiends. Salman cast off the remnants of his shirt and with all the other naked children and the dogs that they had been quick to train to their will, each child adopting a dog, they set out on a regular plunder of villages and towns. When they came to a village a couple of children were sent on to scout and the raid would be carefully planned. The children would pounce on the village with wild cries, the dogs joining along and barking furiously. People would be paralysed, unable to believe their senses, while the children ransacked houses, shops, bakeries and passed on like a hurricane leaving not a crumb behind. Sometimes, the villagers armed themselves and gave chase on horseback, but were driven back by the onslaught of dogs and a hail of stones from the children. And sometimes the children met with tough resistance and were repulsed with clubs and firearms. Many were killed, but they took this in their stride and simply fled, leaving their dead and wounded behind.

The little town they had come to was on a rocky wooded mountain slope. The children had stopped some way off and were laying plans for their raid. The dogs had laid their heads on their paws and seemed to be dozing. The decision to attack had been taken, but for some reason the children were afraid this time. So were the dogs. Salman noticed their eyes rolling fearfully.

The iron shutters of the shops clanged open, raising echoes from the rocky hillside. The children waited awhile, then burst into the town with bloodcurdling shouts. They reached the square in front of the mosque and had already raided the corner bakery, when a volley of shots rang out. Dogs howled as bullets hit them, children screamed. Whichever way they turned they were met with gunfire. The dogs dropped by the dozen, writhing, they fled, blood spurting from their wounds. The children fell over the dead dogs, dying, and the slaughter went on all morning. By midday only a few of the plundering children were left in the town. The dogs had long since abandoned the children.

Salman was running in the forest holding a goat leg and a huge loaf of bread. He was wounded, blood flowed from his left shoulder, his thigh and his head. He never knew how long he ran. Were there other children running with him? Dogs? He did not know. He remembered eating some of the bread, but could not recall what he had done with the goat leg. A fog-bound road, a bridge, incoherent fragments passed before his eyes. But very clear was the image of the bulging, glass-green eyes, the eyes of the man who had fired at him. Only the eyes he saw, as though the man had been bodyless, faceless.

For how long, how many days, years, had Salman roamed like this in the desert with children, with dogs . . . What destruction had he not seen, what bloodshed, what savagery. It had all seemed quite normal to him. One thing he remembered very clearly. All through that time he was with the children and the dogs, he would greet the rising sun, kneeling and kissing the ground three times. He would murmur a prayer that would turn into a chant. At first the naked children stood by and stared in silent wonder. But after a few days they were murmuring the same words as Salman, and it was not long before they, too, on waking up knelt to the rising sun and, as the tip of the sun appeared, prostrated themselves and kissed the earth three times, murmuring their prayer and lifting up their voices in song. This mode of worship spread not only to the children of Salman's band, but to all the vagrant children on the Mesopotamian plain. It was a distinctive thing about them, a special ritual. As for Salman he steadfastly kept up the ritual to this day, sometimes secretly, sometimes quite openly.

"Ah father, if only you knew who I am, if only you knew the real Salman . . . How many times he's been through fortune's wheel . . ."

In all this huge Chukurova no one knew who he was. Not even in the village did anyone know him. There were times when Salman could not help himself from hinting at some incident from his past that he remembered, but that was nothing to show the real Salman. He was doomed to remain a sealed book for everyone, even for himself, to the end of his life.

From what he could recall, from what everyone said here and

all over Mesopotamia and Urfa, his mother had been the most beautiful woman the world had ever seen. And she had looked just like Fair Eminé. That's what everybody here said.

"Her name was Zeynep."

"Salman's mother . . ."

"In the land where the gazelles play . . ."

"Where Arab steeds race through the desert . . ."

"She was the most beautiful woman in all of Arabia."

"Who was it saw her in a dream? Jennet Woman saw her . . . Resplendent, in a ball of light . . ."

"Suddenly I saw her coming from way off."

"I saw she looked like Fair Eminé!"

"Her figure, her countenance . . ."

"Those lovely eyes, exactly like."

"Those long lashes . . ."

"She walked like a gazelle, just like . . ."

"Where she steps the roses bloom . . ."

"Where she steps the ground is velvet green."

"In a blaze of light she comes."

"Zeynep, I said, Zeynep . . ."

"She came to me and took my hand."

"She sat down on this age-old earth . . ."

"Side by side we sat."

"Under a distant long lost sky . . ."

It was raining. Lightning flashed in the distant sky, forked and whirled and shattered and burst in a fulgurating blazing ball in the middle of that distant sky. And the world was bright as though a thousand suns had dawned, a dazzling torrent of light.

"He clapped her into irons."

"Ismail was consumed with jealousy."

"He put heavy chains on her hands, her feet. A spiked collar on her throat. Tied her to a strong oak tree and spread a tent over it of pure silk, yellow . . . No male creature must see her, he said."

"The son of an Arab emir had lost his heart to her."

"Tall, dark, handsome . . ."

"His jet-black beard shimmering . . ."

"His blue eyes sad with longing for Zeynep . . ."

"In chains she was, in chains!"

Dust devils tore through the desert, tall as minarets. A sandstorm broke out, shrouding the whole world in darkness, heaving sandhills from here to there.

From the depths of the desert, from Urfa, from Babylon, from Harran plain they came, the horsemen, waving their bare swords, riding hell for leather on bare-backed horses, without reins or bridles, their white robes undulating. Herds of gazelles, hawks, falcons, all helter-skelter, crying, clamouring, fleeing through the desert. And bare-breasted Arabian girls, tall, dark, borne along with the gazelles under the star-studded desert sky in the blue velvet night in a mad whirling dance. And among the girls . . . He seizes Zeynep and carries her off on his bare-backed steed. Far, far away to Lake Van and snow-capped Mount Süphan. Alone and far, in a land of desolate poplars. And there Salman was born in Ismail Agha's dwelling on the shores of Lake Van. Arab emirs rode up all the way from the desert and they saw Salman in his mother's arms. Alas, they cried, the loveliest girl in Arabia has given herself to this Kurd, alas . . . They spurred their horses away from snow-capped Mount Süphan and returned to the Arabian desert, to their black goat-hair tents. Alas . . . Ismail was jealous of the flying bird, the creeping ant, of anyone, any eye that looked at Zeynep, even his own.

"In chains he held her . . ."

"A spiked collar round her neck . . ."

"All in a yellow silken tent . . ."

"In a princely garden . . ."

"A purling spring nearby . . ."

"Under a spreading plane tree, on the shores of Lake Van, at the foot of lofty Süphan Mountain . . ."

"Sorrowful, forlorn."

"And her son Salman on her lap . . ."

And war broke out. From the snowy mountains people streamed down like the great rivers, the Euphrates, the Tigris, the Karasu, down into Urfa plain, Mardin and Harran, down into the grazing grounds of Halil Ibrahim's gazelles, the prophet Halil Ibrahim, tall, sable-bearded, whose eyes were like the eyes of a gazelle, who tended no other animals, only the gazelles from whom he was descended. Zeynep's yellow tent was left behind, but the chains were still round her neck. And so they wandered through the desert for a year, maybe three years, the chains always round Zeynep's neck. Salman had suckled his mother's breast amid the rattling of these chains . . . And one day the Arab horsemen appeared again, riding bareback without reins or bridles. They came in a cloud of dust from the other end of the desert, from below ancient Nineveh, skirting old Babylon, crossing the Euphrates three times. They found Zeynep, threw her onto a horse and galloped away. But one night she escaped. On a white Arab steed, bareback, clinging to its mane, she rode back to the land of Halil Ibrahim. For days she searched for her husband and her son, and in the end she found them. Again they came, the Arab horsemen and dragged her off by the hair and again she escaped. In the end Ismail and Zeynep hid away with a tribe of devil-worshipping Yezidis. Safe at last . . . And every morning, together with the Yezidis . . .

"Together they faced the dawning sun and when the first rays hit the earth . . ."

"They bent their heads to the ground . . ."

"And sang to the rising sun."

"And one day, along with the others, they went up a sacred hill . . ."

"And from right and left, from the desert, from the Abdülaziz Mountains, from where the sun dawns . . ."

From where the sun dawns, from Lake Van, the plains of Iran, from the high Caucasus, from Erzurum and Pasin plain, they came, the Yezidis, and converged on the sacred hill. Fires were lit in the desert night, the meat of gazelles was roasted on the embers, and the purple wine was quaffed. Thousands gathered there and gave thanks to the dawning sun, to the first light, for the earth was formed with the first light, human beings created in the first light, and they offered praise to the light in great olden epics and danced their ceremonial dances.

And again the horsemen came and surrounded the worshippers with drawn swords. They came from the mountains in the north, from the sources of the Euphrates and the Tigris, and a terrible battle was fought there, on that hill. And they carried away the wives and daughters of the sun worshippers, they decimated their herds of gazelles. All these things Ismail saw.

"Ismail saw the Arab horsemen carrying off Zeynep . . ."

"Alas, alas, he lamented."

And Ismail pursued the Arab. Three Arabs he felled down with his sword, shedding their blood over the hot desert sand. He took Zeynep and rode away. But the other Arabs encircled them. Round and round them they rode, one hand clutching their horse's mane, the other holding the sword, ever more swiftly, and the circle narrowed. Ismail, Zeynep and Salman were trapped in the middle. Sand swirled from the horses' hooves. Bare swords flashed over their heads. Ismail saw there was no escape. He wielded his sword, blood in his eyes now, again and again he struck, piercing deep into the flesh of the Arabs. The chains on Zeynep's arms rattled. Had she been free, a sword in her hand, she would have disposed of a few Arabs herself . . . They broke through the circle and galloped off, leaving the Arabs behind in utter confusion, still circling on the sands, like storks gyrating in the sky when they are making ready to migrate.

Ismail heard a groan. He turned and what should he see! Zeynep was in the throes of death. She was steeped in blood and so was Salman in her arms. And the chains too red with blood but no longer rattling. Ismail reined in and lifted Zeynep down. Salman was crying. Don't leave me in this desert, Zeynep said, where the vultures will devour my dead body, take me to that northern land and bury me beneath that plane tree, beside that purling stream. And look after my son Salman as the apple of your eye.

Ismail took the blood-soaked woman up onto his horse again and with Salman behind, they rode out of the vast desert into the snowy mountains.

The enemy had blocked all the roads. Wounded soldiers, swarms of lost children and refugees poured down into the plain. Far away were the lofty mountains, Süphan, Nemrut, Esrük . . . Far away was Lake Van, its cranes, its partridges. Ismail who had been riding night and day for how long he did not know, stopped at last on some lofty crags. Far below, the red-veined rocks dropped steeply to where the Euphrates flowed, dark green, sluggish, smooth . . . Above the crags was an oak tree, its trunk so large five men could not have held hands around it. Ismail spurred the horse and dismounted near the tree. Zeynep had been dead for some time now. He unfastened her chains. Salman was frozen, blood caked all over him. Ismail dug a grave there, beneath the oak tree and laid Zeynep in it. Then he sat down and keened over her.

"Ismail never keened over Zeynep!"

"Of course not!"

"It's Ismail killed her, not the Arabs."

"Out of jealousy he killed her."

"She was so beautiful that he went mad with jealousy."

"So jealous was he that he put her in chains."

"And that wasn't enough."

"He locked her in."

"Even that wasn't enough."

"He posted guards at her door, armed guards, bushy-moustached Kurds."

"Even that wasn't enough."

"In the end he killed her."

"Even that wasn't enough."

"He was jealous of bird and beast, of snakes and insects . . ."

"So he carried her up to the flinty crags of a mountain."

"There he found an ancient tomb carved into the flinty rock."

"It was the tomb of the desert king's daughter."

"He'd had this tomb made for her so that her body should never become food for snakes and worms."

"Ismail had known of this tomb . . . He lifted the lid and there was the king's daughter as though she had only just been laid to rest, as though she was asleep."

"With all her gold and pearls and emeralds beside her . . ."

"All in a golden bed . . ."

"Under a silken quilt . . ."

"Her black hair spread over the pillow."

"Gently, Ismail laid Zeynep down beside her."

"And then he keened and prayed and danced the *semah* for three days and three nights . . . Inside the tomb . . ."

"It was a large tomb, big as a palace chamber."

"Then Ismail closed back the lid and covered the whole tomb with earth, so it could not be discovered by anyone."

"She was more beautiful than the sleeping princess, Zeynep, more beautiful even than Fair Eminé."

"Fair Eminé . . ."

The midnight cocks were crowing as Salman knocked on Eminé's door. She was at the door at once, a flaming pine torch in her hand that smelled of burnt resin. Her large dark eyes brightened. She smiled, her cheeks dimpling, her perfectly white teeth gleaming. Her breasts swelled under her nightgown. A warm misty woman's smell struck Salman and he swayed. Desire spread through his veins, warmed his heart and at the same time a longing, a trusting, an intoxicating closeness. He felt his legs giving way under him.

"I've been waiting for you," Eminé said. "For ever so long. I knew you would come to me like this one day, one night . . ." She took the pine torch in her left hand and with her right hand drew Salman's yellow head to her breast. "Come," she said. She led him to a couch near the hearth spread with an embroidered cambric coverlet. "Sit here, Salman my dear, I'm glad you came."

He remembered her like something out of a dream. An ancient long-ago dream she was for him, Eminé . . .

When they first settled in the village, Ismail Agha had spent days rambling all over the place with the curiosity of a cat. He had been like this in the old country too. He knew every hill and vale in the vicinity of Lake Van, all the islands and caves, all the churches, villages and forts. Here in the village he was soon familiar with every house and all its inmates.

One day he was walking down from the old castle through the blue-flowering thyme and the white asphodels, alive with the humming of bees and redolent with fragrant odours, and he came to the river at the Sheldrake Rock. The blue flowers of the chaste trees were in full bloom. On the opposite bank, at the foot of the sheer crags where eagles nested grew a profusion of heavy-scented myrtle bushes. Ismail Agha had never seen myrtles before. Here in the Chukurova the myrtle was considered as a holy plant. Olive trees, too, he saw here for the first time. Suddenly, from the bushes beneath Sheldrake Rock, a young girl appeared. Her hair was tied in a bright green silk scarf. Her dress was a lighter green and at the waist was a still lighter green sash. A pair of old-fashioned gold earrings hung from her ears. The girl's large black eyes were bright with longing, the eyes of a woman in love ready to give all she has. Ismail Agha was nonplussed, a tremor shook him from top to toe, a deep sensuous pleasure such as he had never felt before. He lowered his head. The girl's black hair was braided in the forty-plait style, adorned with gold drops and coral and blue beads. Her neck was long and graceful as a swan's. The dimples in her cheeks added to the beauty of her dark-complexioned face, the shapely red mouth, the pointed chin. They remained there for a while without a word. Ismail

Agha was afraid to lift his head, to look at the girl again. Abruptly he turned away and was lost in the maze of tall chaste trees.

He met her again. He was wandering through a cornfield when she suddenly materialised before him. He felt again that sensuous tremor stirring him to the core as she looked at him, her eyes sad, full of love. He bent his head, unable to sustain her gaze. After a while he looked up. Her eyes were still on him, adoring, bewitched.

One third time they met again in the Valley of Hawthorns. Again she did not say anything, she only gazed at him for a long while, then ran off into the trees.

Ismail Agha soon found out who she was. Her father, Süleyman Bey, had been quite old, a stranger to the village. He had arrived one day riding a handsome Arab steed and bringing along his tents, camels and retainers. His wife had rows of gold-coin necklaces hanging down her chest. His sons wore splendidly embroidered cloaks and each had a German rifle on his shoulder. Süleyman Bey settled in the plain below Sheldrake Rock, together with his retainers, his grooms, his cattle, his herds of sheep and droves of horses and not much later built himself a long spacious house. He quickly adapted to the village. The villagers looked up to him, for he belonged to a Turcoman tribe celebrated in song and ballads all over the Chukurova right down to Aleppo. He had been obliged to flee from his homeland. But all the time, he lived in fear. He rarely left the village, and then only accompanied by half a dozen horsemen. At night too, he was well guarded by armed men. But one night towards dawn a great uproar roused the village, fighting had broken out around Süleyman Bey's home, turning the village into a veritable hell. The assailants were on horseback and spoke a strange language and they were all fair-haired, tall and green-eyed. The fighting continued all through the day. Süleyman Bey, his sons and what remained of his retainers were captured, their hands bound, thrown onto the backs of horses and carried away. The villagers cleared the bodies that lay all about the place. Most of them were those of the fair-haired attackers, but among the dead was Süleyman Bey's wife. Somehow Eminé had escaped and so had one of the grooms, Old Tanir. Eminé did not keen or weep. She buried the dead according to the age-old Turcoman ritual, offered the customary funerary repasts, had the Coran read on the fortieth day of their death, and then retired into her house and lived there alone with Old Tanir like a daughter with her father. She never lost hope that her father and brothers would come back one day. The years passed and Eminé's beauty became famous all over the Chukurova. Young scions of noble Turcoman tribes lost their heart to her, but she turned every one of them away, saying that she had sworn on the Coran that no man's hand would touch hers before her father and brothers returned. In time, the lovers gave up, and Eminé was more or less forgotten. Anyway, she was not sociable and was hardly ever seen in the village. Old Tanir, a German carbine in his hand, with never a word to anyone, was always there to guard and protect her. Eminé too had a gun and never went out without it.

Such was Eminé's life until Ismail Agha came to settle in the village.

He could not avoid her. Everywhere he went he met her adoring eyes, her lovelorn face. People saw her hanging about outside Ismail Agha's house whatever the weather and soon the girl's dark passion was on everyone's lips, talked about all over the Chukurova. People pitied her and reproached Ismail Agha. Even Zéro was sorry for her. Why don't you take her to wife, she said, I'll get on with her perfectly. We haven't had any children, maybe she'll give us a child. It can only bode ill to let anyone suffer like that because of us . . . Ismail Agha only bowed his head without a word.

Eminé was not daunted. Even when Ismail Agha went stumping, she turned up every day, looking at him humbly, entreatingly.

"She'll die, this girl."

"Look at her, Ismail. She's wasting away."

"This bodes no good for you, Ismail."

"It'll go ill for you, Ismail, if this girl kills herself . . ."

"In vain she waited for her father to come . . ."

"All of the Chukurova was in love with her."

"So many gallant youths!"

"She never gave any of them a look, Ismail . . ."

One early morning as the east began to pale, Ismail was riding through the Narrow Pass when she appeared before him again. This time she spoke.

"Stop, Ismail," she said.

Ismail reined in.

"I am disgraced, shamed before the whole world. All because of my love for you. Have you nothing to say to me?"

Ismail was silent, his face ashen.

"Don't worry. I'm not going to kill myself. That isn't the way with us Horzum people. Our girls do not kill themselves. They do not kill themselves in order to keep their love alive. It is a sin with us to kill love. Listen to me, Ismail. I can give you a son, a descendant of the Horzums, a great ancestry that goes back to the land of Horasan, even if it is exhausted now."

Ismail Agha's head was bent low.

"Won't you say anything to me, Ismail, not one single word?"

He looked up. There were tears in his eyes.

"I have made a vow," he said, his voice strangling. "I cannot break it here, in this land of exile . . ."

Eminé smiled. She stood aside and Ismail slowly rode on.

After this Eminé stayed away from Ismail Agha. Not until Mustafa was born did she attempt to see him. But on the fortieth day of Mustafa's birth, the villagers were astounded to see Eminé in her finest clothes crossing Ismail Agha's yard and entering the house. She went straight to where the baby lay in its cradle. Ismail and Zéro were frozen. After a long look at the child, she produced a gold *mashallah* charm studded with pearls and blue evil-eye beads and fixed it to the baby's clothes. She smiled and without a look about her turned and left. A week after this, she was married to a rich young man from a neighbouring village. The festivities went on for three days and three nights. But only a few days later she was back without having even divested herself of her wedding gown.

Nobody ever found out why Eminé had done this, neither her husband of three days, nor Old Tanir, nor anyone else.

Salman sat hunched on the couch, his eyes on the ground. Eminé gazed at him in silence for a while. The resinous torch was burning in a corner and shadows played on the brush walls. A few late cocks crowed from the far end of the village. Suddenly, Eminé went to the closet and brought down the bedding. It fell with a plop onto the wide blue Turcoman *kilim*. Salman gave a start. She plumped up the mattress and pillows, then got into the bed and started to take off her clothes. Salman held his breath, his eyes widening. Eminé's body was faultless, her breasts round and firm, her hips curved in two small arcs to her waist. A misty woman's smell spread through the room. She never took her eyes off Salman. His shoulders were shaking. It was the first time he had seen a woman's body like this, warm, expectant. With a great effort he rose, trembling in all his limbs. Eminé's lips parted, her teeth glistened, the little mound beneath the round dimpled belly began to swell. Salman stood there unable to take a single step, his face tense, his eyes glowing, unbelieving. The flames of the pine resin torch flickered, the room darkened and brightened in turns. From out of the night came the call of a night bird. Eminé heard it every night at the same time. It probably nested in the hollows of the tall rock behind the fountain. Who knows for how long, for how many years it had called like this in the night. Eminé lay back on the bed and waited. Come Salman, she said inwardly, afraid to hear herself, ashamed. You will be the first man to lie with me . . .

It had begun to rain. Raindrops pattered on the roof of the house and a strong wind had risen. Dry everlastings had been thrust into the brush wall over the hearth in yellow bitter-smelling bunches.

Eminé's forty-plaited hair was spread over the pillow, the silver and gold sequins glittering, the ancient red beads glowing.

Salman's legs gave way. He dropped back onto the couch. His heart throbbed, tearing at his chest, his head whirled, his eyes darkened. Sweat ran down his face and neck. The sour smell blended with Eminé's misty woman's smell and spread through the air. His nostrils dilated like a horse's. His hands clasped his penis. It was rigid, swelling. Writhing he tried to keep it down. Eminé breathed more quickly. "Come," she moaned. She drew Salman to her and before he knew it his penis was inside her.

They were each savouring their first experience, Eminé her first man and Salman his first woman after the bay filly.

Eminé rose with the dawn. She dressed all in green, tied a green kerchief over her head and put on her necklace of gold coins and her gold earrings. She bent down and kissed Salman again and again, then passed on to Old Tanir's room at the entrance to the house.

Ever since the first day Old Tanir had kept a vigil at night. When Salman knocked on the door last night, he had been ready with his rifle, but had quickly made himself scarce. She found the old man squatting on his bed, his head leaning on the butt of his rifle. He smiled under his sleeve. Eminé's face was changed, it glowed. In all these years he had never seen her like this. "Let her marry him," he thought. "She couldn't marry the father, well, let her at least marry the son . . ." But he had his misgivings. What if the villagers learnt that Salman had spent the night in this house with Eminé and with Old Tanir watching over them, rifle in hand too. How could he look anyone in the face after this? And what if Salman just let the girl pine after him and did nothing about it, like his father had done? Well then, Old Tanir swore on all the saints that he would shoot Salman right in the forehead without a qualm.

Salman was asleep, a deep peaceful sleep, all the bitterness, the hardness was effaced from his face. He slept like a child. Eminé in her green clothes flitted in and out of the house in a whirl of happiness, kissing Salman, running out to the crags, then down to the river, along the pebbly shore, back to the crags to pick mauve spearmint that she strewed over Salman's blanket. Tea was on the boil over the hearth. Eminé milked the cows, prepared the butter churn and as the first rays of the sun appeared from behind the old castle, she put the milk to boil and told Old Tanir to watch lest it boil over while she went to churn the butter. She still felt that exhilarating sensation surging through her veins, making her heart stop, lifting her up into the dreams, the love, the bliss of attaining everything she had ever longed for.

The sun was quarter high when Salman woke up, bewildered, not knowing where he was. Only for a moment, then he met Eminé's loving eyes and smiled.

"Did you sleep well, my Salman?" She cradled him in her arms as though lulling a baby.

"Very well," Salman said timidly.

"Well get up then, wash your face and we'll have some breakfast."

Salman went to the washroom. Eminé followed him with a pitcher of water, a brand-new yellow towel and a pink soap. She poured the water for him and as he looked around she said, "You can't go out, you know. You'll have to relieve yourself in the stable. I'll clear it out afterwards." He smiled and passed into the stable which opened out of Old Tanir's room. He was soon out again and Eminé again waiting with the pitcher.

They sat down to eat.

"Come along, Tanir Agha," Eminé said.

"I'll breakfast later," he said, and went out.

Somehow Salman's hand could not go to the steaming glass of tea before him, the fresh milk in the copper bowl, the bubbling butter, the fragrant honey and bread. His eyes were fixed on Eminé, he was lost in contemplation of her face. She laughed and hugged and kissed him, and as he still looked at her entranced without touching his food, she hugged him again and again enough to break his bones in a transport of delight which spread to Salman and they breakfasted all in a tumble and Eminé soon bolted the door and they found themselves in bed.

For a whole week Salman remained shut up like this, making love with Eminé. And Old Tanir kept watch outside with his rifle in his hand, careful not to let anyone come near the house.

Then one night, it was nearly midnight, Salman said: "I'm going, Eminé."

"Where?"

"To the farm. My father must be anxious about me. Worried, losing his sleep . . ."

"You think so? That he'd lose sleep over you?"

"I know him very well. He would be worried sick but he would never ask anyone where I am."

"Do you love him very much?" Eminé's eyes clouded.

Salman bowed his head. "Very very much. I worship him as the saints and dervishes worship Allah." He looked up and stared questioningly at Eminé.

"But he doesn't love you," she blurted out suddenly, then very low, "neither you, nor me . . ."

Salman took her hand. They walked together to the door and stood there side by side. Then as he opened the door Salman said in a moan "Neither you, nor me. And after this he'll never, never love me . . . Never."

He disappeared into the night.

It was early morning when he came to the farm. The farmhouse was a two-storied building set against some rocks. Its walls were thick as a castle's. The courtyard was wide and in the middle rose a tall pointed rock in which were three deep cave-like hollows, their mouths concealed by cactuses and brambles. Behind the farmhouse some massive carob trees had somehow taken root between the rocks. The entrance to the house was through the middle of three wide archways. The roof tiles were faded by sun and rain. A balcony ran the whole length of the west side of the building.

The gate to the courtyard was unlocked, but the main door of rough-hewn pinewood under the archway was closed.

"Müslüm Agha, Müslüm Agha," Salman called.

Müslüm Agha's bushy-moustached face appeared over the balcony.

"Welcome Salman Bey," he cried excitedly, then ran down the stairs and opened the door. He wore a dark blue jacket, blue silver-filigreed *shalvar*-trousers, and round his waist was a silk sash in which he had thrust his gun. "Where have you been, Salman? Ismail Bey sent word days ago that you were coming. Welcome to the farm. Come in, come in . . ."

Müslüm Agha was obviously a worldly-wise seasoned man. All sorts of stories were told about him, but no one knew who he was or where he had come from. He had turned up one morning at Ismail Agha's door. "I've come to you, Ismail. I've come to seek shelter with you in this land of exile, in this Chukurova. Don't ask who I am, where I'm from. If you like the looks of me, if you take to me, I'll stay here and work for you. If not, you don't need to say anything, I'll wait for a month and then take myself off without your even knowing it." These words pleased Ismail Agha. He laughed. "Right you are, a month, and then we'll see."

Upstairs, the maidservants had already spread the cloth and brought in breakfast. Müslüm Agha drew his watch from the pocket of his blue forty-buttoned Aleppo waistcoat. "We've got plenty of time before the labourers come out to work," he said. The silver watch-chain hung in several rows from one pocket of the waistcoat to another. Salman longed to have such a watch, but could not bring himself to ask his father. Müslüm Agha's waist-coat, too, with its forty buttons, its gilt filigreed collar and pockets, was an object of envy to him, but he had been too ashamed to ask the Arab horse traders who came regularly from Syria to bring him such a waistcoat on one of their trips.

They ate their breakfast in silence and had just finished when the *ezan* call to prayer was heard from up in the crags.

Müslüm Agha smiled. "There's a young imam here among the labourers," he said. "He's got a beautiful voice and he climbs up on those crags yonder and calls to prayer five times a day. At first none of the labourers made the *namaz*. Then they began to imitate him. I do it myself now. Would you like to join me?"

Salman was embarrassed. "I don't know how to make the *namaz*," he said apologetically. "Father never taught me. He didn't ask me to do it either . . ."

"Your father knows best," Müslüm Agha said. "If he never told you to do it, then there must be a good reason."

"But I want to do the *namaz*."

"Well, why don't you?"

"But what would father say?"

"He prays himself, doesn't he, five times a day too, without fail. The *namaz* is good. Your father would be pleased if you did it too."

"Would he?" Salman cried eagerly. "But who's going to teach me how? And the prayers . . ."

"Don't you know any prayers at all?"

"I do, but . . ."

"Well then?"

"My prayers are different. I don't know myself what sort of prayers . . ."

"Well, a prayer's a prayer, whatever kind it may be," Müslüm Agha laughed.

"But mine is strange."

"How strange?"

"It's a song to the sun. A song that's recited to the sun as it rises . . ."

Müslüm Agha hesitated and thought this over. Then he said: "Why not, you can make the *namaz* and sing that song to the sun inwardly. Many people say whatever words they know as they make the *namaz*. So do I . . . Everyone has a prayer to make in this world, a different one for everybody."

"Really?" Salman rejoiced. "Is that really so?"

"Really."

"I thought everybody said the same words during the *namaz*."

"Most people do," Müslüm Agha said. "But what about those who don't know the words?"

"What do they do?"

"They say what comes to them, what they know. That's what I do myself."

"Don't you know the *namaz* prayers either?"

"Well yes, a little. Yet it always pleases me more to say my own prayer."

"Come, let's go and pray together with the labourers, just as the sun rises," Salman cried with the impatience of a child.

"We must perform our ablutions first."

"I know that," Salman said. "I've seen father do it."

With a pitcher of water and a cake of soap, he ran down the stairs and out beneath the carob trees. There he relieved himself, washed carefully and when he returned Müslüm had finished his ablutions too and was drying the back of his ears.

The Imam in front, Müslüm Agha and Salman behind and the labourers following, they stood on the still-damp grass in front of the farmhouse and, as the Imam recited prayers in his beautiful voice, they made the morning *namaz*, bending and straightening according to the ritual. Afterwards Salman felt a glow within him, a peace such as he had never felt before.

The land that stretched from the farmhouse down to the distant river had been sown with wheat. The heavy yellow spikes drooped and glistened like gold in the early morning light. First the harvesters rumbled into the field raising echoes from the mountainside. They were drawn by strong horses. Their shares rose and fell over the golden sea of wheat like the wings of some strange mythical bird. Then the threshers arrived, adding to the noise. In the stonier parts of the field and on the lower reaches of the mountain hundreds of labourers were already at work with sickles. The sun rose like a heap of glowing embers just above the river, the water flashed and glittered and irradiated the whole field. Pinpoints of light danced all over the crags, the glow of the wheatfield also fell over the crags, slicing ribbons of light and passing on like lightning. It was impossible to look with open eyes at the glittering crags, the gleaming wheatfield, the molten silver radiance that was the river. The very weight of the heat muffled the sound of harvesters and threshers and tractors, of the trucks and horse carts and horse-bells that usually were so clear. Even the echoes from the crags were dulled in this intense radiance. Sometimes the cry of a francolin could be heard, very faint. Flushed by the harvesters were a host of hares, francolin, gazelles, black snakes and long thin golden arrow-snakes. Bird nests were crushed under the heavy iron wheels of the machines, eggs and nestlings buried in the earth, though in places tiny speckled eggs and yellow-beaked fledglings remained untouched between the stubble. Young birds, newly trying their wings, flitted vainly up and down and the young of jackals, hares and wolves scattered about in terror.

Salman stood against a rock, dazed by the torrent of light that inundated the plain. The hundreds of flashing sickles, the revolving shares of the harvesters, the fleeing animals, the grasshoppers darting through the air, the thousands of shimmering blue and green and speckled beetles, gossamer wings glinting under the hard wing case, veined with blue, yellow, green, mauve . . . All this seemed like a miracle to him.

Müslüm Agha had gone about his business and left him there alone. A large white kerchief over his head, he rode through the field, supervising the harvesters and threshers, the women who carried the sheaves to the threshers and to the horse-drawn sledges, the loading of wheat into carts for the farm stores.

The sun was almost setting when a long shrill whistle made Salman start. Müslüm Agha was before him, sitting his lathered horse. Sweat had dried on the back of his blue forty-button waistcoat, leaving a white patch. His face was burnt dark, only the eyes and teeth gleamed.

"Forgive me, Salman Bey," he said, alarmed at Salman's wide dazed look. "I left you here like this. Curse my dumb foolish head. May my eyes drop out! I'm afraid you've had nothing to eat either, ever since morning." He spoke to Salman with all the respect he showed Ismail Agha and Salman was immensely gratified. He smiled. Müslüm Agha was relieved. "Here, Bey," he said as he dismounted, "why don't you ride my horse back to the farm?"

Salman declined and they walked back together, leading the horse.

The farmyard was teeming with labourers and mechanics. From the three small ovens in a corner, freshly baked bread was being distributed to the labourers and the odour of warm bread filled the summer night. Fires had been lit right up into the crags and the food set to cook over them. Salman's strong sense of smell could tell just what was simmering in each pot.

Upstairs, they found their meal waiting for them. There was *bulgur* pilaff, smelling good of butter, a summer stew with plenty of eggplants and tomatoes, and in the middle of the meal-cloth on a silver platter, three roasted francolins, shot by the huntsman

Heko that very morning. This silver platter together with some silver plates and bowls and a set of gold forks and spoons had been discovered by Müslüm Agha in a cache under the farm-house and he had ridden all speed to give the good news to Ismail Agha. And Ismail Agha had said, for heaven's sake, Müslüm brother, don't tell about this to anyone, the villagers will invent no end of stories. And I don't want you to bring those things to my house either . . .

Salman loved the meat of francolin. At home he often went hunting for francolin because he knew his father loved them too. When he saw the roasted birds, a lump formed in his throat. His hand simply would not go to the gold spoon that shone under the dull light of the gas lamp. And because Salman was the Bey's son and a guest, Müslüm Agha too, did not start to eat.

"Aren't you hungry, Bey?" Müslüm Agha said at last. "Is anything wrong?"

Salman smiled ruefully. "They won't go down my throat, those francolin," he said. "When I think how much my father loves them . . . How could I forget my father all this time? My brave good father . . . May my eyes drop out!" He said this just like Müslüm Agha had done just a moment ago.

Müslüm Agha burst out laughing. "Why Salman Bey, my dear, is that what's eating you? I'll send Heko out tomorrow and he'll bag a dozen francolins for your father."

"I'll go out shooting too," Salman said, and he picked up the gold spoon. He knew the story of these gold spoons, but it was the first time he ate with one. He remembered how, in spite of all the urging and pressing from Zéro and Hassan, Ismail Agha had absolutely refused to have the gold and silver service in the house. No good can come from a dispossessed bird's nest, he kept repeating. Both Müslüm Agha and Salman had immediately thought, what about the farmhouse itself? Isn't that a nest too? But they had not dared put the question to Ismail Agha.

Salman was hungry. He quickly devoured two of the francolins, picking the bones clean, together with a good helping of pilaff and stew, all washed down with several bowls of *ayran* that had been cooled in the well.

The next morning he was awake before the Imam's call to prayer. He waited under the mosquito-net and when he heard the Imam's voice, he jumped out of bed and ran down to make his ablutions under the carob trees. Müslüm had already done this and, together, they silently went to stand behind the Imam. It seemed as though a greater number of labourers were making the *namaz* this morning. A cool dawn breeze was gently blowing, wafting in pungent scents and bringing peace to men's hearts. The golden yellow wheatfield blended into the luminous deep blue dawn sky, soughing and waving in the wind.

Again Salman spent the whole day in front of the crags under the blinding sun, lost in contemplation of this magic world, and was only shaken out of his trance by Müslüm Agha.

For many days afterwards, every morning he performed the *namaz* swaying to and fro, reciting the prayer and singing the song he remembered so well in that language he did not understand. He stood beneath the crags and gave himself up to the spell of this world of a thousand and one colours, of flashing lights, of teeming animals and birds and insects, forgetting his father, Fair Eminé, the bay filly, everything that had made up his life up to now.

One day all this ended. Suddenly he was on a harvester, whipping up the horses, flinging the cut stalks behind over the stubble. Some days later he was manning a tractor. Then he was among the mowers, wielding his sickle as though he had done this all his life. He took part in every one of the activities in the fields, working himself to death. Some evenings he would fall asleep over his food and Müslüm Agha would have to carry him off to bed.

"You shouldn't work so hard, Salman Bey," Müslüm Agha said. "Beys never work like that. Certainly they don't go harvesting and toting sheaves and driving tractors like any ordinary labourer and turning black as a gypsy like you, and thin as a rake too. If your father sees you like this he'll be no end upset."

Salman made no answer. Sweating, dusty, straw and chaff sticking to his face, his clothes torn, his hands all swollen and scabby, he only smiled happily. Once or twice a week he would send his father a brace of francolins that he had hunted, but always as though these came from Müslüm Agha and not himself.

The harvesting was over and the threshing machines now worked non-stop from before daybreak to midnight. Standing in the shade of a *chardak* that Müslüm Agha had erected for him, Salman never tired of watching these monstrous machines that swallowed the wheatstalks and disgorged chaff and grain.

"Müslüm Agha," he said one evening as they were eating their dinner, "I want you to send a man to the village tomorrow to get my horse, clothes and weapons."

"I can't just send anybody," Müslüm Agha objected. "Never trust your horse, your weapon, your woman to anyone. I'll go myself early tomorrow and get them for you."

The morning prayer was just ending when Salman spied Müslüm Agha in a corner of the courtyard with his own horse, his rifle, daggers, binoculars and carpetbag. He quickly reached the end of his prayer and ran up to Müslüm Agha. Carefully he inspected the horse. "Thank you, Müslüm Agha," he said at last. "I see Süllü's taken really good care of my horse." He led his horse to the big gate of the courtyard and hitched it to a small fig tree there. Then he went upstairs and quickly changed into the clothes he found in the carpetbag. He donned his bandoliers, daggers and revolver, drew on his boots, and with the binoculars hanging from his neck and the rifle slung over his shoulder, he mounted his horse and rode out into the fields. Everywhere he went he greeted the labourers with cordial words and the labourers responded as they would to the agha or the bey of the place. "A blessing and plenty to our agha," all in a chorus, three times as though singing a song. All day long he rode through the farm, enjoying the deference and admiration in everyone's eyes.

For a whole week he wandered like this, not only through their own farm, but in the outlying farms and villages as well and one day he crossed the river and galloped on until he came to the town where he ate a meal of kebab at Sülo's famous kebab restaurant before returning to the farm. Days went by like this aimlessly and then one early morning at daybreak his horse seemed to lead him of itself to Eminé's door. She greeted him with a fervent embrace and he sensed again that maddening woman's smell and, taking her up, he carried her to her bed still warm from the night. Old Tanir was coughing in the other room.

Salman's horse remained tied in front of Eminé's house till nightfall for all the villagers to see. He left in the evening and rode back to the farm. He could not sleep that night. Somehow he felt small now, ashamed . . . He wanted to sink to the bottom of the earth. His father would surely have been told that his horse was at Eminé's door the night before. Maybe he knew of the first night too. No doubt he knew, his father knew everything, though he did not show it. Who knows what he thought of him now, how he despised him. How could a man go to bed with a woman in love with his own father, and passionately at that? He was crushed with shame at the thought. He vowed to himself every morning as he made the *namaz* prayer that he would never see her again. The farm was idle now, only a few farm hands, some servant women and Müslüm Agha were left. Salman had nothing to do but go riding through the countryside, the thought of Eminé never leaving him, the memory of her woman's scent making his penis harden on the horse, rendering him weak with lust, driving him to spur his horse on at a killing pace. The horse, its nostrils wide, panting hoarsely, carried him to the edge of the village, but at the Narrow Pass, he reined in and, however much he longed to go to Eminé, shame overcame him and he galloped back to the farm in a whirl of dust. Every day now he came and went like this, sometimes three, four times a day, until both the horse and himself were worn out, ready to drop.

By now everyone was aware of what was going on. The whole village waited with bated breath for Salman to go to Fair Eminé again.

And Ismail Agha too followed his son's inner struggle with the deepest concern.

The cool autumn winds had begun to blow. The sun was low over the Mediterranean now. That day Salman had ridden hell for leather to the Narrow Pass and back, how many times he did not know. His ears drummed, the rushing wind made him feel very cold. Darkness had fallen and the chirring of night insects sounded loud as he found himself at Eminé's door. He knew he could not turn away any more. This was the end. If he went in now, he would never be able to leave Eminé again. It was then she appeared at the door in her green gown, the pine torch in her hand. He jumped off the horse without another thought and drew her back into the house.

From then on, every couple of days, his horse was to be seen tethered in front of Eminé's house. All this time he heard nothing from his father. Somehow he could not bring himself to ask Müslüm Agha. The latter never said a word to him about Ismail Agha. This infuriated him . . .

One morning as Salman was leaving to go to Eminé, he saw Arif Saim Bey's car approaching in a cloud of dust on the road along the river and entering the farm. Dreading to encounter his father, he mounted his horse and was about to ride away when he heard a booming voice calling to him. He turned and saw Arif Saim Bey getting out of the car. There was no sign of his father. Much relieved, Salman dismounted and stood at attention, hands joined, in front of the Bey.

"Welcome, Bey," he said humbly.

"Is Ismail here?"

"He's at the village."

"Müslüm Agha?"

"He's inside, Bey."

"There's an adopted son of Ismail's here, his son rather, Salman by name."

"That's me, Bey, at your service."

"Is that you, my child?" Arif Saim Bey exclaimed. "I've heard you're a brave lionhearted youth, that you'd go through fire and water for your people. Is it you killed all those eagles in the sky?"

Abashed, Salman squirmed trying to find something to say.

"Take that horse inside and come back here."

"As you please, Bey." Helter-skelter Salman drew the horse into the stable and was back in a trice. "Yes, my Bey . . . ?"

Arif Saim Bey pointed to the seat beside the chauffeur. "Get in."

Timidly Salman got into the front seat while the chauffeur held the door open for him. It was the first time in his life that he was going to ride in a car.

"That's how they are, these people!"

"They're Yezidis."

"They worship the devil."

"They bow down to the sun."

"One day it's Salman who goes to bed with Eminé . . ."

"One day it's Ismail . . ."

"Before the bed's had time to cool!"

"They're both infatuated with that woman."

"She's got Salman twisted round her little finger."

"She can make him burn this whole village if she says the word."

"And shoot the villagers too . . ."

"If she just says the word . . ."

"Ismail knows."

"Ismail's not a man to take this lying down."

"His own true love . . ."

"His dark passion."

"He would never share her with his son."

"Well, what's he doing now then?"

"Taking turns with Salman!"

"Maybe they even watch each other."

"Father and son . . ."

"As they do it . . ."

"Ah, but you don't know Ismail!"

"He's a bloodthirsty man."

"A killer . . ."

In that land from where he comes, beyond those mountains yonder, on the shores of Lake Van . . . The news was brought to the village . . . Up there in the mountain, all by himself, an Armenian was dying of hunger. The villagers brought him down . . . And the Armenian made the vow to Islam. He became a Moslem, the most devout of Moslems. In the Moslem religion the convert is doubly dear. But Ismail . . . When he saw this skeleton of a man, this Armenian who had eaten nothing for days, only wild roots on the mountain . . .

"He gave a wild cry . . ."

"He drew his sword . . ."

"He brandished it in the air . . ."

"Flashing like lightning . . ."

"And what did they see next!"

"The Armenian's gory head rolling on the ground . . ."

"Ah, this Ismail you see here . . ."

"At his *namaz* prayers five times a day . . ."

"Telling his beads all the time . . ."

"This Ismail knew about the Armenian's gold."

"He knew where it was hidden."

"So he took the gold, jars and jars of it . . ."

"And left in a hurry with all his family in the dead of night."

"All this stuff about the Russians coming . . ."

"What business have the Russians there?"

"All lies . . ."

He had a brother, this Ismail, who would spend his days sitting on the shore of Lake Van, murmuring prayers. A sainted man he was, who joined the Holy Forties, who went about in a glowing ball of green light, who walked over the waters of the lake raising up the dust as on dry land . . . Ismail was madly jealous of his saintliness, and also because he was so handsome that all the Kurdish girls fell in love with him and all the fairy maids too.

"So as he was fleeing, with all those jars full of gold, Ismail came to the lake."

"Hüseyin, he called, hey Hüseyin!"

"Hüseyin was sitting deep in thought."

"Deep saintly thoughts . . ."

"Come Hüseyin, we're leaving this place."

"Hüseyin looked at him without a word."

"Ismail shook him by the shoulders and tried to make him rise."

"Take your dirty hands off me, Hüseyin shouted."

"That made Ismail ever so angry."

"He lifted him up by force."

"Walk, he said, we're going."

"The other stood firm."

"They fell to fighting, the two brothers, there on the lake shore."

"Their mother tried to separate them."

"Their father . . ."

"All the villagers could not tear them apart."

"Ismail was strong, Hüseyin weak."

"He grabbed Hüseyin's head and held it in the water."

"Until he was drowned dead . . ."

"He drowned him, Allah's own saint!"

"A man who'd drown his brother . . ."

A man who killed his own brother as he wept and pleaded, a man who strangled a person who'd just accepted the Moslem faith, would he let Salman go scot-free? And this Salman only a waif found dying on the roadside, and who was now trying to take from him his own true love . . . That Eminé . . .

"His woman making love to his own son!"

"Wouldn't he make mincemeat of her?"

"He wouldn't even deign to touch them himself."

"He'd just order his men . . ."

"Süllü, Müslüm Agha . . ."

"He's got plenty of people to do this kind of work!"

"He could ask Zalimoglu . . ."

"That sanguinary eagle of the mountains . . ."

"And one night they would snatch Salman and Eminé from their warm bed . . ."

Salman was back a few days later from his outing with Arif Saim Bey. He seemed preoccupied, unwilling to look or talk to anyone. In this abstracted mood, he wandered in and out of the rooms, through the courtyard, down to the river, up into the crags, not even making a move to go to Eminé's house. Every morning he rose very early, went out into the crags and knelt before the dawning sun, murmuring his prayer that turned into a song very low at first, then louder, echoing from the crags into the countryside.

Then, a week later, he jumped onto his horse and made straight for Eminé. He stabled the horse and settled in the house for good, spending his time curled up against Eminé, his head between her breasts, reluctant to get up even to eat or relieve himself. If it wasn't for Eminé's cooking special delicacies for him, bringing them to him on a platter, insisting he should eat, Salman would surely have let himself die of hunger. His face was set in a frozen mask, his eyes glassy. Only from time to time he was seized with frenzied desire and for hours on end he made love to Eminé, sweating of all his pores, until they were both exhausted, their eyes sunk into their sockets, dark as though they had been punched. Eminé was alarmed now, but she did not dare to say anything. One morning, after they had made love all night, Salman rose smiling and made straight for the barbershop and asked to be shaved. Then he walked through the village, talking to people, as he used to, going in and out of houses, spending hours listening to every gossipmongering old woman. He found that everyone was more than ready to talk to him.

Once in a while he would go out into the mountain to shoot, aiming at every living thing he saw, never missing his mark however small. Soon the crags behind the farm were strewn with dead eagles, hawks, and vultures. Down in the plain he killed hares and foxes and jackals and no less than three gazelles. He had taken Müslüm Agha's double-barrelled shotgun along and used it for shooting at birds. Three gazelle kids, too, he felled. But all these animals that he killed he left where they had fallen, without another look at them. At night he either went galloping full speed along the plain or he rambled up on the crags or among the ancient ruins.

The rain that suddenly burst out of the clouds in the west, falling in large heavy drops and raising the dust, put an end to all this. He was soaking wet when he came to the farm, his teeth chattering. Müslüm Agha quickly stripped and dried him, took some new underclothes from the walnut chest, made him put them on, lit the fireplace, spread a pallet in front of it pushed Salman onto it and threw a blanket over him. After a while, Salman stopped shivering. He began casting anxious glances about him like a wounded animal. He rose, went to the balcony, returned, stood gazing at the glowing embers, went down the stairs and up again, mechanically, all in a dreamlike trance.

Müslüm Agha finally held his arm. "Salman Bey, my dear," he said, "what's the matter with you? There's something wrong these last days. I can see it."

Salman gave him a blank glassy stare.

"Say something to me, Salman Bey . . ." Müslüm Agha's voice was kind, affectionate.

"What?"

"Say something to me . . . To me, Müslüm . . ."

"To Müslüm?"

"To me! To me!"

Suddenly, Salman's face changed. He smiled. "I'm sorry, Müslüm Agha," he blurted out. He looked at him pleadingly, his neck stretched out expectantly.

"Salman Bey, tell me, are you in some kind of trouble?"

"Yes!" Salman shouted. "Oh yes . . ." He grabbed Müslüm Agha's arm and dragged him to a corner as far from the balcony as possible. "We must get away from here," he said.

"Why?"

"They're coming."

"Who?"

"Those people who are after you. They're coming from the desert . . . From Arabia. I know. Fifteen armed men, your enemies. They've found you out and are on their way from below Payas. They're going to cut you up with a butcher's knife."

A shade of doubt crossed Müslüm Agha's face. Only for a moment. "Who told you that?" he asked.

"It's on everyone's lips in the village. The whole of the Chukurova knows it. Your enemies are after you." He spoke quickly, his mouth dry with excitement. "Huge knives in their hands . . . Let's get away, Müslüm Agha."

"Well," Müslüm Agha said slowly. "I thought I'd killed them all."

"You killed them?"

"Every one of them," Müslüm Agha said. "I wiped them all out, root and stem. Wouldn't you do the same to those who killed your son and his wife in their sleep on their summer *chardak*, so young, so lovely in their peaceful dawn sleep, your own dear hearts, killed with bullets right through their eyes . . . Wouldn't you do the same?"

"Then they're sure to come, we have to escape."

"I've killed them all," Müslüm Agha said in a cold incisive voice. "Wiped them out stock and stem. They can't rise from the grave."

Salman rushed off down the stairs. He was up again in a moment. Quickly he put on his blue *shalvar*-trousers, his waist-coat and boots and decked himself in all his paraphernalia of weapons, bandoliers, and field glasses. His horse, still saddled, was at the manger. He slipped on the bit, drew the horse out into the yard and, oblivious of the heavy rain, spurred it on into the cloud-capped mauve mountains.

Müslüm Agha was left with a strange feeling of sadness. Poor lad, he thought. He's afraid of something. Life has frightened him.

"It'll pass," he muttered to himself. "It'll pass, *inshallah*. Salman's a good lad. What a pity though . . . This fear is driving him out of his mind."

Müslüm Agha had known fear in his life, fear that made him crazy, that took him beyond death. Maybe this was the real death, this stark fear that was worse than death itself, to find one-self beyond all feeling, beyond love, emotion, joy, friendship, beauty, beyond pity and pain and devotion. This fear that had struck Salman at his heart's core would either drive him to some crazy action or it would carry him beyond death, washed clean, as Müslüm Agha had been.

As he paced up and down the balcony with these thoughts, Salman came riding up, his horse's hooves squelching in the mud. He was wet through again. His eyes glinted strangely like a cornered wolf's.

"Müslüm Agha," he said flatly when he came to the balcony, "They're going to kill me."

The cold irrefutable conviction in his voice made even seasoned old Müslüm Agha shiver. "Who wants to kill you?"

"Those people . . . They kill with butcher knives, with naked swords . . . Slashing to right and left, they kill . . . Didn't you hear, Müslüm Agha?"

Müslüm Agha drew a deep sigh. "I heard. I saw. Would that my eyes had been blinded and I not see this. Would that my ears had been deaf . . ."

"They'll find me here. They'll kill me . . ."

Müslüm Agha shook his head. "No, they won't," he said. "I also waited a long time for my enemies to come . . . Though they were dead, had been dead for a long long time. I knew how they died, how they turned to dust in this black earth, but still I spent nights awake, mortally afraid, a gun in my hand, waiting for them. And somehow, even now, though I know they're long dead, I still wait for them to come one day . . ."

"But they will come," Salman cried, "and father will never see me again."

He suddenly felt a wrenching longing for his father. That he should never see his father again, that his father should never look him in the face again, then he would really be left a desolate derelict in this wide, wide world. Suddenly the image of Mustafa rose in his mind, Mustafa's frightened, timid face, the foxy look in his eyes . . . That boy didn't love his father at all . . . A wave of anger shook Salman's whole body. It was always the same with him when he thought of Mustafa. He was even afraid he might kill him one day in one of his crazy fits, pounding his bones to smithereens. But what would his father do then? Wouldn't he kill him too? He had pondered this often. No, his father would never kill him. He would just give him a cold icy look, as though looking at a worm, as though looking at something that wasn't there and leave him behind, unnoticed, to wish for a thousand deaths . . .

During the next couple of days Müslüm Agha talked to him patiently, trying to draw him out of his strange mood.

"Your father's the most generous of men, kind, understanding. Go to him, talk to him. You'll see how he loves you. You're his son that he tended all these years like a delicate plant. Would he ever abandon you and leave you to those wild beasts who come from the desert? Go to him as though nothing had happened."

"Is that true? You really believe that?"

"Of course it is," Müslüm Agha said. He understood full well the lad's misgivings.

"Then I'll go to him tomorrow. I'll go and kiss his hand."

"Do that," Müslüm Agha urged him. "You'll see how he'll greet you with open arms. You'll see how he's missed you, a thousand times more than you have."

"Tomorrow then, tomorrow . . ."

The next morning Salman would be all set to go, when suddenly he would get off the horse and lay aside his weapons. "A fellow can't go to his father armed to the teeth like this, can he?" he would say to Müslüm Agha. He would remain there in the yard, motionless, lost in thought, turn to Müslüm Agha who had been watching him anxiously, "I can't do it," he would say and off he would go to shut himself up in his room.

On such days Müslüm Agha was careful to stay away from him and only sent up his food with one of the woman servants.

Dawn was breaking. Eagles could be heard screeching on the high crags. Müslüm Agha was out in the courtyard pacing up and down pensively. Salman had not been seen for a whole week.

There was a sound of footsteps coming down the steps and in a minute Salman appeared at the main entrance of the farm-house, fully dressed and equipped with all his weapons. He was clean-shaven and his yellow boots were polished bright. He started at the sight of Müslüm Agha as though caught red-handed, then hung his head.

"Müslüm Agha," he whispered, "d'you know, they're going to kill my father."

A shadow of fear crossed Müslüm Agha's face. Then he said coldly: "Who would want to kill your father, Salman Bey, my dear?"

"They'll kill him, they'll kill him," Salman repeated quietly over and over again.

"But who do you mean?"

Salman's voice strangled. "Those men, those men . . ."

Müslüm Agha was suddenly really perturbed. His brow wrinkled and his nostrils quivered. "It's the evil eye, Salman Bey, my dear," he said dully. He took care never to forget calling

Salman, Bey. "It's the evil eye will be the loss of your brave, generous, gallant father."

Salman clenched his fists. "They're going to kill him," he hissed through his teeth.

"It's the eye, the evil eye of this Chukurova that'll be the death of him. Your father, the most handsome, the goodliest of men . . ." The words poured out of Müslüm Agha like a keening lament. "Like a tiger he is, your father, a leopard in the craggy hills. His eyes are soft and velvety as the desert gazelle's, brimming with love and kindness, his fingers are slim as reeds, his waist so narrow you can join your two hands around it. Give him a gun and he will hold a whole army at bay, he will shoot the fleeing hare in the hind leg, the flying crane in the eye . . . Ah, Salman Bey, my dear, your father is the noblest among his peers. I know him from his homeland beside Lake Van, he doesn't know me . . . Ah, Salman Bey, my dear, it's the evil eye will be the death of your lion of a father, the evil eye of the Chukurova . . . People are envious of his courage, his generosity, his manliness . . . I beg of Allah to take my life before your father's, so my eyes should not see him lying dead in this land of exile, in this torrid, mosquito-ridden Chukurova plain."

He flung his head up like an angry horse and spoke with cold determination, stressing every word. "Whoever touches a hair of his head . . . That man I will not leave alive. Even if he flees to the depth of hell, I'll chase him and catch him and tear him to pieces." Then in a softer tone, but with a strange, wary look at Salman: "Besides, Salman Bey, my dear, if your father were to die, I could not live another day. This world would not be worth living in without our noble Ismail Bey. And you, Salman Bey, my dear, you, his son, could you ever live on after him, after such a father? No, my child, Salman Bey, you too, you never could live on after him."

His steely gaze fixed on Salman, he waited for an answer.

"But they're going to kill him, my father!" Salman cried. He ran to the stable, drew out his horse, mounted it and rode out of the yard.

The winds streamed to right and left of him, like a wild torrent, whipping his face, booming, whistling, and before him swallows in hundreds zoomed like arrows, whizz, whizz . . .

Before his narrowed eyes, fleeting, sharp as a razor's edge, a thin gleaming streak, yellow fields of man-tall, heavy-eared wheat, swishing, swishing. Millions of insects, hard cases speckled black, red, green, mauve, yellow, white, orange . . . Gossamer wings glittering bluely . . . Children and dogs, tongues lolling, rushing from village to village, from town to town, screaming. Flashing, swords, swish swish . . . Sandhills aswarm with huddled frightened people, horsemen galloping bareback, drawn swords plunging into soft flesh, in, out, in, out, blood spurting, denting the desert sand, swish swish . . . A mauve expense of thornbushes, teeming with snakes, children and dogs lying low . . . swish swish . . . Fair Eminé, her breasts bare, like a beautiful nefarious alluring bloom, but festering, putrid, crawling with worms, stark death, agonising. Swish swish . . . Memik Agha mourning, running, his screams shattering the village . . . Severed arms, legs, gouged out eyes . . . Swish swish, flashing sickles, harvesters, great wings flapping, threshers churning up chaff and straw, pungent odours of grass, greasy workers, swish swish, streams of butterflies, blue, orange, yellow, a bright yellow, colouring the sky, flaming pinpoints . . . Zalimoglu, foxy-faced Memik Agha, Müslüm Agha, kindly, rolling his eyes at him, swish swish. Mustafa's eyes, wide with fear, widening, a face all eyes, swish swish . . . They're going to kill my father . . . Bluebirds flung out of their cages, clear blue streaks in the air, each bluebird a slice of blue. My father, oh my father . . . And the falling rain and the sun, a huge ball, flashing, plunging into the plain, bursting . . . Lizards, green, red, tongues flickering, pouring out of the sky, swish swish, my father, oh my father! A dust devil, a thousand dust devils springing from the seashore, from Toprakkalé way, a speeding whirling coruscating sun, tossing stars, grasses, stubble, insects in thousands, helter-skelter, dogs, children strewn over the crags, tumbling crags, swish swish, flooding, drying cracking crags, swish swish, my father, oh my father . . . All flowing along with Salman, swish swish . . .

The horse carried Salman up to the castle ruins. It was all in a lather, its sweat steaming, smelling strongly. Below, in front of the village houses, white mosquito-nets fluttered in the breeze. Far in the distance, beyond the pale blue ranges of foothills, Mount Düldül rose out of the blue, its snowy peak swathed in a coppery haze. A bee is flitting over the drying marjoram, alighting, rubbing its wings and flying off again. A snail crawls slowly on a mauve rock leaving a white trail in its wake.

Salman was sweating. Suddenly a cold rain-heralding gust whipped up the dust. He looked towards the west. The sun was about to set, only a slim slice was left over Dumlu hill. Salman spurred the horse towards the village.

Swish swish . . . Only the horse's head above the tall wheat, the sea of wheat, wind-blown, flowing in a torrent of light, dazzling, refulgent. Swish swish . . . Eagles above the wheat, shedding their shadows over the bright mirror of the crops, the wide undulating field . . . The rain is coming. Spiked wheat spilling to the ground . . . Naked children, dogs, labourers, wheat spikes broken, engulfed, drowned in light, lost to sight, lost in the blowing light. Mustafa, swords, blood, Ismail Agha, sad, hurt . . . swish swish. The horse, cleaving through the wall of wheat, stopped at Eminé's door together with the flowing crops, insects, birds, the glowing lights . . . Salman dismounted, she threw her arms around him, swish swish. Old Tanir, his long sparse beard, his long face, a maze of wrinkles, his forehead resting on the rifle that he never lets go . . . Eminé, like a lush verdant meadow . . . My father, they're going to kill my father! I must go to him at once. Spider webs hung along the bushes, wet with dew, swinging in the wind, the spiders lying low in their corner, flies and bees caught in the webs, buzzing, dead. A huge trembling web on a cactus plant and in the middle three green flies, glinting, their wings still vibrating, struggling, dying. My father, oh my father! On the threshold he laid down his rifle, his revolvers, his daggers, his bandoliers. The field glasses dangled from his neck. He took them off. He stood there a while, walked over to the cactus with the spider web, turned back and picked up one of the daggers from the threshold. He thrust it into his waist. Then he faced Eminé.

"I'm going to my father," he said. He looked at her, a long long look as though he would never see her again. "I must."

"Don't go," Eminé said. "Salman, don't go. Your father will never forgive you, never, neither you nor me. Never, Salman, never not until he dies . . ."

Salman turned away.

When he came to the big house, Süllü was standing at the courtyard gate. "Salman!"

"My father," Salman said. "Is my father at home?"

Süllü pointed to the crags behind the pomegranate tree. Ismail

Agha was sitting there with some villagers in the last light of day, telling his *tespih* beads.

Salman began to walk that way. Then his eyes fell on Mustafa who was playing with some children under a cactus hedge, laughing and shouting with joy, so thoroughly engrossed that he did not see him. Salman stopped short, crazed with anger. Only a moment, then he hurried up to the crags and stood before Ismail Agha. Ismail Agha smiled, Salman murmured something unintelligible. Father and son faced each other, but suddenly Ismail Agha's eyes widened with astonishment. And in the same instant Salman was upon him, dagger drawn. With a grating of bones the double-edged Circassian dagger plunged three times straight into Ismail Agha's heart. As Salman ran off into the crags still holding his bloody dagger, Ismail Agha rose, his tall figure swaying, his hand clutching his collar, his eyes huge. Then he sank to the ground, his eyes still staring, aghast, frozen.

Also by Yashar Kemal

Memed, My Hawk

"Yashmar Kemal achieves the Russian quality – an intimacy of detail which makes his etching indelible, more selected and therefore more obvious than life . . . The book is a small, sharp, moving epic of the Turkish soil"
Sunday Telegraph

"A remarkable novel, reminiscent of Hardy in its power and scope"
Queen

To Crush the Serpent

"Prose of unrelenting immediacy"
Independent

"Part *Hamlet*, part *Blood Wedding*, wound tightly to novella-length"
Observer

The Wind from the Plain

"He speaks for those people for whom no one else is speaking"
James Baldwin

Iron Earth, Copper Sky

"This strange and lyrical book, beautifully translated by Thilda Kemal, has the compulsive power of a tale told to a wondering audience beside a flickering fire"
Daily Telegraph

The Undying Grass

"A narrative sweep as strong as the winds off the Taurus"
Observer